FINANCIAL PLANNING AND MONITORING

David Sutton
Daphne Turner
Peter Turner

MACMILLAN

First published 1995 by
MACMILLAN PRESS LTD
Houndmills, Basingstoke, Hampshire RG21 2XS
and London
Companies and representatives
throughout the world

ISBN 0–333–62488–2

A catalogue record for this book is available from the British Library.

10   9   8   7   6   5   4   3   2   1
04 03 02 01 00 99 98 97 96 95

Copy-edited and typeset by Povey–Edmondson
Okehampton and Rochdale, England

Printed in Malaysia

Contents

List of figures

Preface

As result of recent developments in both the private and public sectors, budgeting, the control of financial resources and the processes of financial decision making have emerged as topics of crucial importance. The purpose of this book is to focus attention on the basic techniques and procedures involved, and to explain these in as simple and 'user-friendly' way as possible with clear illustrations and ample opportunity for practical work.

The work has been based primarily on the advanced GNVQ Unit 11 syllabus of BTEC. Parts I–IV of the book cover that syllabus specifically. The practical work – in particular the major assignments – have been carefully designed to meet all the performance criteria involved. Part V has, however, been added in order to complete the picture, making the book suitable for use as a supplementary reader for the foundation examinations of the professional bodies and for first-year university courses. The book should also be of considerable value for anyone involved with budgeting and financial control.

DAVID SUTTON
DAPHNE TURNER
PETER TURNER

About the authors

After experience in local government, the civil service and the leisure industry, *David Sutton* entered teaching and has taught accountancy in a number of colleges. He is now in charge of accountancy training at Selby College, is an A-level examiner in accounting and a moderator for a number of GCSE boards. He has been deeply involved with BTEC work since its inception.

After a background in teaching at home and overseas, *Daphne Turner* joined the Schools Council Project for statistical education and then entered local government. Previous to her retirement, she was Senior Education Officer with a large local authority with specific responsibility for finance. She has undertaken a number of projects for industry and for the Office of Population Censuses and Surveys. She continues to work for the Open University and is an experienced author.

Following experience in hospital finance and in journalism, *Peter Turner* taught for many years both in England and overseas. He also served as a technical assistance expert in accountancy training with the Ministry of Overseas Development and was subsequently Head of Business and Management Studies at Barnsley College of Technology. He has written a number of books dealing with accounting, economics, business studies and with management in developing countries.

Acknowledgements

The authors wish to record their sincere thanks to those who helped them with this book and who provided technical information on which the examples and assignments have been based. In particular, they wish to record their gratitude to:

Mr M Connor, Director of Finance, Selby District Council, North Yorkshire

Mrs P Davies, Practice Manager, The Health Centre, Pontardawe, Swansea

Mr A Denbigh White and Mr J B Clarke, Burmatex Ltd, Osset, West Yorkshire

Mr M Harrop, Director of Finance, Pontefract Hospital NHS Trust, West Yorkshire

Mrs Judith Johnson, IT Consultant, Eggborough, North Humberside

Mr Simon Ridley, St John's Studios, Scarborough

Mr Andrew Robinson, Partner, Davison and Robinson, Castleford, West Yorkshire

Mrs J Sutton, Proprietor, St Olive's Hotel, Scarborough

Mr Brendan Crossan and Mr Andy Talbot, Selby College, North Yorkshire

PART I FINANCIAL INFORMATION AND PLANNING

TOPIC OVERVIEW

All organisations, whether large or small, public or private, commercial or otherwise, must have adequate 'information systems' through which relevant data can be channelled to those who manage them and who make the decisions. This is the concern of Part I. Chapter 1 considers the role that financial data plays in such information systems, the sources of the information, who needs it and its relationship with the planning and monitoring processes. Chapter 2 looks at the problems involved in decision making once the data has been obtained whilst Chapter 3 considers how finance departments in different sectors of the economy are adapting their structures in order to meet the changing needs of time.

Part II considers the problems of budgeting. Budgeting is concerned with the monitoring and assessment of progress within a pre-set framework, and is the link between planning and policy making on the one hand, and the achievement of objectives on the other.

Part III is concerned with the estimate of likely costs, and the tracking of actual costs, involved in the production of goods or the provision of services.

Effective financial planning and monitoring is impossible with adequate cost information. Part IV concentrates on some particular techniques used in assessing financial performance and in making decisions. Part V takes a detailed look at the problem of reading meaning into final accounts – an essential preliminary to effective monitoring.

1 THE NATURE OF FINANCIAL INFORMATION

Think about this . . . _Assume that you have been put in charge of planning a holiday in Germany for yourself and three friends. Draw up a list of the information you would need for planning purposes and state the sources from which you could obtain it._

1.1 MANAGEMENT INFORMATION SYSTEMS

No organisation can be run efficiently without proper information on which routine operations, longer-term planning and important decisions can be based. The information must be adequate, relevant and presented in a form which can be easily understood by those receiving it. The information may be _qualitative_ (i.e. non-numerical), such as descriptions of trading conditions and regulations in oversea markets, or _quantitative_ (i.e. numerical), such as costing data, sales statistics and financial forecasts.

A commercial organisation will normally have a network of information systems which may provide information on such issues as economic trends and commercial developments, market changes, product data, costs, the personnel situation, and likely competition. The ideal situation is a fully integrated _management information system_, but this is not always possible or feasible. Indeed, there is often an unfortunate significant _lack_ of integration between the systems which results in left hands not knowing what right hands are doing.

Any data produced by an information system should be:

- _Cost effective_
  This means that the information produced should be worth the cost of acquiring, processing, analysing and distributing it.
- _Relevant_
  This means that it should be of a nature as to meet the _needs of the user_, and be in a form which can be understood by him. The traditional base from which accounting has developed has

3

resulted, all too often, in financial data being presented in a highly conventional style and format which has not always been the most suitable for its intended purpose.

- *Accurate*

  That is, the information should be accurate and up to date. This as true of accounting information as of any other. However, its accuracy need be no more accurate than that needed by the user. For example, for audit purposes, it will probably be necessary to have balance sheets totalled to the last penny. For issue to club members or to shareholders, however, it will probably be sufficient to show the final accounts correct to the nearest pound – or in many cases, correct to the nearest hundred or thousand pounds. The published balance sheets of large multi-nationals are often only correct to the nearest million. Unnecessary detail can often cloud the issue, not clarify it.

TASK 1.1   Assume you have been appointed director of a new tourist agency in your town, specialising in promoting continental holidays. Describe the management information system which you would require in order to do your job.

1.2 FINANCIAL INFORMATION SYSTEMS

Financial data is the one type of information which almost all organisations have available to them, though the system for providing this is often far from adequate. The information flow in respect of it is usually the most complex and developed of any in the network and its effectiveness is crucial to almost all aspects of the organisation's operations. At its core lies the accounting system. This structure is based on long tradition and well-established principle. It is quantitative in its approach and attempts to be highly objective. Unfortunately, unthinking obedience to convention means that, in some enterprises, the structure in use is archaic, unresponsive to changing needs, and serves to discourage initiative rather than to encourage development. The emphasis on quantitative values sometimes gives the impression of a greater degree of validity and precision than the data warrants. Also, the information with which it deals is primarily historical – i.e. based on past events such as costs already incurred, sales made during the previous financial period, assets which have already been purchased – at, of course, the cost at which they were purchased.

The finance function has a much wider base, and is more inclusive, than the accounting sub-function which is part of it. Finance consists primarily of three aspects:

- *Financial planning*
  That is, considering the financial implications of the plans being made by management and ensuring that the necessary funding will be available when required.
- *Administration of finance*
  That is, the recording, storing and retrieving of financial information and the proper handling of funds. This, of course, is the pure accounting aspect.
- *Financial control*
  That is, ensuring that finance is managed in a way compatible with the planned operations of the organisation, that deviations are properly and promptly enquired into, and appropriate action taken.

1.3 WHO NEEDS THE INFORMATION?

The primary purpose of any management information system – as the name suggests – is to provide information to management. This will be needed for proper appraisal of the current functioning of the organisation, for the assessment of future plans, and for guidance in the essential role of decision making.

The need for financial data is not limited to management. In a commercial organisation, relevant information is also needed by:

- *Shareholders*
  Whose main interest will be the present and anticipated earnings of the organisation, and the security of their investment.
- *Creditors*
  Whose concern will be primarily with the short-term solvency of the organisation.
- *Public bodies*
  Such as the Companies Registration Office whose staff must satisfy themselves that the firm complies with the requirements of law, and the Inland Revenue which is, of course, concerned with tax assessments.
- *Auditors*
  Who will need to examine the records in detail.

- *Employees and trade union representatives*
  Who have an obvious interest in the financial stability and prosperity of the firm.
- *Financial press and agencies*
  Much financial information about commercial firms is published in the various newspapers and journals which study financial matters.

Even competitors will have considerable interest in (although perhaps no right to) the information for the purpose of inter-firm comparisons – and sometimes for other more dubious reasons. One of the big problems in company accounting is how to strike the balance between the release of information to those who have valid reasons for wanting it, and the withholding of it from those who might use it to the firm's disadvantage.

Local authorities also have a range of people interested in data relating to their financing. Councillors and the senior professional officers are in much the same position as the higher levels of management in a commercial concern. Council tax payers have a valid concern in how their tax payments are being spent. Central government maintains a watching brief to ensure that limits set by Parliament are not exceeded, and the Audit Commission is there to check not only on the proper recording of receipts and expenditure, but also on efficiency and authority. All local government departments have to work within the very closely constrained limits of their respective budgets, and employees and unions have much the same concern as in commercial concerns. Over recent years, the situation has become increasingly complex with the new demands which have arisen from compulsory competitive tendering, local management of schools and delegated budgets to various institutions.

1.4 SOURCES OF FINANCIAL INFORMATION

In normal commercial organisations, financial information is built up from a wide variety of sources. These include a number of external sources such as the Stock Exchange lists, government reports and statements, trade association publications, publications by various national and international organisations, and financial press reports. Internally, data will be obtained from departmental sources, such as past and projected sales trends, production plans, personnel forecasts and departmental budgets.

TASK 1.2   Visit the reference section of a good central library. Search out and list the publications which give information which could be of value to the finance department of an organisation trading internationally. Summarise the information available.

The main source of financial data, however, is the organisation's own accounting system. The day books, ledger and cash book provide detailed information regarding routine receipts and payments. The profit and loss account (or its equivalent such as an income and expenditure account) shows the profit for the previous period or periods – remember that accounting data is *historical* in nature. Specialised sub-sections of the profit and loss – such as manufacturing and trading accounts – show detailed breakdowns of those particular operations. These will again be historical in nature.

Finally, the balance sheet gives a detailed breakdown of the assets and liabilities as they stood at a particular (historical) date.

1.5 FINANCIAL PLANNING AND MONITORING

The financial requirements of any modern organisation go far beyond those provided by its everyday accounts and the flow of other data immediately available to it.

Management objectives will only be achieved if there is a careful assessment of the financial implications of those objectives beforehand, and a detailed 'plan' prepared outlining how these should be achieved. This often involves the comparative assessment of projects which are competing for the same capital funds (such questions arise, for example, as to whether a firm should manufacture product 'A' or product 'B', assuming there is insufficient capital available to finance both). Equally important is the identification in detail of costs as they occur and their comparison with what had been expected.

This is, essentially, the field of financial planning and monitoring. The purpose of this book is to examine some of the principal techniques which are used. It considers, in the remaining chapters of Part I, the structure of financial departments and the elements of decision making. These elements are the foundation stones of financial policy making.

PRACTICAL ASSIGNMENTS

1 Find out as much as you can about the financial structure and procedures of either
   (i) a public body (such as your health, water or electricity authority), or
   (ii) a fair-sized commercial concern.
   Draw up a report summarising the different groups of people and organisations who may have a valid interest in it. As far as you are able to tell, is the information available sufficient for their purposes?

2 Summarise the differences you would expect to find between the financial information system of a small club and that of a large company.

Investers
Public bodies
Employees
Auditors
Press
Creditors

2 DECISION MAKING – THE BASIC PRINCIPLES

Think about this . . . *Think of the plans you have for your personal future. How many different types of plan can you identify?*

2.1 TYPES OF DECISIONS

Strategic
Planning

Plans, together with the relevant decisions, can be broadly categorised into three types. At the highest level, there is long-term – or *strategic* – planning. This involves decisions which are primarily concerned with *what* objectives an organisation should attempt to achieve and are made by top management. Examples include such major issues as capital investment, financing, resourcing, product choice and marketing policy.

How long a period is covered by strategic decisions depends on the type of industry concerned and the nature of its objectives. In the case of some businesses – such as retail shops – it may be as little as a year or even less; in others – such as oil exploration companies – it may be as long as twenty or thirty years. They usually involve considerable sums of money, and often there is a high-risk element involved. Such decisions determine the whole character and nature of the enterprise, and one particular feature of them is the amount of thought and consideration which has to be given to the options involved – options which, in themselves, are often highly contentious. Another is the length of time necessary for their implementation.

Tactical
Planning

Then there is medium-term – or *tactical* – planning. This involves decisions which are concerned with *how* given objectives should be achieved. They are taken at a lower level of management than those stemming from strategic planning. Typical examples involve decisions on minor capital investment, product modification and general marketing plans. In other words, whereas strategic decisions are concerned with the ultimate objectives of the organisation, tactical ones are more concerned with keeping the enterprise 'on course' to meet them.

Operational Planning

Finally, there is short-term – or *operational* – planning. These plans are largely of a routine nature and are usually delegated to middle management and supervisory levels. Examples include the re-stocking procedures, credit control in connection with customers, and routine marketing and distribution issues.

TASK 2.1   Can you sort your personal plans into strategic, tactical and operational ones?

The 'Programming' of Decisions

Programmed decisions

Decisions can also be classified into programmed and non-programmed ones. *Programmed decisions* refer to those for which a standard response has already been formulated given a particular set of circumstances and are typical of the decisions at the operational level. The action to be taken is included in the normal routine work procedures and, once the standard response has been formulated, hardly involve any real 'decision making' at all. It is only when unusual circumstances arise, or the standard responses appear unsuitable – that is, the 'exceptional' situation – that real managerial attention has to be given to the problem. This is known as *management by exception*.

Non programmed decision

Any Projects taking place

Non-programmed decisions are those requiring the exercise of critical judgement and skill. They apply to all exceptional (i.e. non-routine) situations and are typical of the higher-level tactical and all strategic decisions. The greater the degree of judgement required, the higher up the management structure will the decision have to be made. An example is whether or not to invest a large amount of capital in a new factory. This will demand a very careful and highly expert appraisal of such issues as the relevant cost-benefit factors, what commercial opportunities which will be opened up, the nature of the opportunity-cost involved, and the economic and social environment in which the new factory will be operating. The decision will demand judgement and skill of the highest order.

Figures for ratio analysis – Shareholders Public Sectors Employees

Corporate Planning

A particular type of strategic plan is the *corporate* plan. The word 'corporate' means 'body'. Therefore, a corporate plan is one for the whole body – i.e. the whole enterprise concerned. It is not one just for an individual department or group of departments. It provides the 'framework' within which all other plans must fit. Corporate planning helps to focus attention on:

- *The business opportunities open to a firm* – for example, the scope for new products.
- *The firm's weaknesses* – for example, possible labour or raw material shortages.
- *The firm's strengths* – for example, the specialised skills and equipment available to the firm, or its present 'hold' on the market.
- *Avoidance of inter-departmental rivalries* – and conflict between their individual departmental plans.
- *Encouragement of workers* – at all levels and in all departments – to work together towards the same overall objectives.
- *Identification of the external commercial factors* affecting the business – such, for example, as the strength of competitors, likely changes in law, new import controls and licensing regulations.
- *Identification of external social factors* – such as pollution control and 'green' issues generally, regard for employment levels and community development schemes.

Undue emphasis on corporate planning may, however, lead to inflexibility and can limit the speed with which firms can take advantage of unexpected opportunities. Above all else, corporate plans need a speedy and effective 'feed-back' to management of progress achieved, and of the problems which emerge from time to time – in other words, of an effective management information system (see p. 3).

TASK 2.2   Choose a school, college, club or firm with which you are familiar. Consider the nature of the various types of decision which have to be taken, and whether they amount to strategic, tactical or operational decisions. At what level of management are the decisions taken? For how many of them can a programmed response be formulated? Could any of them be classified as part of a *corporate* plan?

2.2 DECISION MAKING PROCEDURES

There are two ways of arriving at decisions. One is based on the assumption that the decision maker will act in a rational and sensible manner and that s/he will consciously sum up all the possible solutions and choose the option which best meets the needs, plans and objectives of the organisation. This is known as the *economic model* of decision making. There are a number of well-established steps in this process and these are outlined in Figure 2.1. As regards any particular decision, it may be possible to omit some of the steps.

Figure 2.1
Steps in Decision
Making

1. *Clarify the problem* or objective in connection with which the decision is to be taken.
2. *Establish the 'decision areas' involved* – for example, decisions concerning a new product will affect (at least) the design, production and marketing departments as well as the finance division. All will be involved and will have to work closely together. It would be of no use for the design staff to devise one type of product and the marketing department to plan for another, and little point also if the finance for it cannot be raised.
3. *Break the problem down* into its constituent parts. Resolve conflicts between departments.
4. *Establish information needs.* All decisions need to be based on adequate information and background data. This often takes time to research and obtain.
5. *Ensure proper information flows.* It is one problem to obtain the information required, it is another to ensure that it is received by – or at least is available to – those who will need it.
6. *Identify a range of possible solutions.* Calculate the possibilities and implications for the firm of the most likely solutions.
7. *Choose the best solution* from the list of possibilities.
8. *Communicate the decision* to all those who will be affected by it.
9. *Review resources available* and decide what additional ones – e.g. what additional finance, manpower, skills, stocks – will be required.
10. *Implement the decision.* It is pointless to spend a considerable amount of time in reaching a decision and then not put it into operation. In many badly-run organisations, many decisions are never properly and effectively implemented.
11. *Monitor the result.* There must be effective feed-back so that decisions-makers can judge the result and, if necessary, modify the original decision.

The second approach is the *behaviourial model.* Often, the response to a particular problem or suggested plan is an immediate reaction without a full review of the various options. The decision maker has the immediate short-tem effects primarily in mind, together with the wish to avoid conflict and to 'find the easiest way out' of a difficult situation. In practice, many decisions are taken in this way.

Decision-making efficiency depends on

- a good organisational structure so that it is clear who *should*, and who *should not*, make particular decisions; and
- a satisfactory communication system and a proper flow of information.

Decision Making and 'Crisis Management'

Many decisions have to be taken when events occur which could not possibly have been anticipated, and there is not time to follow through the normal process of decision making. Decisions have to be taken quickly and often without consultation and there is no question of being able to go through the steps shown in Figure 2.1. This is sometimes called *crisis management*, but this is a misleading name. Many of the decisions refer to events which arise in everyday management. They may not be predictable, but this does not mean that the situation is out of hand and that the management is staggering from one crisis to another.

TASK 2.3   Assume your firm is considering the replacement of its present fleet of ten delivery vans. Prepare a report, based upon as much actual detail as you are able to obtain, of the issues involved, of the matters to be considered, and of the recommendation which you would make.

2.3 STYLES OF DECISION MAKING

People make decisions in different ways. The manner in which it is done will depend, in the first instance, on the nature of the problem involved. One problem may have to be tackled one way; another problem in a different way. It will also depend upon the nature, character and temperament of the decision maker. Many of the most successful entrepreneurs habitually defy all the rules of management – but this is not to say that us lesser mortals should copy them.

Three main 'personal' styles of decision-making have been identified:

1. *Autocratic*
   Autocratic decision makers tend to make decisions on their own without consulting subordinates. A modified form of the autocratic style exists when advice and views are asked for, but little notice taken of what is given.
2. *Consultative*
   Here, the problem is discussed with others, either individually or as a group. The decision maker then considers the views which have been expressed before making the decision – a decision which may (or may not) reflect the opinions of those consulted.

3. *Group*

In this case, the problem is put to a group, the 'decision-maker' acting more as a chairman than as a dominant leader. The group considers and assesses the options and a decision is arrived at based on the majority view prevailing within the group. This is sometimes known as the *democratic model* of decision making.

TASK 2.4 Think of some managers and leaders who you know. Is their customary style of decision making autocratic, consultative or democratic? Do you think their style is suitable to the type of organisation concerned?

2.4 DECISION TREES

A *decision tree* is a visual representation showing the possible options which could be followed in response to a particular problem or decision. The options are shown as 'branches' leading out from the original problem like the branches of a tree (except that the representation is horizontal, not vertical). Each of the options itself leads to the necessity for further decisions, the options again being shown as branches. This is illustrated in Figure 2.2. The original problem is *what to do for a holiday*. The initial options (i.e. 'branches') are then shown as either going somewhere overseas, going somewhere 'at home', or of having no holiday at all. If the overseas option is chosen, the question then has to be whether it should be a 'winter cut-price' break, or whether it should be a 'full price' summer-season holiday. If the winter break is chosen, then it is a question of whether it should be a sun-seeking type of holiday or a winter-sports vacation. Having decided that one, then it is not difficult to list the further options, e.g. should it be Africa, Greece, South America ... or where?

Note that at each stage, the possible answers are true options – meaning that *only one of them* can be chosen.

Decision trees make it possible to appreciate at least the major options available, and illustrate that the answer to one problem often creates additional problems to which further answers must be found. Decision trees thus focus attention on the *implications* of decisions.

TASK 2.5 Figure 2.2 was intended only as a very simple example of a decision tree. The sequence of options has not been fully explored. See how far you can take each of the 'branches'.

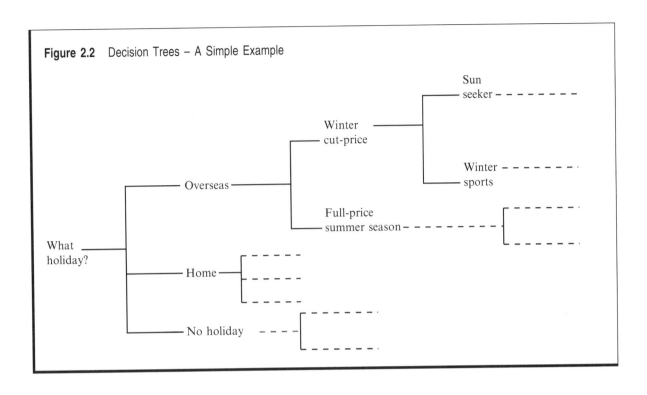

Figure 2.2   Decision Trees – A Simple Example

PRACTICAL ASSIGNMENTS |1| Newham Ltd is a company which manufactures and sells frozen foodstuffs for the home market. Their products consist of frozen chips, pizza and prepared meals. Martin Newham is the managing director and he has appointed directors to be responsible for the following functions in the business:

(i)   purchasing
(ii)   sales
(iii)   production

(iv)   marketing
(v)   personnel
(vi)   finance.

REQUIRED:
For each of the above areas, identify:

(a)   A key operation carried out by that function.
(b)   The decision which must be made to enable that operation to take place.
(c)   The information required for the decision.

Present your answer by completing a table similar to the one below. Purchasing has been completed as an example.

FUNCTION	OPERATION	DECISION	INFORMATION NEEDED
Purchasing	Purchase of raw materials	Use an existing supplier or choose a new one	Quality, price discounts, credit terms, delivery
Sales			
Production			
etc.			

2 Susan Gage is the managing director of Gage Ltd, a small manufacturing company. She is very concerned about the company's performance over the last six months and believes that there are a number of important decisions to be made. She has called a board meeting of her co-directors for which the accountant has provided the following data (all figures in £000):

Month	Sales	Cost of sales	Overheads and expenses
July	600	310	190
August	650	335	208
September	800	420	280
October	500	270	190
November	410	235	165
December	400	250	160

REQUIRED:
(a) Using suitable methods of data presentation, re-draft the above information in formats suitable for presentation to senior management for their use in decision making. Susan is very concerned about the following:

(i)   gross profits
(ii) net profits
(iii) gross profit margins
(iv) net profit on turnover ratio.

(b) From the charts and diagrams which you have produced for the senior management, identify *TWO* areas where immediate decisions should be made. What further information will be required before decisions can be made?

(c) Susan Gage is a self-made person who is confident and very ambitious. Some of her senior managers have suggested that she is sometimes unable to listen and take advice.

What style of management do you think Susan is likely to adopt? To what extent do you think it would be (i) possible, and (ii) beneficial to the company, for her to adopt any other style?

3 Choose a problem which could arise in a commercial situation (*possible* examples include (i) a manufacturing company which is undecided whether to distribute its goods by direct sale to the public or through the normal chain of wholesalers and retailers, (ii) whether to buy an expensive machine with lower running costs, or an inexpensive one with higher running costs, (iii) whether to advertise nationally or locally).

Draft a decision tree in respect of the problem you have chosen.

③ ORGANISATION OF FINANCE DEPARTMENTS

Think about this . . . *Assume that you have undertaken the responsibility for the initial organisation of a sports club in your local town (suppose that no such club exists at the moment). Consider how you would structure the organisation and divide out the responsibilities. Draw a plan to illustrate your ideas.*

3.1 GENERAL BUSINESS ORGANISATION

Just as a person needs a skeleton of bones to support him, so a business needs a proper structure of departments and staff to enable it to function properly. One of management's major responsibilities is to see that the structure of an organisation enables it to do its work in the most efficient way possible.

An organisation is usually divided into a number of departments, each department being responsible for a specific range of work such as production, finance, personnel, marketing. The *finance department* is the key to any modern organisation. It must be structured on sound business lines and must establish a proper web of relationships with other key departments.

Organisation and Personnel Charts

The structure of the departments and sub-departments can be shown in an *organisation chart*. This shows the departments, how these are related to each other and the lines of communication between them.

Organisation charts differ from *personnel charts*. These show the posts held by individuals, their job titles and, sometimes, the span of control (see below). The charts, therefore, indicate how responsibilities are divided between different individuals, and who is responsible to whom.

Despite their advantages, such charts have three serious limitations.

18

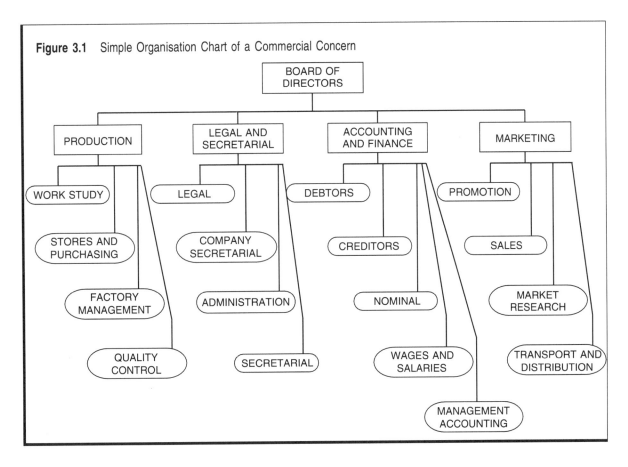

Figure 3.1 Simple Organisation Chart of a Commercial Concern

1. They only show the 'formal working groups' as specified by management and do not give any indication of *informal groups*, the unofficial contacts and relationships which develop whenever people are brought together. These can have a very powerful influence on the workings of a business – both good and bad. It is therefore important that senior managers recognise the existence of such groups and ensure that they work 'for' the firm rather than against it.
2. Such charts emphasise the lines of *demarcation* (i.e. the lines of separation) between departments and individuals to such an extent that co-operation and 'give-and-take' between them can be hindered. Care must therefore be taken to develop good communications within and between departments.
3. Very few organisations are static, since they often have to respond to unforeseen events or external influences. The charts therefore often become quickly *out of date* because changes in the structures are not recorded.

The preparation of an organisation chart requires a careful analysis of the work to be done (known as *job analysis*), and its division into

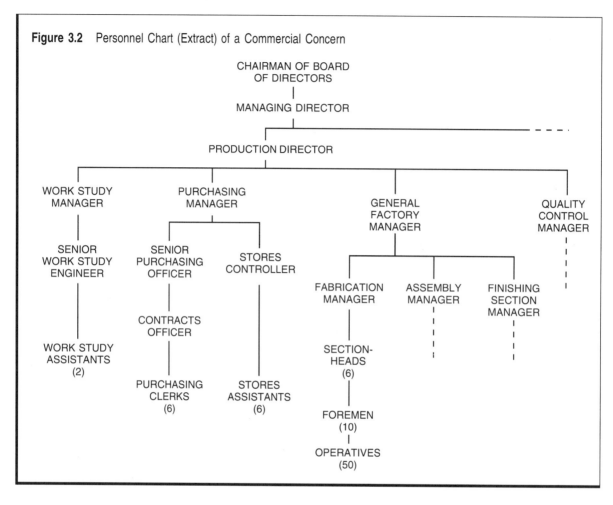

Figure 3.2   Personnel Chart (Extract) of a Commercial Concern

separate posts. A detailed list of the duties and operations required for the performance of a particular post is known as a *job description*. A summary of the qualities, qualification and experience required of a candidate for the post is a *job specification* (i.e. it 'specifies' the person to do the job which has been described). Unfortunately, the terms 'job description' and 'job specification' are used very loosely, and care should be taken in any particular instance as to what, precisely, is meant.

Line and Staff Relationships

Both organisation and personal charts usually indicate the 'lines of authority' – that is, the relationships which exist between individuals or between departments. A *line* relationship is one where responsibility and authority flows directly downwards from manager to supervisor to worker. A *staff* relationship (sometimes called a *functional* relationship) is one which crosses the organisation chart from side to side. A senior warehouse official, for example, may have a staff relationship with a marketing executive. They have to work together and co-ordinate their efforts but neither is superior to the other. A costing clerk (who is directly answerable to the chief accountant and therefore in a line relationship to him) may have a staff relationship with a senior production engineer. Line and staff relationships sometimes become confused and difficult situations develop. Strictly, however, the existence of staff relationships should not be allowed to undermine the basic principle of line authority, namely that no one individual should report to more than one superior on any single function. This is known as the *unit of command*.

The number of workers that a manager or supervisor is expected to control is known as the *span of control*. The span is limited by the time the supervisor has available, his energy and personality, and the nature of the work which is being undertaken. Managers and supervisors vary considerably in the number of workers they are directly able to control. For most, the norm is only about five or six.

Delegation

The amount of work involved in running a large organisation is usually too much for the senior managers to cope with entirely on their own. This means that responsibilities, authority and duties have to be passed 'down the line' to others – i.e. to middle management and first-line management. This is known as *delegation*. One of the arts of management is to know to whom particular tasks can be delegated – and to whom they should not. Proper delegation means the spreading of the work load. It also means that particular tasks can be delegated to those who have special experience or qualifications to deal with them. However, there is always the chance that the person a task is delegated to will prove incompetent. There is also the risk that unless there is proper 'reporting back', the senior manager will not know what is going on.

Delegation does not allow a senior manager to shirk his ultimate responsibility, however. Should the organisation be found to be in breach of the law, then it is the person at the top who is held responsible, not the junior who did the work.

Matrix Management

Matrix management gives the appearance of being a mixture between line, functional and committee organisation. It was developed in response to particular problems which developed in the aircraft manufacturing industry. The massive developments which have taken place within that industry resulted in technological problems and difficulties of a size and scale far beyond those experienced by any firm: consider, for example, the huge problems of supersonic flight. Such difficulties, it was found, could only be solved by bringing together, as a group, various specialists from different departments each of whom had an expert knowledge of some aspect of the particular problem concerned. These specialists would still retain their place in the normal 'line' structure, but their work and responsibility within the specialist group would be independent of this.

> The word matrix means *an enclosed unit within which something develops.* In matrix management, the specialist group is the enclosed unit. The thing which it is hoped will develop is the solution to the problem concerned.

The person in charge of a matrix group should be the person best qualified to deal with the special problem concerned. S/he may well be fairly junior in status but, within the group, ranks above senior staff who also happen to be members. The group normally reports directly to a very high level within the company. The matrix group may be dissolved once it has reached a solution to the particular problem in respect of which it was set up. Alternatively, it may be given a permanent place within the structure of the organisation.

3.2 ORGANISATION OF FINANCE DEPARTMENTS

Whatever type of structure an organisation has, it will need a finance department, the structure and organisation of which has to reflect the type of organisation concerned and the responsibilities it is expected to fulfil. The structure of many departments has not materially changed over recent years, but the responsibilities with which most of them have had to cope have changed almost out of recognition. This is true not only of the private sector, but also of all branches of the public sector. Private organisations will always need a structure to support their need to buy and sell, to make a profit and to meet their legal responsibilities. By contrast, public-sector accounting was once concerned mainly with spending money that it had been allotted, or had raised by revenue from the rates, but there have been many changes which has set them in a much more commercial orientation.

3.3 RESPONSIBILITIES OF PRIVATE-SECTOR FINANCE DEPARTMENTS

Figure 3.3 summarises the principal functions for which finance departments in commercial concerns have responsibility. The relative importance of the functions will vary from concern to concern. In a wholly-owned subsidiary, for example, accounting for the issue and transfer of shares will not be so important as in a major public company whose securities are actively traded in on the Stock Exchange. Similarly, a private limited company will not be as concerned as a PLC with the regulations of the Accounting Standards Board (see below) whilst partnerships and sole proprietors will not be concerned at all. A number of the functions overlap and the separate listing of them does not suggest that they must be carried out by separate individuals.

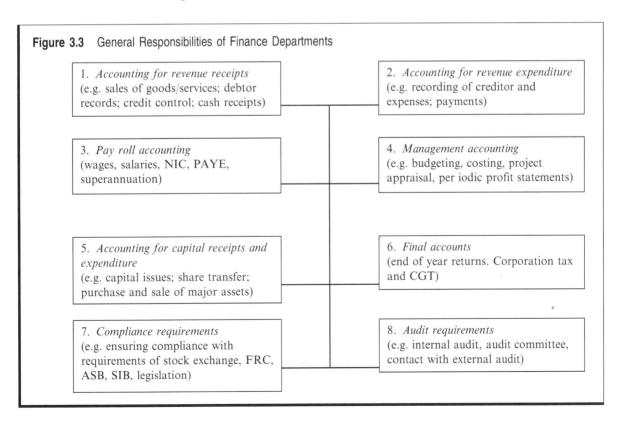

Figure 3.3 General Responsibilities of Finance Departments

1. *Accounting for revenue receipts* (e.g. sales of goods/services; debtor records; credit control; cash receipts)

2. *Accounting for revenue expenditure* (e.g. recording of creditor and expenses; payments)

3. *Pay roll accounting* (wages, salaries, NIC, PAYE, superannuation)

4. *Management accounting* (e.g. budgeting, costing, project appraisal, per iodic profit statements)

5. *Accounting for capital receipts and expenditure* (e.g. capital issues; share transfer; purchase and sale of major assets)

6. *Final accounts* (end of year returns. Corporation tax and CGT)

7. *Compliance requirements* (e.g. ensuring compliance with requirements of stock exchange, FRC, ASB, SIB, legislation)

8. *Audit requirements* (e.g. internal audit, audit committee, contact with external audit)

A recent development of crucial importance in terms of accounting responsibilities has been the effect of 'Cadbury'. The Cadbury Report was prepared by a high-powered committee set up in May 1991 by the Financial Reporting Council, the London Stock Exchange and the accountancy professions. Its brief was to examine the financial aspects of corporate governance. The final report, incorporating a *Code of Best Practice* was published in December 1992 and is gradually being implemented. All 'listed' companies (i.e. those quoted on the Stock Exchange) have to comply with the code, and all unlisted companies are 'encouraged' to do so. A further committee will be set up in June 1995 to check on progress.

The responsibilities of finance departments in the private sector have, since 1991, also been sharpened and greatly extended by the new regulatory framework consisting of the *Financial Reporting Council* (FRC) and its related organisations, the *Accounting Standards Board* (ASB) – which replaced the old Accounting Standards Committee – the *Urgent Issues Task Force* (UITF), and the *Financial Reporting Review Panel*. The ASB has been extremely active in publishing exposure (i.e. discussion) documents (FREDs), and *Financial Reporting Statements* (FRSs) which supersede the old Statements of Standard Accounting Practice (SSAPs).

3.4 RESPONSIBILITIES OF PUBLIC-SECTOR FINANCE DEPARTMENTS

As a result of legislation resulting in such initiatives as local management for schools (LMS), compulsory competitive tendering (CCT) for such tasks as refuse collection and school meals, the formation of trust hospitals and fund-holding General Practitioners in the National Health Service, the traditional structure of public-sector finance departments has had to change substantially.

Local Authorities

The number and structure of departments within local authorities must necessarily reflect the responsibilities of that authority. At the time of writing, there were three types of local authority: District Councils, County Councils and Metropolitan District Councils. Metropolitan District Councils combine the responsibilities of the other two for areas of high population density.

Section 151 of the Local Government Act 1972 says:

> every local authority shall make arrangements for the proper administration of their financial affairs and shall secure that one of their officers has responsibility for and the administration of those affairs.

All local authorities, therefore, have a statutory requirement to appoint a Director of Finance to ensure that the financial dealings of the Council meet the requirements of law. There is also a requirement for that person to:

> maintain an adequate and effective external audit of the accounts of the body and he, or his authorised representative, shall have a right of access at all times to such documents of the body which relate to the accounts of the body (Accounts and Audit Regulations 1983: Regulation 4).

All local authorities have always maintained a clear division between capital and revenue transactions, but the division is becoming increasingly blurred by the way central government imposes control on both types of expenditure. The opportunities for income generation by a local authority are extremely limited and there is no profit motive as in a business organisation.

A typical structure for a Local Authority District Council's Finance Department is shown in Figure 3.4. For a Council with greater responsibilities the structure would be much larger and would include a greater number of qualified accountants, to whom the Director of Finance would be able to delegate responsibilities.

Within a local authority as a whole, other departments also have financial responsibilities and many of them also have to use that money to meet other legislative requirements. The importance of close co-operation between departments cannot therefore be under-estimated.

The officers of all authorities, of whatever type, must must provide advice to the elected members, who ultimately make the decisions about how to spend the money.

National Health Service

NHS hospital trusts

In the past, hospitals have been allocated money through a local health authority which they have then spent up to that limit. The day-to-day financial transactions were carried out by a small number of officers within the hospital while the monitoring of the expenditure was carried out by the health authority.

26

Figure 3.4(A) Organisation Chart of a District Council

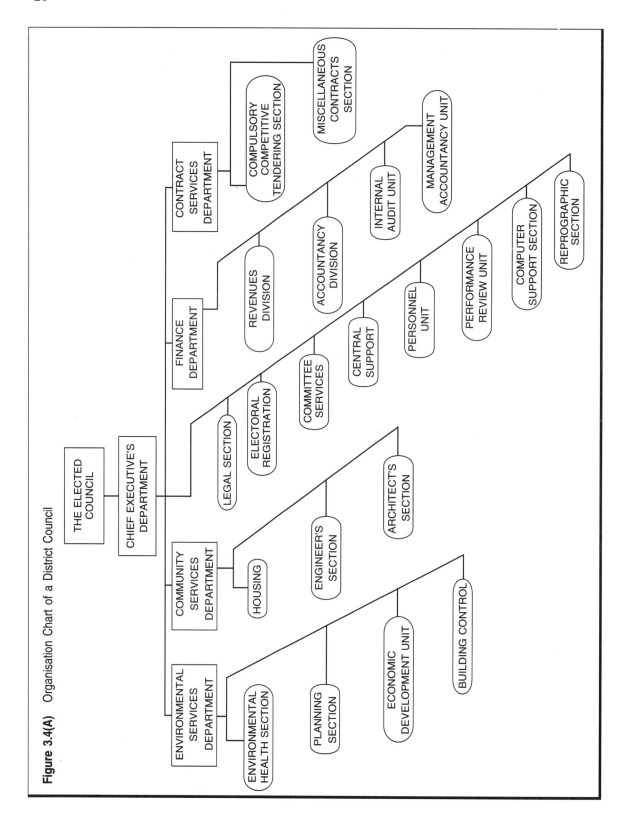

Figure 3.4(B) Organisation Chart of a District Council's Finance Department

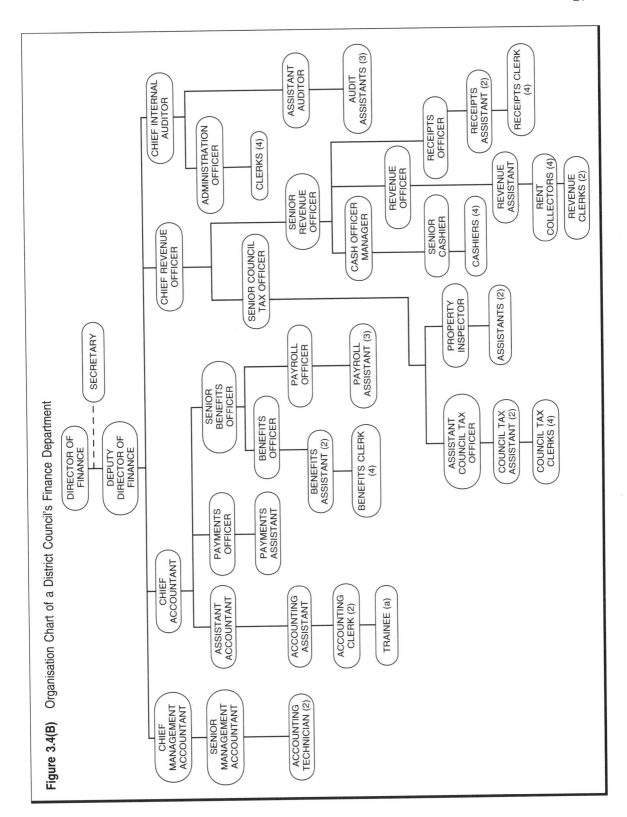

Many hospitals have now been given 'trust' status. This has meant a fundamental change in their financial responsibilities and procedures. Such hospitals must have a Trust Board, similar to the board of directors of a commercial company, and have to 'sell' their services to 'customers'. These include health authorities, which enter into block contracts for the services to be provided, fund-holding general practitioners who may pay on a cost-per-case basis, and other hospitals or organisations which wish to purchase particular services. The areas of freedom and constraints under which a trust hospital can operate are strictly laid down by central government and have to be rigidly adhered to.

These requirements and changes have led to the need for larger finance departments, an example of which is shown in Figure 3.5

Not all the new appointments are additional personnel. Some recruits have been transferred from the relevant health authority. Others already existed within the hospital but have had their jobs redesignated. A number of management teams, each of which includes a member of the finance department and a consultant, have had to be established to make financial decisions. In many ways, these teams have a matrix-type relationship within the hospital structure.

The Director of Finance plays a key role in the running of the hospital. He or she is a member of the Trust Board and of the hospital's management team, as well as having the responsibility for the financial affairs of the hospital.

Fund-holding GPs

An entirely new departure in accounting responsibilities in the 1990s has been the development of fund-holding general practitioners within the National Health Service. The stated objectives of the 'funding' are to make the health service more cost-conscious, provide 'better value for money', increase the quality of patient care, rationalise the use of hospital resources and improve communication between GPs, hospitals and the paramedic services.

At the time of writing (1994), a practice must care for at least 9000 patients in order to become fund-holding. The practice must have staff with expertise in budgeting, information technology and management. The staff must also be able to administer and monitor the practice fund (sums in excess of £2 million are commonly involved). The fund is expected to cover staff costs, the provision of drugs and charges for using hospital resources and community services (such as health visitors and district nurses).

The practice manager has direct responsibility for the control of the financial resources, for contract negotiation, for quality control

Figure 3.5 Organisation Chart of a NHS Trust Hospital Finance Department

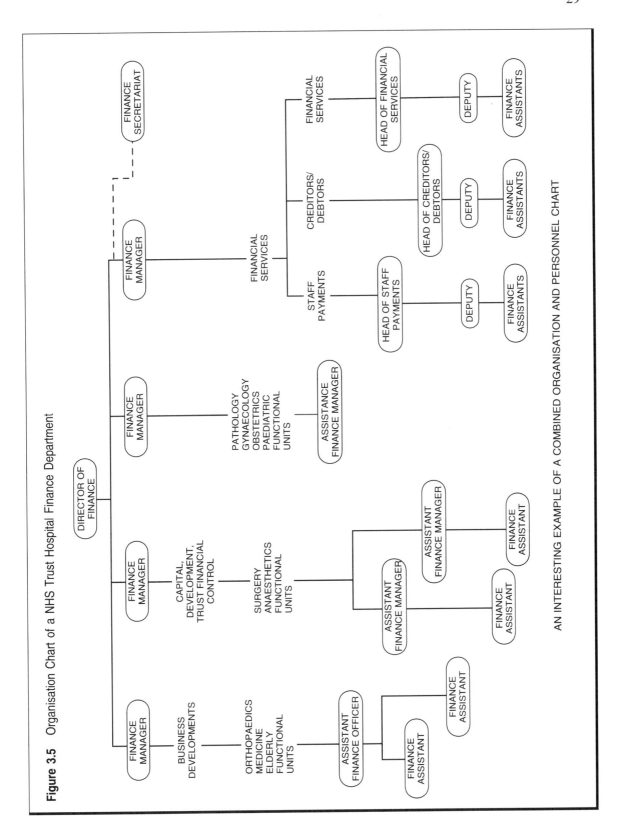

AN INTERESTING EXAMPLE OF A COMBINED ORGANISATION AND PERSONNEL CHART

and for monitoring the waiting-list situation in compliance with the Patients' Charter. Responsibilities also exist for the validation of invoices and other charges, and for the authorisation of payments. There is also responsibility for the fund-holding database and the timely production of monthly financial reports, copies of which have to be submitted to the Family Health Services Authority. The insistence on proper budgetary procedures and management appraisal techniques, and the correct interpretation of what the fund-holding reports are telling the managers, are intended to lead to the implementation of carefully planned policies regarding drug costs, the utilisation of central services and the recognition of areas where patients can benefit from the provision of additional services, both 'in-house' and hospital-based.

The Overall Picture

As a result of recent legislative changes, therefore, more people in the public sector are now required to have financial expertise. In additon to the examples given above, the advent of delegated budgets to schools has required school managers to have a far greater awareness of and responsibility for their own financial affairs. As we have seen, the introduction of trust hospitals has meant that within one hospital medical staff generally have had to become increasingly aware of the financial implications of their work. Financial knowledge and understanding is thus required by a far wider spectrum of people than in the past.

PRACTICAL ASSIGNMENTS

1. An extract from a job description for a Director of Finance of a trust hospital is given below. Study it carefully and then discuss any areas of similarity and any major differences between this officer and one in a private-sector company.

   The Director of Finance will be responsible for:

   - the financial management of the Trust and the production of all statutory accounts
   - ensuring financial probity and compliance with financial standing orders
   - the formulation, execution and monitoring the effectiveness of the financial control system
   - advising the Trust Board on all financial issues including banking, insurance, investment and risk management
   - the production of the necessary financial management information at regular intervals to ensure that financial targets are understood and achieved.

S/he will be required to:
- participate in the Trust's contracting strategy
- ensure that effective internal and external audit procedures exist.

2 (i) Study the structure of an organisation with which you are familiar or about which you can obtain information – your school, college, firm for which you or someone you know works.

(ii) Draw a plan of the organisational structure, showing the line, staff and other relationships which exist. Identify within that structure all those that have some financial responsibility.

(iii) Discover if, and how that responsibility is overseen by the person with ultimate financial responsibility for the organisation.

(iv) Can you suggest any improvements or alternatives?

(v) Compare your findings with those of a friend or another student.

REVISION QUESTIONS: PART I

In each of the following items, state which option best answers the question

1   Decisions of a medium-term nature are primarily:
(a) strategic decisions
(b) tactical decisions
(c) non-programmed decisions
(d) operational decisions.

2   A management information system is a fully integrated network which provides
(a) data on a wide range of topics
(b) non-financial information to management
(c) financial and statistical data only
(d) specialist management data only.

3   The 'style' of a manager who regularly discusses problems with all concerned before making a decision is said to be:
(a) autocratic
(b) democratic
(c) group
(d) consultative.

4   A job description describes
(a) the type of person needed for a particular post
(b) the responsibilities and duties connected with a post
(c) the code or reference which identifies the particular job
(d) the demands a job will make on a person.

5   A financial information system
(a) is an alternative name for double-entry accounting
(b) excludes routine book-keeping data
(c) includes financial data from all sources
(d) consists of selected accounting information.

6   Decisions based on rational thought, judgement and good sense are described as being of the
(a) economic model
(b) programmed model
(c) behaviourial model
(d) psychological model.

7   The relationship between a subordinate and his immediate superior is known as a
(a) functional relationship
(b) matrix relationship
(c) staff relationship
(d) line relationship.

8   A chart illustrating the way a particular decision leads on to the need for further decisions is known as a decision
(a) plan
(b) matrix
(c) map
(d) tree.

9   Estimates of future staffing needs are known as
(a) manpower plans
(b) staffing analyses
(c) personnel projections
(d) organisation charts.

10   Strategic decisions are primarily concerned with the
(a) long term
(b) medium term
(c) short term
(d) immediate situation.

11   A financial information system is concerned with financial
(a) planning

(b) control and planning
(c) administration, control and planning
(d) management.

12 Management by exception is usually associated with
(a) strategic and tactical decisions
(b) tactical and operational decisions
(c) operational and programmed decisions
(d) operational and non-programmed decisions.

13 A description of the qualifications and experience that a candidate for a particular post would be expected to have is known as a job
(a) analysis
(b) specification

(c) outline
(d) description.

14 Crisis management decisions are usually taken
(a) without rational thought or planning
(b) in the heat of the moment
(c) with only limited consultation
(d) by poor managers who lack foresight.

15 Using accounting information to plan future activities is known as
(a) management accounting
(b) creative accounting
(c) progressive accounting
(d) policy accounting.

MAJOR ASSIGNMENT: PART I

INTRODUCTION

Kelley Ltd is an established manufacturing company making plastic products for sale at home and abroad. Paul Kelley is the managing director of this medium- sized private limited company and Thelma Roberts is the new financial director.

The company is very keen to expand and diversify into new areas. At a recent board meeting, Thelma Roberts proposed that the company should consider buying one of two other companies which were available for sale and which were sited on the nearby industrial estate. Both the companies are involved in light engineering and are established family concerns. Thelma has provided the following data in relation to them:

STIRKE ENGINEERING CO. LTD

Phil Stirke is the managing director of the firm and holds 75% of the shares. The remainder are owned by his daughter Barbara Stirke. The Stirke family would be prepared to sell the firm of £3 million to Kelley Ltd.

The following financial summary, produced by the company's accountants, covers the most recent five years for which data is available:

Year	Turnover (£m) (£m)	Cost of Sales (£m)	Overheads and Expenses (£m)	Capital Employed
19–1	3.8	1.3	1.6	4.0
19–2	3.7	1.4	1.7	4.2
19–3	4.0	1.6	1.65	4.2
19–4	4.2	1.5	2.1	4.4
19–5	5.0	1.75	2.2	4.8

A local firm of valuers has placed the net asset value of Stirke Engineering as £2.5 million. The capital employed of £4.8 million consists of long-term bank loans and amounts owed for £2.3 million. Kelley Ltd would be prepared to take over all the assets and liabilities for the purchase consideration of £3.0 million.

Stirk Ltd presently employs an average of 100 workers. The company employment structure is as follows:

Managing director	Phil Stirke
Financial director	Helen Stirke
Production director	Norman Gee
Marketing director	Karen Smith

Personnel director	Harry Pollard
Chief accountant	Paul Bang
Office manager	Sarah Colclough
Assistant accountant	Cheryl Cooper
Production manager	Harvey Barnes
Sales manager	Barry Rhodes
Personnel assistant	Peter Lee

In addition, there are 5 office staff, 4 plant supervisors, 2 regional sales managers, 6 sales representatives, 2 maintenance operatives, 5 full-time plant operatives.

Stirke Engineering Ltd have full order books for the next eighteen months and are hopeful of securing new contracts in the Middle East and in Asia,

POYNTER PRODUCTS LTD

Managing director Barry Poynter, financial director Carol Richardson and local investor Ian Proudfoot own an equal shareholding in this company. At a recent board meeting, they agreed that they would be prepared to consider an offer of £1.5 million for the company.

A local firm of valuers has placed the net asset value of Poynter Products Ltd at £950 000. The company has a total capital employed of £1.8 million consisting of bank loans and short-term debts of £850 000. Kelley Ltd would be prepared to take over all the assets and liabilities of the company. The following data is available in respect of the company for the past five years.

Year	Turnover (£000)	Cost of Sales (£000)	Overheads and Expenses (£000)	Capital Employed (£000)
19–1	550	275	150	800
19–2	600	310	170	830
19–3	1000	520	230	1000
19–4	1200	630	400	1500
19–5	1250	650	520	1800

The company as a number of new product lines and already a third of their business is in the export market. Barry Poynter believes that turnover will expand by 25% over the next three years because of the firm base the company has established in Europe.

Poynter Products Ltd presently employs an average of 70 workers. The company structure is as follows:

| Managing director | Barry Poynter |
| Financial director | Carol Richardson |

Production director	Andy Talbot
Marketing director	Carol Handley
Accountant	Jane Campion
Administration manager	Brendan Smith

In addition, the company employs 3 office managers, 8 full-time office staff, 3 sales managers, 6 sales representatives, 1 plant manager, 4 plant supervisors and 40 full-time and part-time plant operatives.

REQUIRED:

Prepare a report to the board of directors of Kelley Ltd on the proposals put forward by Thelma Roberts. Your report should compare the organisation and management structures of the firms, and discuss the financial and other matters relevant to the evaluation of the proposals. Illustrate your report with suitable methods of data presentation.

PART II BUDGETARY PLANNING AND CONTROL

TOPIC OVERVIEW

Most people know what they intend to do with their next wage packet or instalment of grant or pocket money long before they receive it. They also know by Friday how they intend to spend the week-end and, by Easter, ideas for the summer holiday have been considered. The plans may not have been made consciously, but they are there 'in the back of the mind'.

Business organisations also have to plan their activities and the way they intend to spend their future income. Without a definite plan to work to and against which to compare results, an organisation is like a rudderless ship and is likely to run into difficulties very quickly indeed. This process of planning is known as *budgeting*. Part II of this book examines the principal techniques and problems concerned with budgeting and how these are handled in the business situation.

Chapter 4 sets out the framework within which all budgets are prepared, and looks in detail at the preparation of cash budgets whilst Chapter 5 applies the principles to certain other types of budgets.

If budgeting is to be of real value, there must be an effective appraisal of the outcome and proper action taken where this is necessary – either by controlling the expense item concerned, boosting a revenue-earning item, varying the budget allocation to the item, or by examining the implications for the rest of budget. This appraisal, and possible subsequent action, is part of the process of budgetary *control* and is independent of budgetary *planning*: just because there is good budgetary planning, it does not follow that there is effective budgetary control. Chapter 6 considers the importance of effective control and the principal methods.

Chapter 7 is concerned with some of the more sophisticated budgetary techniques whilst Chapter 8 examines the application of spreadsheet analysis to budgets. The whole budgetary procedure is one which lends itself admirably to this technique.

4 BUDGETING AND THE CONTROL OF CASH RESOURCES

Think about this . . . *Why make plans for the future?*

4.1 NATURE OF BUDGETS

A budget is a 'plan for the future'. It consists of a statement summarising the anticipated activities of an organisation for the foreseeable future. Separate budgets are usually prepared for each of the main operating departments of an organisation: a commercial firm, for example, may prepare separate budgets for sales, stocks, production, personnel, cash, debtors and creditors, purchases, and materials usage. These budgets may be either

- *quantitative* – e.g. based on *tonnes* of materials, *number* of workers, *operating hours* of machines, *volume* of sales); or
- *financial* – e.g. based on *costs* of materials, wages, electrical power, or *income* from sales); or
- a combination of both.

Obviously there is a close link between the two, but there can be independent variations. A considerable rise in the *price* of raw materials can cover up savings on the *quantity* of raw materials actually used. Also, many of the individual budgets are interlinked. Materials usage budgets have obvious links with the stock, purchases and the production budgets. Almost all budgets have to link with the cash budget. In addition, principal budgets can be broken down into sub-budgets: cash, for instance, can be split into sub-budgets for capital expenditure, revenue income and expenditure, debtors and creditors (which are also linked to sales and purchases budgets). The revenue costs budget itself can be further divided into sub-budgets for selling and distribution costs, administration costs, and direct costs.

Individual budgets are summarised in a *master budget*. Usually, there is a *key factor* (sometimes known as a *principal budget factor*) to which all other budgets have to relate. This will determine the 'operating level' – or *level of attainment* – at which the budget is set. What it is will depend upon the circumstances and nature of the organisation concerned. Anticipated sales volume and income is a common key factor. This usually determines such items as the volume of production, desired stock levels and the cash available to service departments. However, productive capacity (where this is limited in relation to the demand for the product) may equally well prove to be the key factor, as can also labour availability. In central and local government, revenue (i.e. the maximum amount politicians are prepared to raise through taxation) is likely to be the crucial factor.

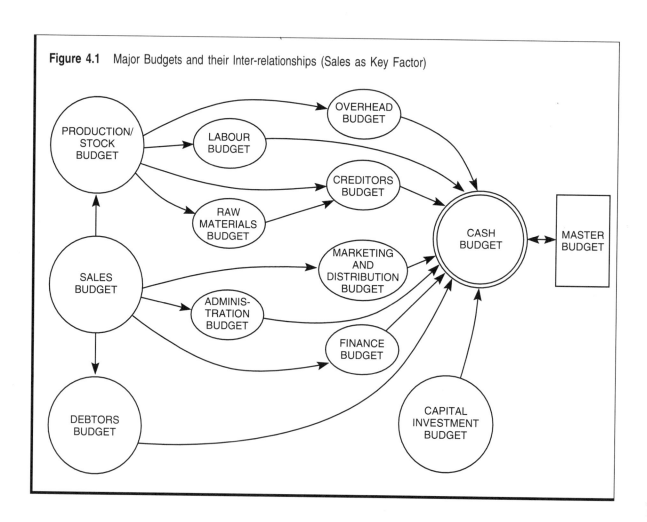

Figure 4.1   Major Budgets and their Inter-relationships (Sales as Key Factor)

4.2 THE BUDGET PROCESS

Data for budgets is obtained partly from past records and partly from estimates of future trends and possibilities. The main steps are shown in Figure 4.2.

Figure 4.2
The Budgetary
Process
	1. Before the financial year begins:
	    (a) Identification of the key factor or factors.
	    (b) Production of 'quantity' budgets by the individual departments.
	    (c) Conversion of quantity budgets into financial budgets within the framework set by the key factor.
	    (d) Transfer of departmental budgets to the master budget with modifications to individual budgets where necessary. This is likely to be a drawn-out process involving many meetings and considerable negotiation with and between departments. Disagreements – often arguments – between departments are likely to arise, and it can be several months before the problems are resolved.
	    (e) Approval procedures by 'top management' before implementation

	2. During the financial year concerned
	    (a) Periodic comparison of actual performance against budget with regard to both volume and finance. The difference between the actual and the expected (budgeted) to the date in question is known as a *variance*.
	    (b) Investigation of the variances – undertaking where necessary:
	        (i) remedial action
	        (ii) revision of sub-budgets affected.
	        For example, if sales are falling far short of target, why is this? Can a sales drive remedy the position? If not, should there be cut-backs in the production and other related budgets? Variances are considered in more detail in Chapter 7.

Note that the above means that at any one time the process means that the staff concerned are likely to be involved with three budgets – the out-turn figures for the previous financial year, the implementation of the budget for the current year, and the preparation of the budget for the forthcoming financial year.	3. After end of financial year (a) Review of the past year and the final variances in terms of 'out-turn' figures – i.e. the final actual – and consideration of the implications of these for the present and future years' budgets.

4.3 CASH BUDGETS

The format of a budget (i.e. the way in which it is set out) will depend largely on the type of budget concerned. In its simplest form, it consists of a tabular presentation with a column for the budgeted figure and a column for the actual figure to date. One of the most common budgets is that for cash. Cash budgets are usually broken

EXAMPLE 4.1

Draw up the cash budget for A. Wholesaler who, on 1 January, had £34 000 as cash-in-hand and at-bank. His anticipated cash receipts and payments for each quarter of the year following are:

(£000)	Jan–Mar	Apr–Jun	Jul–Sep	Oct–Dec
Cash sales	102	200	155	450
Receipts from debtors (previous credit sales)	151	123	62	98
Cash purchases	23	12	20	15
Payments to creditors	121	168	255	180
Sundry trade expenses	14	12	16	20
Repairs, maintenance	2	2	2	2
Rent	6	–	–	6
Tax	30	–	30	–
Purchase of new assets	–	200	70	–

SOLUTION

Quarter	Jan–Mar Budget £000	Jan–Mar Actual £000	Apr–Jun Budget £000	Apr–Jun Actual £000	Jul–Sep Budget £000	Jul–Sep Actual £000	Oct–Dec Budget £000	Oct–Dec Actual £000
Opening balance	34		93		24		(156)	
Receipts:								
Cash	102		200		155		458	
Debtors	151		123		62		98	
Other								
TOTAL INFLOWS	287		416		241		400	
Payments:								
Cash purchases	23		12		20		15	
Creditors	121		168		255		180	
Trade expenses	14		12		16		20	
Rent	6		–		6		–	
Tax	10		–		10		–	
Drawings	20		–		20		–	
New assets	–		200		70		–	
Other								
TOTAL OUTFLOWS	194		392		397		215	
Closing Balance	93		24		(156)		185	

Notes:

(i)   The columns for the 'actual' receipts and payments will be entered up as soon as the amounts are known.

(ii)   The units used in each column – e.g. £, £000, tonnes – should be clearly stated and care should be taken when extracting such data from the table.

down into short periods (say, into months) which are listed across the page. Each column commences, where appropriate, with the opening balance in hand (either in terms of money values or quantities). Allowances are then made for additions and deductions during the period, and it ends with the closing balance. The final balance for one period, or sub-period, will be the opening balance of the next. A budget statement set out in this way is sometimes called *commitment accounting*, since it refers to anticipated commitments. This terminology is in wide use in local authority accounting since its use in this way is approved by the Chartered Institute of Public Finance and Accounting (CIPFA). This, however, can lead to confusion as the term can also be used to debts already incurred but which have not yet been paid, these amounts being added on to actual expenditure (and deducted from the original budgeted figure) in order to give the balance still available, or 'uncommitted'. It is obviously important that any fund-holder should be aware of the amount of such 'uncommitted' funds.

TASK 4.1 Examine the budget of A Wholesaler above. What action does it indicate should be taken, and when?

TASK 4.2 On 1 January. A. Hopeful – a retailer – had a cash balance in hand of £3800. His anticipated monthly receipts from cash sales in the first three months are £12 000, £13 000 and £14 000 respectively and receipts from debtors £15 000, £14 000 and £13 000.

Cash purchases in each of the three months are expected to be £1500, £4500 and £2000 respectively and payments to creditors £11 000, £15 000 and £24 000 respectively. Wage costs will amount to £800 per month and PAYE to £150 per month. Schedule D tax of £3000 will be payable in January. Electricity costs of £650 are expected to be payable in March and office expenses in each of the three months are expected to be £100, £250 and £200 respectively. Rent and rates of £2000 will be payable in March. Advertising in each of the three months is expected to cost £250, £200 and £100 and a new cash till will be purchased in February at an anticipated cost of £1000.

A. Hopeful's actual income in January was £10 000 from cash sales and £13 000 from debtors. His actual expenditure was £2200 for cash purchases, £9000 to creditors, £800 for wages and £150 for PAYE, £150 for office expenses and £100 for advertising. He paid the Schedule D tax when due.

REQUIRED:
1. A cash budget for the three months.
2. Identification of what action may need to be taken, and at what time.
3. Insertion of the actual amounts for January and a statement of any further action which might be advisable.

4.4 THE BENEFITS AND PROBLEMS OF BUDGETING

Major benefits result from carefully planned and properly administered budgets, but a number of difficult problems have to be faced. The benefits and the problems are summarised in Figure 4.3.

Figure 4.3

Budgeting: benefits and problems

Possible Benefits

- A budget provides a plan for the whole organisation to work to and should lead to 'goal congruence' (i.e. all departments work for the same ends).
- It sets a standard against which to measure actual performance.
- Budgets enable the 'actual' figures to be compared against the anticipated ones. Variances are shown up and remedial action can be taken.
- A 'management by exception' approach tends to develop, i.e. it becomes clear where the problems are on which managers should concentrate.
- Budgets *should* serve to encourage and develop communication between departments.
- Individuals may become involved in corporate planning, thus improving morale and increasing motivation.
- A 'forward-looking' attitude among staff tends to develop.
- Potential problems are often identified in good time.
  Note in Example 4.1 that the trader can foresee that he is likely to run into a cash shortage in March and must therefore take action (e.g. arrange a short-term loan) in good time.
- Budgets are indicative of good management practice.

Some of the Problems

- Accurate estimation of the figures to be included, particularly in times of fluctuating or sharply rising cost levels.
- Ensuring that departments limit their requests (for items such as staff and finance) to levels which they reasonably need – and which are within the framework of the resources likely to be available (see the section on zero based budgeting in Chapter 7).
- Obtaining the necessary co-operation and communication between departments that effective budgeting makes necessary. Far from encouraging communication, the budgeting process often leads to conflict between departments.
- The danger of 'over-budgeting' – i.e. breaking down of budgeted figures into so many sub-heads of expenditure that it becomes restrictive.
  The problem can be overcome in part by allowing budget-holders limited powers of transfer of funds between sub-heads of expenditure – a process known as 'VIREMENT'. The power to vire is particularly limited in central and local government work where the expenditure on particular items must, by law, be limited to that previously approved by Parliament or Council.
- Carelessly-framed budgets, in which amounts allocated to heads of expenditure are in excess of requirements, can cover inefficiencies and wasteful expenditure.
- The amount of preparatory work involved and the (usually) limited time-span within which to do it
  Remember that the staff concerned usually have other responsibilities as well and may at any one time be concerned with three different budgets – the 'outcome' of the one for last year, the implementation of the one for this year, and the preparation of the one for next year.

TASK 4.3   Consider an organisation with which you are familiar – club, school, college, business firm – and identify the precise problems which you think would arise in attempting to prepare a realistic budget for next year.

4.5 ASSIGNMENTS ON CASH BUDGETS

Be careful of the following points when tackling assignments:

- Cash budgets must include *all* cash receipts and *all* cash payments *these must be included in the periods actually received or paid, not when earned or incurred.*
- Notional expenses are *not* included in a cash budget.
  Examples include depreciation, bad debts and bad debts provision. Such items are sometimes included in cash budget questions as a 'catch'.
- Calculation of some of the items may be required.
  The wording of the question must be given careful consideration to determine exactly what is needed.
- Care should be taken to determine the period during which an item is received or paid.
  Again careful reading of the question is required as the period concerned may not be immediately clear.

PRACTICAL ASSIGNMENTS

[1] Howard Clayton has agreed to purchase the business of Simon Ridley with effect from 1 January. Ridley's assets and liabilities have been agreed at:

	£		£
stock at cost	26 000	creditors	20 000
debtors	50 000	bank overdraft	25 000

Howard intends to improve the liquidity position of the business by introducing £15 000 capital immediately. It is expected that 10% of Simon's debtors will prove to be bad but that the remaining debtors will settle their accounts by the end of January subject to a cash discount of 2½% The creditors will be paid during the first week of January. Sales for the first months of Howard's ownership are forecast as £32 000, £30 000, £32 000 and £28 000 respectively. All sales will be on credit with customers being allowed a two-month credit period. Howard expects his purchases to be: January £18 000; February £22 000; March £20 000; April £18 000. He expects to receive one month's credit from his suppliers. General cash expenses will be £200 a month and there will be personal drawings of £500 per month.

REQUIRED:
A cash budget for the first four months of Howard's ownership, showing clearly the balance at the end of each month.

2 At the close of business on 30 June, a retail firm had cash and bank balances amounting to £50 000. It is anticipated that cash income from sales over the next six months will be (£000) 500, 600, 400, 360, 210, and 340 respectively. In addition, arrangements have been made for a loan of £100 000 which will be received in August.

Purchases from suppliers during the months June to December will amount to (£000) 450, 500, 460, 390, 380, 730, 1080 respectively. It is the policy of the firm to pay creditors on the 15th of the month following purchase.

Arrangements have been made for the disposal during August of some old equipment which originally cost £20 000 and against which a depreciation provision of £8000 has been built up. A trade-in allowance of £10 000 is to be allowed against the purchase price of £30 000 for the replacement equipment. This will be paid on 15 October.

General running expenses of the firm are estimated at £20 000 per month.

The firm has agreed to pay a commission of 10% on sales to its staff as from the beginning of July. It is to be paid quarterly in arrears at the end of the month following the end of the quarter concerned.

Rent is payable quarterly in advance. The firm's policy is to pay it on the 15th of the month before it is due. Rent for the quarter July–September is £15 000. Thereafter, it will be £20 000 a quarter.

REQUIRED:
(a) A cash budget for the period 1 July to 31 December.
(b) A statement of what action may be necessary, and at what points in time.

3 Jean Roberts owns and manages a block of flats in the seaside town of Scarborough. The block contains eight small flats and a luxury flat. The property has a market value of £160 000. Jean has decided that from 1 January of next year, five of the smaller flats will let all year round to local tenants. Three small flats and the luxury flat will be let as holiday accommodation. Jean has produced the following forecast information for the year as from 1 January next:

(i)   *Bank balance* as at 1 January £2000
(ii)   *Price per week for the holiday flats*
(iii) *Anticipated bookings*

Period	Luxury flat (£)	Small flats (£)
Easter (i.e. April)	120	70
May	130	75
June	175	100
July	200	130
August	250	130
September	180	100
October	175	80

(a) Holiday flats

Jean, who has built the business up over the last seven years, forecasts the following bookings for the holiday flats:

Luxury flat: 2 weeks at Easter.

4 weeks in each of the months May–September inclusive.

2 weeks in October.

A special booking has been made by a local business man for the period 1 November to 31 December at £300 per month payable at the end of each month.

Small flats: All three flats for 2 weeks at Easter.

All three flats for 4 weeks in each of the months May–September.

Two flats for 3 weeks in October.

A 10% deposit is payable on each holiday booking and the balance is payable on arrival. Jean expects that 10% of all deposits will be received in February, 40% in March and 50% in April

(b) Other flats.

The other (five) flats are let all year round for £50 per week. Payment is made weekly on Fridays in cash. It is expected that an average of 2 weeks' rent will be lost on each flat as a result of the turnover in tenants.

(iv) *Expenses*

Repairs will be undertaken by David Jones, a local builder and joiner, during February at an estimated cost of £900. *Advertising* in the *Scarborough Guide* will cost £500, payable in July. The *business rate*, amounting to £1300 for the year, is payable in two equal instalments in January and July. *General expenses* of £50 per month are payable at the end of each month. *Redecoration*, costing £600, will be carried out in March and paid for in April. A *schedule D tax liability* for £550 is outstanding and is payable in two equal instalments in January and July. As regards *heating and lighting,* all flats are metered and paid by tenants. Jean pays for lighting, etc. in the hallways in the month following the quarter concerned. She estimates that amounts payable will be £300 (in April), £500 (in July), £600 (in October) and £550 (in January of the following year).

One cleaner is employed throughout the year at a wage of £25 a week. The other is employed for a total of 24 weeks between 1 April and 30 September at £18 a week.

(v) *Drawings*

Jean plans to draw £600 a month from the business for her own personal use.

REQUIRED:

(a) A detailed cash budget for the business covering the period from 1 January to 31 December.
(b) A forecast profit statement for the year ending 31 December.
(c) Jean is considering selling the block of flats and investing the capital sum of £160 000 in securities. What return would be required on the capital to maintain her present income?

4   Derek Olsen owns and manages a picture-framing business. He also buys and sells prints. He owns the shop premises and a two-bedroom flat above which have been valued at £75 000. On 1 January, he had a balance on his business bank account of £1500. He believes that times are hard and that he will have to struggle in order to survive. He has produced the following forecast information for the next eight-month period:

(£)	Nov	Dec	Jan	Feb	Mar	Apr	May	Jun
Income Earned								
Sale of prints	1800	2000	1500	2000	1200	900	1300	1800
Framing	850	700	800	1000	600	800	900	1100
Expenditure incurred								
Purchase of prints	650	650	500	1500	300	800	600	1000
Framing materials	250	250	250	250	250	250	250	250

All prints are sold for cash. For picture framing and restoration, customers pay a 10% cash deposit and the balance the following month. Prints are purchased from suppliers on credit terms of two months. Picture framing materials are paid in cash for which a 12% discount is received.

The flat above the shop is let at £200 per month. This is always received on the last day of the preceding month. The business rate for the premises is £2000 payable in two equal instalments in May and November. Wages of £40 a week are paid to a part-time assistant. Electricity charges are paid by direct debit each month in the sum of £100 and the estimated phone bill is £800 per annum, payable in January, April, July and October. General expenses, including cleaning and insurance, are calculated at £30 per week and a schedule D tax assessment of £600 must be paid in equal instalments in January and July. Derek is a keen footballer and has agreed to a business sponsorship scheme for his local club which will cost him £200, payable in February.

Derek intends to draw £600 monthly from the business account for his own purposes.

REQUIRED:
(a) A cash budget for the period January to June inclusive.
(b) Derek is considering purchasing a new machine for picture framing at a cost of £3500. This, he believes, will increase his turnover by 15%. Derek is concerned how he should finance the purchase. Advise him on his options.
(c) Advise Derek on the advantages of producing detailed cash budgets. Do you think his worries are justified concerning his business position?

5 Callcar Ltd was formed with an authorised capital of 250 000 ordinary shares of £1 of which 100 000 were issued at par for cash and fully subscribed. An initial operational plan was drawn up to cover the first sixteen weeks of the company's working, it being divided into four periods of four weeks each.

Six cars were purchased for cash at the beginning of period 1 at a price of £18 000 each *less* 10% trade discount. The plan assumed that four of these cars would be on general hire Monday to Friday as from the beginning of week 2 of period 1 at the weekday rate of £30 per car per day. All six would be on hire on Saturdays and Sundays at the weekend rate of £54 per day per car. Market research has convinced the directors of a full take-up by customers.

A contract has been signed with a local firm for the two cars not on general hire to be made available on a chauffeur-driven basis Mondays to Fridays inclusive at a rate of £180 per day per car. Payment for each period is to be made at the end of the first week of the subsequent period.

A contract has been signed with a local garage for the supply of fuel. It is expected that 200 gallons will be consumed in the first period, 400 gallons in the second and third, and 500 gallons in the fourth. The cost has been agreed at £2.50 per gallon with payment on one month's credit.

Depreciation at 25% per annum on the diminishing balance method will be allowed on each of the vehicles.

It is anticipated that there will be fixed costs of £600 per period. Full-time staff wages of £4080 will have to be met in periods 1 and 2, and of £5280 in periods 3 and 4. Part-time staff wages of £1080 per period will have to be met commencing in the first week of period 2.

Servicing costs of £900 per period will have to be met commencing in period 1. Initially, servicing will be carried out overnight but it is planned to buy two additional cars at the start of period 4 for £19500 cash each subject to 10% trade discount. These cars will enable vehicles to be temporarily withdrawn from operation for servicing and other purposes.

REQUIRED:
(a) An explanation of the terms (i) authorised capital, (ii) issued capital and (iii) issue of shares at par.
(b) A statement explaining the advantages to a firm of preparing cash budgets.
(c) A cash budget for Callcar Ltd for the first four periods of their projected operation.
(d) A description of any difficulties which the budget reveals and a statement of the various options open to the company in meeting them.

5 BUDGETING – THE WIDER PICTURE

Think about this . . .
A common practice in departments when drawing up their budgets is to take last year's figures, and simply add on a percentage to each of the various items to allow for likely increases in costs. What problems can you see arising from this practice, and how can they be overcome?

5.1 SALES BUDGETS

Although cash budgets lie at the heart of any organisation or division, sales budgets are usually crucial – at least to commercial organisations – since sales are usually the 'key factor' on which other budgets depend.

Sales budgets may be concerned with sales *volume*, sales *costs*, or sales *revenue* – or with all three. The sales volume budget is important because of its implications for the production budget, whilst the sales cost and sales revenue budgets are important because of their implications for the cash budget and the indication they give of gross profit margins.

Sales budgets are often broken down by region, product or by 'responsibility' – for example, by individual sales representative or particular branch. Sales costs can also be analysed into

- sales expenses (e.g. sales representatives' salaries, commissions, travelling and hotel allowances);
- sales administration charges (e.g. secretarial and office expenses connected with sales including postage and stationery);
- routine advertising (e.g. press, radio, TV, posters, general sales literature and promotions);
- market research costs;
- distribution costs (e.g. product handling, packing, transport, warehousing costs);
- product launch costs.

Product launch is concerned with the costs of establishing a new product on the market. Such launches involve exceptional expenditure on advertising and promotional activities. Usually a special budget is provided which is distinct from that concerned with routine advertising and promotion.

Sales budgets are based on information drawn from a variety of sources. which include:

- Historical records of demand levels and trends.
- Forecasts of business and economic trends, and employment trends in sales areas concerned.
- Possible effects of sales campaigns.
- Market research information, including reports from sales staff.
- Level of competition.
- Size and quality of the sales force and the effectiveness of the distribution system.
- 'Customer appeal' and suitability of product design (including packaging) in relation to changing market conditions.

EXAMPLE 5.1   For the months January–March of next year, Juxta Ltd anticipates monthly sales of 4500, 3000 and 2000 units respectively. Fixed costs have been estimated at £12 000 and there will be a unit variable of £10. Unit selling price has been agreed at £20. The following represents a simple sales budget based on this data:

| Month | Projected sales (units) | Sales costs | | | Sales Revenue (£) | Net Revenue (£) |
		Fixed costs (£)	Variable costs (£)	Total costs (£)		
January	4500	12 000	45 000	57 000	90 000	33 000
February	3000	12 000	30 000	42 000	60 000	18 000
March	2000	12 000	20 000	32 000	40 000	8000
Quarterly total	9500	36 000	95 000	131 000	190 000	59 000

TASK 5.1   Juxta Ltd intend to undertake an intensive sales campaign in March and estimate that, as a result, monthly sales of 6500, 5500 and 5000 units will be achieved in the second quarter of the year. The increased production will increase fixed costs to £14 000 per month, and the unit variable will rise to £12 as a result of an agreed pay award. Selling price is to be reduced to £17.99

REQUIRED: 1.   A sales budget for the second quarter of the year.
2.   A comment stating, with reasons, whether the company should go ahead with the sales initiative. Is there any additional information you would like before coming to a final decision?

5.2 STOCK BUDGETS

Stock – or 'materials'- budgets follow the same broad principles as cash budgets but may be based upon the *quantities* of the stock involved as well as on the financial values. In most organisations, there will be various stock budgets, each dealing with a different department and even for particular items within departments. There may, for example, be budgets for stationery (possibly sub-divided into the stocks required by individual sections), raw material stocks, fixtures and fittings, equipment, furniture and furnishings and general consumables. The budgets may relate to items which are for direct consumption within the organisation or may be in respect of items which are intended for resale. In the latter case, if financial valuations are to be included, care must be taken not to confuse purchase costs with sales revenues without adjustment for the profit element involved.

EXAMPLE 5.2   The following is an extract from a consumable stock budget for the data processing section of a small office:

Ref No	Description	Unit	Opening stock	Consumption	Desired closing stock	Purchase requirement	Unit Cost	Total Cost
			(units)	(units)	(units)	(units)	(£)	(£)
Z170	Paper	Carton	50	80	60	90	30	2700
P460	Laser labels	Box	100	60	100	60	5	300
H216	3.5" disk	Box	200	80	150	30	15	450
C235	Ribbons	Carton	140	200	100	160	20	3200

If the 'usage' element of the budget differs from the 'purchases' element, there will obviously be a variation in the closing stock.

5.3 PRODUCTION BUDGETS

A production budget is a forecast of future production levels. The budget will have to take into account productive capacity (i.e. how much the existing or potential factory, labour and raw material resources are capable of producing), the levels of stocks it is wished to maintain, the storage – or 'shelf' – life of the product (note that it may be worthwhile to 'manufacture for stock' if a product can be stored and sales are likely to rise in the future) and the anticipated sales trends (this, of course, will have been set out in the sales budget). Production budgets are, for the most part, based on a simple equation, namely:

$$\text{opening stock} + \text{production} = \text{sales} + \text{closing stock}$$

Given three of these four factors, it is of course possible to calculate the remaining one.

EXAMPLE 5.3   *The sales of Spa Novelties Ltd take place mainly in June and July (to meet the August and September demands from retailers) and in October and November (to meet the Christmas needs of retailers). The managers consider that 1500 units is the minimum stock level which they should hold of one of their product-lines.*

The firm commenced April with this minimum stock holding and sales forecasts indicated that unit sales for the following six-month period were likely to be: April 3000; May 40 000; June 8000; July 9000; August 4000; September 2000. The management was anxious to maintain a steady flow of production and decided to produce 6000 units per month of the six-month period.

The production budget for the six-month period, showing the closing stock at each month-end, is as follows:

(units)	April	May	June	July	August	September
Opening stock	1500	4500	6500	4500	1500	2500
Planned production	6000	6000	6000	6000	500	2000
Stock available	7500	10 500	12 500	10 500	6500	4500
Anticipated sales	3000	4000	8000	9000	400	2000
Closing stock	4500	6500	4500	1500	2500	2500

Note:
1. The planned production builds up sufficient closing stocks to maintain the minimum stock-holding during July – the month when summer sales peak.
2. After August, the planned production rate exceeds anticipated demand – hence the progressive build-up in closing stocks. This may – or may not – be desirable depending upon likely demand after September.

TASK 5.2   Assume, in Example 5.3, that the management decide that they wish to keep the closing stock level at 2500 units in September and thereafter since market research indicates that the Christmas demand is likely to swing to other products.

Produce a revised production budget for August and September giving effect to this decision. What other budgets are likely to be affected by the altered figures?

5.4 PERSONNEL BUDGETS

A personnel budget is usually made up of a number of sub-budgets, each dealing with a different grade of labour or different skill required. Direct labour budgets for each skill needed will reflect anticipated output and must therefore dovetail into the production budgets. The budgets have to be prepared with considerable care. On the one hand, they have to take into account such complications as the incidence of holidays, sickness, resignations and the time needed to train the staff concerned. On the other hand, no cost-conscious firm can afford to employ more workers than necessary, labour often being the most costly element in the manufacturing process. The form of the budget will reflect the needs and problems of the firm concerned and the type of work in which it is engaged. The following illustration is a highly simplified example of a direct labour budget.

EXAMPLE 5.4 *A firm's production budget anticipates an output of 100 000 units of a particular product during the forthcoming year. Each unit normally requires 10 hours of direct labour. The firm currently has available 500 workers of the grade and type needed. Normal working practice calls for a 40-hour working week, and the factory operates a 48-week year. Experience has shown that absences due to sickness and other reasons reduces labour availability by 10%. The following is the direct labour budget for the operation:*

Anticipated production (units)	100 000
Labour hours required (hours) 100 000 × 10	1 000 000
Present labour available 500 × 40 hrs × 48 wks × 90%	864 000
Labour shortfall (hrs)	136 000
Proposals for meeting the shortfall:	

TASK 5.3
1. Example 5.4 was stated to be a highly simplified example. Consider the various factors which could complicate such a budget.
2. The Example 5.4 did not include proposals for meeting the shortfall. Map out your own suggestions, and comment on any difficulties or problems which may be involved.

The main factor determining the direct labour requirement is the level of *production* at which it is intended to operate. However, allowance may have to be made for 'idle time' since, even in the most efficiently organised establishments, it is seldom possible to keep men and machines at full activity all the time.

EXAMPLE 5.5   *A production run of 800 000 units is planned. Normal production is 100 units per man-hour, but machines are normally idle for 10% of the time. The man-hours required are:*

$$\frac{800\,000}{100} \times 110\% = 8800 \text{ man-hours}$$

PRACTICAL ASSIGNMENTS

1 A firm's estimated sales are as follows:

	units		units
July	9000	November	12 600
August	10 500	December	8000
September	12 000	January	7000
October	9900		

Each unit of the product requires 20 kg of material A (cost £1 per kg) and 40 kg of material B (cost £1.50 per kg). Stocks on hand at 1 July: 160 kg of material A and 390 000 kg of material B. The management of the firm has decided that, as from 1 July, the firm's policy should be to have enough stocks of material in hand at the end of each month to meet exactly the requirements for the following month's anticipated sales.

REQUIRED:
A materials purchase budget for the months July to December, showing both the quantities and the costs of materials to be purchased each month.

2 The sales director of a company anticipates that sales of a new line during the forthcoming January will be 500 units at a unit price of £120. He expects demand to increase by 15% in February and to remain at that level despite a 12% increase in selling price on 1 April. As a result of an advertising campaign in May, it is expected that monthly unit sales will rise to 750 units in June and subsequently.

The monthly fixed expense allocation has been agreed at £10 000 and the unit variable will remain constant for the foreseeable future at £40.

REQUIRED:
A sales budget for the period 1 January to 31 July.

3 A firm produced the following forecast information regarding two new products which it proposes to introduce in the new year. These will replace its existing products.

Product A

The estimated monthly sale for January, February and March are 800 units. It is expected that in April sales turnover will increase by 20% and by a further 15% for the months of May and June. The unit selling price will initially be £25 but this will be decreased by 8% from 1 June. The product's share of overheads will be £3000 monthly, and the unit variable will be £20.

Product B

Sales for product B are expected to be 600 units in January increasing by 8% for the months February to May inclusive. The proposed price increase in June, however, is expected to reduce demand by approximately 7.4%. The initial unit selling price will be £18, but this will be increased to £19 on 1 June. The product's share of overheads will be £7000 monthly with a unit variable of £5.

The sales volumes and revenues for the month of June is expected to remain constant for both products for the rest of the year.

REQUIRED:
(a) A sales budget for the period 1 January to 30 June.
(b) Which product is likely to achieve the largest net revenue over the initial six-month period?
(c) It has been suggested that the firm should consider cancelling the production of the product which proves to be the least profitable at the end of the year. Suggest reasons why this might be unwise.

4 Taskers Ltd manufacture a number of products including artificial Christmas trees. A new design is being introduced for sale both at home and abroad. Production will begin in July and the product will be available for sale to 'the trade' from August onwards.

The production manager has been with the company for a number of years. He is a man of 'fixed' ideas and has a reputation for 'not being easy to get on with'. He states that monthly production during July and August will be limited to 40 000 trees because of holiday rostas. Thereafter, production will be at 80 000 trees a month except for December when, again due to holidays, production will drop to 40 000 trees. He argues that to produce more than 80 000 units would mean increasing his fixed costs out of all proportion.

A young marketing executive has recently been appointed and, provided there is the sales promotion scheme which he has planned for the spring and summer, he is satisfied that he will be able to obtain orders for 30 000 trees in July, 40 000 in August, 60 000 in September, 120 000 in October, 80 000 in November, and 10 000 in December.

REQUIRED:
(a) The managing director is worried that there may be a large amount of stock left on hand at the end of the year if the production plans go

ahead as suggested. Prepare a statement of the balance which will be left on hand at the end of the year *if* production and sales data listed above prove accurate, and suggest ways of coping with the problem.

(b) A detailed month-by-month production and sales budget based on the above data.

(c) A note of any problems which the budget reveals, together with suggestions how the problems could be overcome.

BUDGETARY CONTROL

Think about this . . . *The cost of raw materials used by a firm during a particular period was well in excess of the budgeted amount. What could have been the reasons for this and, in each case, could the situation have been avoided?*

6.1 THE NEED FOR CONTROL

Ineffective monitoring and control of budgets can result in:

- Failure to realise that budget allowances are being exceeded until it is too late to take remedial action.
- Inefficiencies as a result of faulty budget pre-planning not being identified.
- Failure to reveal 'over-budgeting' – this is a situation in which the framework of a budget is so detailed and restrictive that it acts as a straightjacket on the firm's operations.
- A rash of unnecessary expenditure. This often arises at the end of the financial year when budget holders spend unused allocations to prevent them 'going back into the kitty', or because they feel that underspending will result in a reduction in the succeeding year's allocation.

This must be distinguished from a situation in which budget-holders act cautiously throughout the year and delay 'postponable' (but necessary) expenditure until late in the year as a guard against unanticipated contingencies which might arise.

6.2 BASIC CONTROL TECHNIQUES

The first essential in good budgetary practice is the preparation – in the first instance – of a carefully planned and properly structured budget (see Chapters 4 and 5). Budgetary *planning* is, however, no substitute for budgetary *control*. Budgetary control is an entirely independent – but equally vital – exercise. Unless there is effective control as well as sound planning, the time and resources spent on budgeting will be completely wasted.

Budgetary control consists primarily of comparing actual income or expenditure with the budgeted amount. This exercise is usually undertaken periodically throughout the financial year as well as after the end of it.

Periodic Checks

In the simplest form of periodic check, the budgeted figure is compared with the actual incurred (or received) to date. This comparison, when viewed along with balances from other budgets, may be of use in indicating the current cash position, but is of limited value to the budget-holder. The data is of more use if, in the case of expenditure, amounts which are 'committed' (e.g. in respect of goods ordered) are added to the amounts actually expended. The balances then inform the budget-holder of the uncommitted funds which he can still spend. Note that this is using the term 'committed' in its other sense (see p. 43 for the two ways in which this word can be used, and be careful to guard against the confusion which can arise).

EXAMPLE 6.1   *The following shows a simple expenditure budget for a small branch office:*

Financial Year ending 31.12.-1

Department/Branch No: 106

Date: 31.3.-1

	Budget	Funds Spent	Funds Committed	Funds Spent & Committed	Funds Uncom- mitted
Wages	200 000	49 000	–	49 000	151 000
Rent	10 000	2500	–	2500	7500
Insurance	15 000	10 000	–	10 000	5000
Stationery	60 000	20 000	12 000	32 000	28 000
Maintenance	9000	5000	1000	6000	3000
Electricity	13 000	4000	–	4000	9000
Transport	5000	1500	500	2000	3000
Repairs	6000	2000	1200	3200	2800
Telephone	3000	2500	–	2500	500
	321 000	96 500	14 700	111 200	209 800

TASK 6.1 Examine the budget in Example 6.1. Comment on any matters of significance revealed by the figures. Discuss what further information might be helpful and suggest possible lines of action.

The 'Out-Turn' Figures

The actual figures for any period, as opposed to the budgeted figures, are known as the *out-turn* figures. They are usually presented in columnar form showing the budgeted amounts, the actual expenditures (the out-turn figures), and the difference between the two. The summary of out-turn figures can be for any particular period, but obviously the most important one is that for the full accounting year. A major problem with out-turn figures is that they are usually not available until some weeks – often several months – after the end of the period concerned.

The difference between budgeted and out-turn figures is known as the *variance*. A *favourable* variance exists when actual expenditure is less than the budget (or when actual income is greater than the budgeted figure); an *adverse* variance exists when actual expenditure exceeds the budgeted (or when actual income is less than the budgeted.) The *Think about this . . .* section at the start of this chapter suggested, of course, an adverse balance on the cost of raw materials.

Variances form the basis of the *feed-back* to management, which is the information arising from out-turn figures which may indicate the need for management action. The feed-back is said to be *negative* if the action it promotes is aimed at reducing the effect of the variance. If, for instance, the feed-back suggests wastage of materials in production, then action should be considered which will reduce that wastage. It is described as *positive* where action is indicated which may increase the variance – such, for instance, as when better quality raw materials are needed which can only be acquired at a higher price.

6.3 INVESTIGATION OF VARIANCES

Variances require investigation in case action needs to be taken. The important factors which have to be considered are:

- significance
- trend
- controllability.

Significance

Budgets at the best are only *estimates*, and estimates are always subject to a margin of error. Small variations between the budgeted and the actual figure usually have little significance and a certain degree of 'tolerance' can be allowed before the variance is regarded as *significant*.

Trend

Even if the variance is within the permitted tolerance, a watchful eye should be kept on the *trend*. If, for example, the amount of an adverse variance in (say) direct labour costs as a *percentage* of output is steadily increasing, then action may be called for even though the variance – as yet – is still within the tolerance limits. It is always better to foresee problems (and to take appropriate action) before they arise than to solve them after the event.

Controllability

Look back to the *Think about this* . . . section at the start of the chapter. No doubt you were able to suggest a number of possible reasons for the increasing expenditure on raw materials – increases in the purchase price per unit, purchase of inferior quality materials, wastage through faults in the material, wastage due to bad workmanship, new designs needing larger quantities of materials are some examples. Which reasons would be within the control of the firm itself?

Obviously, wastage due to inefficient processing is clearly something which is within the control of the firm. Increases in the unit cost of electricity is something which is not so clearly within the control of the firm, though the level of consumption *may* be within its control. Costs which are outside the control of the firm are usually known as 'non-controllable' costs.

Variances – whether controllable or not – may be significant, not only in themselves, but for the implications they may have for the rest of the budget. A significant rise in the cost of raw materials, though outside the control of the firm, could mean that the selling price of the product may have to be revised.

Figure 6.1 illustrates, in flow-chart form, a basic procedure which can be followed in investigating variances.

Variances in controllable costs must be interpreted carefully. A favourable variance in the cost of materials may be the result of the

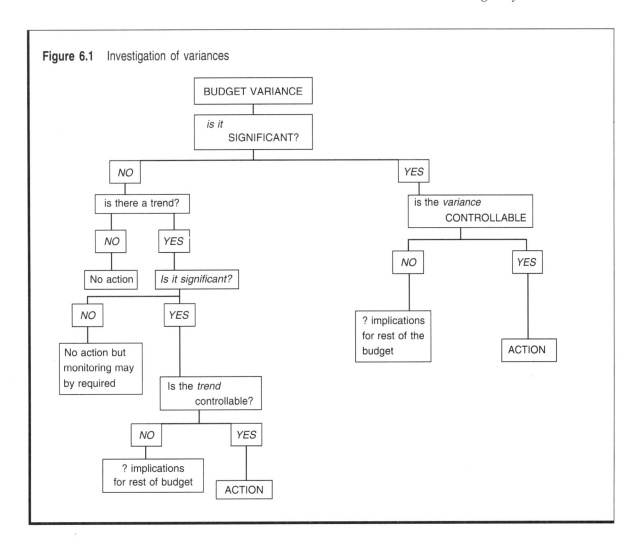

Figure 6.1 Investigation of variances

purchase of sub-standard materials, or a glut in the supply causing a temporary reduction in price, rather than the more efficient use of materials. An adverse variance may be due to an increase in the purchase price beyond the control of the firm – unless cheaper supplies are available from alternative suppliers.

PRACTICAL ASSIGNMENT

1   In year 1, A&M Ltd budgeted as follows (all figures in £000):

sales 500; cost of sales 200; administrative expenses 20; wages and salaries 40; rent 70; advertising 50; distribution costs 60; miscellaneous expenses 10.

The out-turn figures for the year were:

sales 510; cost of sales 190; administrative expenses 25; wages and salaries 50; rent 70; advertising 45; distribution costs 50; miscellaneous expenses 15 In year 2, the budgeted figures were:

sales 600; cost of sales 240; administrative expenses 25; wages and salaries 50; rent 80; advertising 70; distribution costs 65; miscellaneous expenses 10. The out-turn figures for the year were:

sales 580; cost of sales 250; administrative expenses 30; wages and salaries 65; rent 95; advertising 50; distribution costs 60; miscellaneous expenses 20.

REQUIRED:

A suitable tabular statement of the variances in each of the two years together. Add comments on the significance of each and suggest what action, if any, might have to be taken. State what further information you would like.

7 FURTHER TECHNIQUES IN BUDGETING

Think about this . . . *The expenses of an organisation often vary with the level of a particular activity – e.g. sales or manufacturing in commercial concerns. How are fluctuations in the activity likely to affect the rest of the budget and what complications is this going to cause in control?*

7.1 FLEXIBLE BUDGETING

Budgets do not normally allow for adjustments should levels of output or activity differ from those originally anticipatcd. *Flexible budgets* are designed so that the budgeted figures can be adjusted to the levels which should occur at the actual level of production. This requires:

- each cost item to be classified according to its 'cost behaviour' (see below);
- each item to be adjusted according to a 'basic variable' (such as output in terms of hours worked or units produced).

This is a complicated process since costs are seldom either wholly fixed or directly variable. The main patterns of cost behaviour are:

(a) directly variable   (b) semi-variable (linear)
(c) variable (curvi-linear)   (c) semi-variable (curvi-linear)

Directly Variable

The relationship is that costs are simply some multiple of the cost of the basic variable. The cost of directly variable items at any level of production can be found by simple proportion, e.g. if 3000 units incur a cost of £600 in a directly variable item, then 9000 units should incur a cost of:

$$£600 \times \frac{9000}{3000} = £1800$$

Alternatively, it may be easier if calculations are required for a number of different output levels to calculate cost per unit. In the above case:

$$\text{Cost per unit} = \frac{£600}{3000} = £0.2$$

$$\text{So } £9000 \times £0.2 = £1800$$

An example of this type of cost is raw materials.

Semi-Variable (Linear)

Strictly, these costs should be described as fixed-variable as they consist of a fixed element plus a factor × production element. An example could be wages in a situation where a basic wage is paid, plus an additional payment per unit produced. Suppose that the basic wage cost £5000 and that an additional £2 is paid for each unit produced, then the wage cost for a production run of 3000 units would be

$$£5000 + £(2 \times 3000) = £11\,000$$

The wage cost for an output of 1 500 units on the same basis would therefore be

$$£5000 + £(2 \times 1500) = £8000$$

and for 9000 units

$$£5000 + £(2 \times 9000) = £23\,000$$

Variable (Curvi-Linear)

These costs increase parabolically, i.e the cost varies according to the square of the number of units produced. A factor must be calculated which represents the curve of the sequence and this is multiplied by the square of the output. Suppose that in a particular case this gives us a factor of 0.00006. The item cost for an output of 3000 units would therefore be

$$£(0.00006 \times 3000^2) = £(0.00006 \times 9000\,000) = £540$$

For an output level of 1500 units the cost would be $£(0.00006 \times 1500^2) = £135$

and for an output of 9000 units $£(0.00006 \times 9000^2) = £4860$.

Semi-Variable (Curvi-Linear)

These costs have a fixed element together with an element which varies exponentially to output. Maintenance costs might possibly vary in this way. Some maintenance work has to be carried out on machines even if they stand idle; beyond a certain level of operation, maintenance costs can begin to rise very sharply. The arithmetic computation involves taking the fixed element and adding to it the parabolic element calculated in the same manner as for curvi-linear variables. Suppose that the curve is represented by a factor of 0.001 and that the fixed element amounts to £200. The maintenance cost for the production of 3000 units would therefore be:

$$£2000 + (0.001 \times 3000^2) = £11\,000$$

and for 1500 units

$$£2000 + (0.001 \times 1500^2) = £4250$$

and for 9000 units

$$£2000 + (0.001 \times 9000^2) = £83\,000.$$

EXAMPLE 7.1 *For a budgeted output of 2000 units, it is estimated that direct materials cost will be £5000, wages £10 000, maintenance costs £1700, lubricants £400 and managerial salaries £4000.*

Materials are directly variable to production. Wages are semi- variable/ linear with a fixed element of £6000. Maintenance is semi- variable/curvi-linear with a fixed element of £1600 and a factor of 0.00005 and lubricants are variable/curvi-linear with a factor of 0.0001. Managerial salaries are a fixed cost. Show the budgeted costs for outputs of 1500 units, 2000 units and 3000 units.

OUTPUT (units)	2000 £	1 500 £	3 000 £
Materials (unit cost of £2.5)	5 000	3 750	7 500
(directly variable)			
Wages (fixed cost £6000 + unit cost £2)	10 000	9 000	12 000
(semi-variable/linear)			
Maintenance (£1600 + units^2 × 0.00005)	1 800	1 712.5	2 050
(semi-variable/curvi-linear)			
Lubricants (units^2 × 0.0001)	400	225	900
(variable/curvi-linear)			
Managerial salaries	4 000	4 000	4 000
(fixed)			
TOTAL COSTS	21 200	18 687.5	26 450

7.2   ZERO BASED BUDGETS (ZBB)

Budgets are usually prepared by taking the figures for the previous period and adjusting them for inflation or any anticipated changes in output. This assumes that the amount allowed previously can continue to be justified – which is not always the case. ZBB overcomes this by allocating 'nil' to each department under each head of its budget, and then requiring justification 'from scratch' for any amount requested. The advantage of ZBB is that it *should* ensure that departments need every coin asked for; the disadvantage is the work and the time to prepare, check – and argue about – the figures to be included.

7.3   BUDGETED PROFIT STATEMENTS

A slightly different type of 'budget' than the ones considered so far are profit and loss (P&L) forecasts. These differ from cash budgets in that they follow the same general format and principles as conventional trading and profit and loss accounts except that they are based on estimated figures instead of known 'historical' figures as in the case of conventional accounts. This means that P&L forecasts:

- are based on revenue items only; capital receipts and payments are excluded;
- make allowances for accruals and prepayments; cash budgets take account only of amounts actually received or paid out;
- include such notional items as depreciation and bad debts provisions which cash budgets do not;
- do *not* commence with an opening cash balance brought forward;
- show the *profit* or *loss* for the period; this is quite different from the net cash flow;
- do *not* include appropriations in respect of tax and dividend payments (these are charged to the appropriation section); cash budgets include the actual payments made during the period concerned;
- are *not* affected by changes in stock-holding levels and changes in credit terms and practices – but cash budgets are to the extent that the changes affect cash payments during the period;
- are often for complete quarters, half-years or for the full year; they are not broken down into such short periods as cash budgets.

EXAMPLE 7.2   *The purpose of this illustration is to compare a three-month cash budget with a P&L forecast for the same period.*

The following information relates to Green Ltd for four months from June to September inclusive (irrelevant data has been omitted)

(£000)	June	July	Aug	Sept
Cash balance in hand	50			
Cash sales		60	20	40
Credit sales	400	410	390	420
Purchases (all credit)	185	173	180	148
Cost of sales		184	172	186
Wages, salaries, commissions		84	82	100
Depreciation		18	18	18
Purchase of new equipment		210		
Rent	5	5	5	5
Office expenses	36	74	78	96
Advertising	26	24	28	20
Provision for redemption of debentures	2	2	2	2
Anticipated bad debts provision				20
General expenses		8	8	10

Trade creditors are allowed one month's credit. The new equipment will be paid for two months after its installation in July. All purchases are on credit and are paid for in the month following. Office expenses and advertising are also paid in the month following that in which they are incurred. All other expenses are paid for in the month in which they arise.

The *cash budget* for the three months July–September inclusive would be as follows:

(£000)	July	Aug	Sept
Cash balance	50	166	230
Receipts: cash sales	60	20	40
credit sales	400	410	390
Total cash inflow:	510	596	660
Payments:			
Purchases	185	173	180
Wages, etc.	84	82	100
Rent	5	5	5
Office expenses	36	74	78
Advertising	26	24	28
General expenses	8	8	10
New equipment			310
Total cash outflow	344	366	711
Cash balance carried forward	166	230	(51)

P&L forecast for the three months ending 30 September 19–

	(£000)	(£000)
Sales		1340
Cost of sales		512
Gross profit		828
Wages, salaries, commissions	266	
Depreciation	54	
Rent	15	
Office expenses	248	
Advertising	72	
Bad debts provision	20	
General expenses	26	701
Net profit		127

Note: The allocations to debenture redemption provision are an appropriation of profit and therefore are not charged to the P&L as such.

Calculations in respect of some expense items may involve projections based upon their 'cost behaviour' (see 7.1 section on *flexible budgeting*). It may also be necessary to calculate missing data. It is often useful to remember in this connection the basic form of the trading account, i.e.

(a) opening stock plus purchases less closing stock = cost of sales; and
(b) cost of sales plus gross profit = sales.

If any one item is missing from the account, it is possible to calculate it.

TASK 7.1   A firm expects to commence the year with an opening stock of £30m. It anticipates sales of £160m and plans to end the year with a closing stock of £33m. It works on a gross profit margin of 40%.

Calculate: 1. The desired gross profit.
2. The cost of sales (i.e. sales *less* gross profit)
3. The amount of purchases necessary, given the opening and closing stocks as above.

Questions can arise when it is desired to maintain a steady rate of turnover (i.e. sales at cost divided by average stock). Given the initial data, it is then possible to calculate the desired closing stock. Given also the desired gross profit margin, it is also possible to calculate the purchases necessary to achieve that figure.

EXAMPLE 7.3 *The sales objective of a firm for the forthcoming year is £200m with a profit margin (profit as a % of sales) of 25%. It will be commencing with stock of £20m and it wishes to maintain an average rate of turnover of 6.*

(Call the closing stock 'x')

Sales at cost $= 200 \times 75\% = £150\,m$

$$\text{Rate of turnover} = 6 = \frac{150\,m}{\frac{(20\,m + x)}{2}}$$

$$6 \times \frac{(20\,m + x)}{2} = 150\,m$$

$$\frac{120\,m + 6x}{2} = 150\,m$$

$$\frac{6x}{2} = 150\,m - \frac{120\,m}{2} \qquad \text{i.e. } 3x = 90\,m$$

$$x = 30\,m$$

TASK 7.2 A firm anticipates sales will be £300m. It desires a profit margin (profit as a percentage of sales) of 20%. It has an opening stock of £12m and wishes to have a rate of turnover of 10. Calculate the level of closing stock and the amount of the purchases.

Remember: (a) *cost of sales = sales less the profit margin*
(b) *opening stock plus purchases less closing stock = cost of sales*

PRACTICAL ASSIGNMENTS

1 R.N. commenced business on 1 November 19-8 taking over the assets and liabilities of Carr Ltd at the following book values on that date:

	£
Fixed assets at cost	8000
Depreciation – fixed assets	4000
Stock at cost	2000
Debtors	4000
Creditors	3000
Bank overdraft	1000
General expenses accrued	100
Rent prepaid	2000

The debtors and the creditors figures relate to sales and purchases for the month of October 19-8.

R.N. paid £10 000 into the business bank account on 1 November 19–8 and paid the liquidator of Carr Ltd the net value of the assets taken over.

R.N. forecasts and plans for the four months to 28 February 19–9 were:

(i)   Gross profit will be at a constant rate of $33\frac{1}{3}\%$ of sales.

(ii)   All sales are on credit and are expected to be £6000 a month in November and December, £13 500 in January and £12 000 in February. Although in the past sales have been on one month's credit, R.N. will extend the credit period to two months on all sales from 1 November 19-8

(iii) R.N. proposes to exercise a strict control over stock levels and to organise his purchases so that his rate of stock turnover for each month is 2. All purchases will be made on terms of one month's credit.

(iv)   Wages will be £500 per month payable on the last day of the month.

(v)   General expenses will be £400 per month : one-eighth of the general expenses are outstanding at the end of each month.

(vi)   Rent for the year commencing 1 March 19–9 will be £7200 paid on 15 February 19–9.

(vii) R.N. decided to continue depreciation at the rate of 10% per annum on cost on all assets in use at the end of the financial year.

(viii) During December new fixed assets will be purchased for £3000 cash and an existing asset, original cost £800, on which two years' depreciation had already been allowed will be sold for £200 cash.

REQUIRED:

(a)   A stock budget for the four months ending 28 February 19–2 showing clearly the stock held at the end of each month.

(b)   A cash budget for the four months ending 28 February 19–2 showing clearly the bank balance at the end of each month.

(c)   A forecast trading and profit and loss account for the four months ending 28 February 19–2 for R.N.

(d)   Comment on the situation of the firm as revealed by the cash budget and by the profit an loss account.

2 The balance sheet of Handley Ltd at 31 December last was as follows:

(£)		Cost	Deprec-iation	Net
Fixed assets:	Equipment	75 000	27 000	48 000
Current assets:	Stock	66 000		
	Debtors	84 000		
	Bank	79 500	229 500	
Current liabilities:	Creditors	135 000		
	Accrued debenture interest	750		
	Proposed dividend	18 750	154 500	75 000
				123 000
Long-term liabilities:	10% Debenture issue (2020)			30 000
				93 000
Financed by:				
	Ordinary shares of £1			60 000
	Retained earnings			33 000
				93 000

Notes:
(i) The actual sales for December, and the anticipated for the first quarter of the new year are:

(£)	Credit sales	Cash sales
December (actual)	84 000	42 000
January	100 500	60 000
February	123 000	67 500
March	120 000	68 000

Trade debtors pay on average one month following date of purchase.

(ii) The purchases (all on credit) for the above four months are £135 000, £142 500, £150 000 and £156 000 respectively. All are paid in the month following the purchases.

(iii) The debenture interest is paid quarterly in arrears at the beginning of January, April, July and October of each year.

(iv) Arrangements have been made to sell equipment on 31 January which originally cost £30 000 (depreciation provision £12 000) for £10 000. Replacement equipment costing £90 000 will be purchased during February.

(v) Depreciation is allowed on a monthly basis at 20% p.a. on cost.

(vi) Wages of £13 500 and general expenses £5500 will be paid monthly. Rent of £27 000 per annum is payable on 1 January each year for the year to the following 31 December.

(vii) The proposed dividend will be paid during March.

(ix) The gross profit margin on sales is 20%.

REQUIRED:

(a) A cash budget for each month of the first quarter of the new year.

(b) A forecast trading and P&L account for the three months to 31 March.

BUDGETING WITH A SPREADSHEET

In yesteryear, accounting was primarily book-keeping – that is, 'writing up the books' manually. In what ways have IT applications superseded the old routines? Can you suggest, with reasons, one particular area ideally suitable for computerisation?

8.1 BUDGETING AND COMPUTERS

The benefits of computerised spreadsheets for monitoring current performance and predicting likely outcomes in budgets cannot be underestimated.

Personal computers (PCs) are increasingly being used for this purpose. Their use is by no means limited to word processing. One of the most popular programs available on a PC is, in fact, a spreadsheet, and this is particularly useful as a budgeting tool. It allows forward plans to be drawn up for whatever time periods are required, actual figures to be inserted and provides the opportunity to compare forecast with actual figures. Once the spreadsheet is set up, calculations are quickly carried out, and it is therefore possible to explore a number of 'what if' situations.

This chapter looks at an example of the use of a spreadsheet for budget purposes. If you have access to a spreadsheet package you will find it helpful to use it for the investigations required. Because of its highly practical nature, the chapter itself should be looked upon as an assignment.

8.2 THE TIME FACTOR

The periods of time used in any budget analysis can vary according to the nature of the detail required. Annually, quarterly or monthly are the most usual, but some firms work on 13 four-weekly periods. Weekly figures are also used, but it is important to note that, because of the way the calendar works, some years have 53 weeks. Comparisons year on year are usually made, so it is important to ensure that like periods of activity are compared.

8.3 A PRACTICAL APPLICATION

In Chapter 4 a budget was established for A. Wholesaler, showing his opening balance, his expected income and expenditure, and the balance expected to be carried forward at the end of each quarters of the year. What amounted to a spreadsheet was then set up to contain these figures, and to allow the totals for the actual transactions and the individual variances to be shown. The initial spreadsheet is shown in Figure 8.1.

In order to have some idea of how his business was functioning, A. Wholesaler then kept a record of his transactions. His first quarter's figures are shown in Figure 8.2, together with a variance figure – the difference between the actual and the budgeted amounts.

Figure 8.1 Cash Budget for A. Wholesaler

QUARTER	Annual budget	Jan-Mar budget	actual	variance	Apr-Jun budget	actual	variance	Jul-Sep budget	actual	variance	Oct-Dec budget	actual	variance
	£000	£000	£000	£000	£000	£000	£000	£000	£000	£000	£000	£000	£000
Opening balance	34	34			93			24			-156		
Receipts:													
Cash	915	102			200			155			458		
Debtors	434	151			123			62			98		
Other	0	0			0			0			0		
TOTAL INFLOWS	1383	287			416			241			400		
Payments:													
Cash Purchases	70	23			12			20			15		
Creditors	724	121			168			255			180		
Trade expenses	62	14			12			16			20		
Rent	12	6			0			6			0		
Tax	20	10			0			10			0		
Drawings	40	20			0			20			0		
New assets	270	0			200			70			0		
Other	0	0			0			0			0		
TOTAL OUTFLOWS	1198	194			392			397			215		
Closing balance	185	93			24			-156			185		

Figure 8.2 Cash Budget and Period 1 Actuals for A. Wholesaler

QUARTER	Annual budget	Jan-Mar budget	actual	variance	Apr-Jun budget	*actual	variance	Jul-Sep budget	*actual	variance	Oct-Dec budget	*actual
	£000	£000	£000	£000	£000	£000	£000	£000	£000	£000	£000	£000
pening balance	34	34	34	0	93	44	-49	24	-25	-49	-156	-205
Receipts:												
Cash	915	102	120	18	200			155			458	
Debtors	434	151	136	-15	123			62			98	
Other	0	0	0	0	0			0			0	
TOTAL INFLOWS	1383	287	290	3	416			241			400	
Payments:												
Cash Purchases	70	23	50	27	12			20			15	
Creditors	724	121	110	-11	168			255			180	
Trade expenses	62	14	30	16	12			16			20	
Rent	12	6	6	0	0			6			0	
Tax	20	10	10	0	0			10			0	
Drawings	40	20	40	20	0			20			0	
New assets	270	0	0	0	200			70			0	
Other	0	0	0	0	0			0			0	
TOTAL OUTFLOWS	1198	194	246	52	392			397			215	
Closing balance	185	93	44	-49	24	-25	-49	-156	-205	-49	185	136

*budget figures have been used where actuals not known

The variance column in Figure 8.2 has been calculated systematically by subtracting the actual figure from the budgeted figure. In the receipts a negative figure means that less has been received than was expected and for payments a negative figure means that less money has been paid out than was expected. By comparing Figures 8.1 and 8.2 you can see that the spreadsheet has been set up to show the closing balance from the first quarter's actual figures as a revised actual opening balance for the next quarter, although the remaining actual amounts in that quarter are not yet known. This figure has also been used to project the 'actual' opening balance for the remaining quarters, on the assumption that the budget figures for those quarters are correct.

TASK 8.1 In the light of these figures, what problems is A. Wholesaler likely to have to face? What action do you think he should take?

Assume that, in fact, A. Wholesaler did nothing and the figures for the second quarter were as follows (all figures in £000):

Cash receipts: 210; Debtors 110; Cash purchases 10; Creditors 150; Trade expenses 10; Purchase of new assets 180.

These amounts were also entered into the spreadsheet, which is shown in Figure 8.3. Notice that once again the opening balance figures for the next two quarters have changed, that for the third quarter becoming £14 000 and the projected opening balance for the fourth quarter –£166 000.

Figure 8.3   Cash Budget and Actuals for the First Two Periods for A. Wholesaler

QUARTER	Annual budget £000	Jan-Mar budget £000	actual £000	variance £000	Apr-Jun budget £000	*actual £000	variance £000	Jul-Sep budget £000	*actual £000	variance £000	Oct-Dec budget £000	*actual £000	variance £000
Opening balance	34	34	34	0	93	44	-49	24	14	-10	-156	-166	-10
Receipts:													
Cash	915	102	120	18	200	210	10	155			458		
Debtors	434	151	136	-15	123	110	-13	62			98		
Other	0	0	0	0	0	0	0	0			0		
TOTAL INFLOWS	1383	287	290	3	416	364	-52	241			400		
Payments:													
Cash Purchases	70	23	50	27	12	10	-2	20			15		
Creditors	724	121	110	-11	168	150	-18	255			180		
Trade expenses	62	14	30	16	12	10	-2	16			20		
Rent	12	6	6	0	0	0	0	6			0		
Tax	20	10	10	0	0	0	0	10			0		
Drawings	40	20	40	20	0	0	0	20			0		
New assets	270	0	0	0	200	180	-20	70			0		
Other	0	0	0	0	0	0	0	0			0		
TOTAL OUTFLOWS	1198	194	246	52	392	350	-42	397			215		
Closing balance	185	93	44	-49	24	14	-10	-156	-166	-10	185	175	-10

*budget figures have been used where actuals not known

The variance figures give an indication of possible trends.

TASK 8.2   Using the figures in Figure 8.3, what conclusions can you draw about possible trends? In the light of these trends, what advice would you give to A. Wholesaler?

Assume that the actual figures for the third quarter were (£000):
Receipts 170; Debtors 50; Cash purchases 30; Creditors 20; Trade expenses 20; Rent 6; Tax 10; Drawings 30; New assets 20.

TASK 8.3
(a) Insert these figures into the spreadsheet and hence find the actual opening balance for the last quarter.
(b) State, with justification, what you think A. Wholesaler's likely closing balance for the year will be.
(c) In the light of these actual figures, do you feel your conclusions about trends are still justified?

Information gained throughout the year is not only important for that year but as a help towards *forward planning*. It is therefore customary to draw up a draft budget for the following year about three months before the current year end. To leave it much later would mean the information on which the conclusions were based would be more accurate, but the time scale may then be too short to allow them to have much influence.

TASK 8.4
Using the new table that you have produced, and using the budget figures as actuals for the fourth quarter, produce a draft cash budget for A. Wholesaler for the next year's trading.

Now assume that, in the fourth quarter, A. Wholesaler faced an unfortunate emergency. His premises happen to be near a river, and unexpectedly heavy rain caused the river to flood and burst its banks. He had to hire a removal firm to shift what stock he could salvage to alternative premises. The cost of the removal was £5000, and the hire of the temporary premises was £4000. Although he was covered by insurance, the national scale of the disaster meant that there was some delay in agreeing the sums involved, and he had to meet the initial outlay himself.

TASK 8.5
Assuming that the remainder of his budget provision was correct, calculate the new opening balance for the following year. In what ways do you feel this should make it necessary to amend next year's draft budget?
What difference would it make if your assumptions about possible trends were assumed to be correct?

REVISION QUESTIONS: PART II

In questions 1–10, state whether the statement is true (T) or false (F).

1   If there is efficient and effective budget planning, there should be no need for budgetary control.

2   In a commercial concern, the quantity of goods likely to be sold is most likely to be the key factor.

3   A budget-holder is likely to be concerned with the budgets for three separate periods at the same time.

4   Budgets are concerned with cash flows, not with quantitative values.

5   A problem with budgets is that the allocation to expenses heads can lead to an increase in expenditure.

6   The direct labour hours budget is un-affected by idle time.

7   An adverse variance in connection with sales shows that the actual was greater than the budgeted.

8   A cash budget is not concerned with provisions set aside out of profits to cover bad debts.

9   Inefficiencies will not be covered up by faulty budgeting.

10   Monitoring of a variance may be required even if the variance itself is insignificant.

In questions 11–25, answer:
A if responses a, b and c are all correct
B if responses a and b only are correct
C if responses b and c only are correct
D if response a only is correct

E if response b only is correct
F if response c only is correct

11   Budgets may be prepared in
(a) quantitative terms only
(b) financial terms only
(c) quantitative and financial terms.

12   The key factor is
(a) any variable on which all budget items depend
(b) always the volume of sales
(c) the amount of resources available.

13   A budget-holder is usually concerned with
(a) last-year's out-turn figures and the current budget only
(b) the current budget and next year's planned budget only
(c) last year's out-turn figures, next year's planned budget, and the current budget.

14   Management by exception means
(a) considering all items in which the actual differs from the budgeted
(b) focusing attention on items exhibiting significant variances
(c) ignoring variances within the tolerance.

15   A master budget
(a) is a co-ordinated framework set by the key factor
(b) integrates subsidiary budgets into an overall plan
(c) supersedes subsidiary budgets which cease to be relevant.

16   The operational norm determined by the budget is known as a
(a) functional level
(b) level of attainment
(c) efficiency level.

17 If the stock usage element and the stock purchase element differ,
(a) a stock shortage will arise
(b) opening stock will exceed closing stock
(c) closing stock will exceed opening stock.

18 A product requires 20 man/hours work. Normal output is 190 000 units a month. Machines are idle on average for 3 minutes each hour. The man/hours required each month will be
(a) 3 990 000
(b) 3 610 000
(c) 3 800 000

19 A profit forecast does not allow for
(a) provisions for bad debts
(b) cash receipts and payments
(c) allowances for depreciation.

20 Flexible budgeting requircs
(a) revision of allocations to reflect the cost behaviour of the expenditure head concerned
(b) adjustment of allocations in line with a particular variable
(c) variation of allocations between the different heads of expenditure.

21 Budgetary control can involve
(a) periodic checks of uncommitted balances
(b) appraisal of out-turn variances
(c) use of particular techniques such as ZBB.

22 Closing stock in a materials budget may be obtained by
(a) adding opening stock and materials consumed, and deducting materials purchased
(b) adding materials purchased and opening stock and deducting materials consumed
(c) Adding materials purchased and consumed, and deducting opening stock.

23 Over-budgeting means
(a) allocating too much money to each head of expenditure
(b) breaking allocations down into too many sub-heads
(c) the overlapping of different budgets.

24 In budgeting, a variance is
(a) an agreed variation in a budget figure
(b) a departure from a budgeted figure
(c) a difference between the actual and the anticipated figure.

25 The movement of approved funding from one budget head to another is known as the
(a) transfer of funds
(b) appropriation of funds
(c) virement of funds.

MAJOR ASSIGNMENT: PART II

The directors of Osborne Ltd, a manufacturing company, have recently decided to up-date the company's financial control procedures. The accountant believes that a sound budgetary control system must be introduced as soon as possible. The following is the balance sheet of the company as 31 December last:

(£)	Cost	Accumulated depreciation	Net
Fixed assets			
Plant and machinery	60 000	21 000	39 000
Motor vehicles	24 000	9000	15 000
Office equipment	3000	1200	1800
	87 000	31 200	55 800
Current assets			
Stocks: finished goods	22 800		
raw materials	10 800		
	33 600		
Debtors	13 500		
Cash and bank	2100	49 200	
Current liabilities			
Creditors		9900	39 300
			95 100
Represented by:			
Issued capital: 90 000 Ordinary £1			90 000
Reserves: Retained profits			5100
			95 100

Notes:
(a)   The debtors (£13 500) are in respect of sales in December.
(b)   The creditors are made up of: £
             Creditors for fixed expenses   900
             Creditors for raw materials   9000
                   (of which £4200 was incurred in November
                   and £4800 in December)

Forecasted data for the six-month period following the balance sheet is:

(i)   The selling price will be £150 per unit. Anticipated unit sales are:

January	240	April	450
February	210	May	390
March	360	June	300

(ii) The planned production runs are 300 units in each of the months January to March inclusive, and 120 units in the months April to June inclusive.

(iii) Anticipated unit production costs are:

	£
Direct labour	36
Direct material	60
Variable overhead	18
	114

(iv) Direct labour and variable overhead will be paid in the month in which incurred. Fixed expenses of £900 per month are paid during the month following.

(v)   Purchases of material will be on credit. Suppliers allow two months' credit, and this is taken. The anticipated cost of purchases is:

January	£6000	April	£8400
February	5400	May	7800
March	6600	June	7200

(vi) The company plans to purchase a new machine in March for £12 000, subject to credit terms of one month.

(vii) The depreciation charges for the sixth-month period will be:

plant and machinery £4200; motor vehicles £2400; office equipment £150.

REQUIRED:

1. Prepare the following budgets for the company for the six-month period following the balance sheet:

(a) debtors' budget
(b) creditors' budget
(c) raw materials budget
(d) cash budget

2. Prepare a forecast trading and profit and loss account for the six-month period concerned.

3. Prepare a forecast balance sheet of the company's position as at the close of business on the last day of the six-month period.

4. (a) Prepare a short report on the advantages of budgetary control.
    (b) *(For students who already have a knowledge of standard costing. Other students may complete this section after completing Part III of this book.)*

Add a comment in your report on the advantages that the company would obtain by introducing a standard costing system. What factors should be borne in mind when using standard costs?

PART III COSTING AND THE MONITORING OF FINANCIAL RESOURCES

TOPIC OVERVIEW

In one sense, *all* accounting is 'costing' in that the objective is to identify and record costs. Cost accounting as such, however, is a specialised branch of accounting which has developed consisting of techniques designed to look at actual and potential costs in much more detail, and to project these figures into the future. Some aspects of costing (such as manufacturing and contract accounts) can be fully integrated into the normal double-entry process and, as such, fit snugly within the conventional double-entry framework. Other techniques – such as budgeting, break-even analysis and capital appraisal – are supplementary to the normal accounting process and structure.

Costing techniques form the basis of good financial planning and control and enables accountants to 'look to the future' as well as to take note of the past.

Chapter 9 takes a 'bird's eye view' of costing and examines one particular area – namely absorption costing whilst chapter 10 looks at another particular technique, namely marginal costing, which is fundamental to most costing calculations. Chapters 11 and 12 consider manufacturing accounts, an important costing application which is integrated with the normal double-entry process. Finally, Chapters 13 and 14 are concerned with standard costing which, through the process of variance analysis, links costing with budgetary control.

$\textcircled{9}$ ELEMENTS OF COSTING

Think about this . . . *To what extent (if at all) do you consider that historical costs (i.e. those incurred in the recent past) are of use in planning future activities?*

9.1 THE NATURE OF COSTING

Costing is the analysis of costs incurred and of income earned in relation to a specified activity so that the component elements of each can be allocated to the particular phase of production, market, product, department or branch concerned or involved. The objective is to identify precisely where profits are being made or losses incurred

Costing usually involves the extensive use of appropriate analysis columns in accounts and statements. It also involves the calculation of percentages and ratios of related data. Consideration has to be given to the different bases for *apportioning* (i.e. splitting) data between a number of heads. Costing is not only concerned with future projections of income and cost curves, with decision making in relation not only to real or sustainable accounting data, but also with non-accounting data such as population statistics, political policies, environmental issues and economic trends.

9.2 COSTING TERMINOLOGY

Costing has its own specific terminology and, during recent years, there has been considerable standardisation in cost accounting terms. The principal terms now in use are set out in Figure 9.1, and care should be taken to use them only within the precise definitions given. Figure 9.2 summarises the elements of cost accounting in flow chart form.

Figure 9.1   Principal Terms Used in Costing

Cost unit	The matching of a particular cost against a suitable unit of output, e.g. production costs per tonne produced, transport costs per mile (or per passenger-mile), hospital costs per patient-day, electricity costs per hour of operation, rent per square foot of floor space.
Cost centre	A general heading under which various costs can be collected, e.g. contract, department, stage of process.
Apportionment	The division of a particular cost between cost centres on the basis of a relevant cost unit.
Allocation	The allocation of a cost, without splitting, direct to a cost unit or centre.
Recovery	The transfer of an overhead cost from a non-production department to a production one.

Within this framework, it is possible to talk of

Differential costs	The difference in costs between two alternative policies.
Incremental costs	The additional cost of producing a further unit (i.e. the marginal cost.
Joint costs	Costs which are involved in the production of two or more products which cannot be segregated, i.e. both have to be produced. Joint costs may only exist up to a 'split-off' point.
Common costs	Costs in relation to two or more products which can be segregated.
Avoidable costs	Any cost which will be avoided by closing down production, i.e. those not necessary 'keep the factory doors open' – usually any variable and some of the fixed.
Controllable costs	Controllable costs are those over which management has some element of control, e.g. wages, advertising, discounts. Uncontrollable costs are the 'external' costs which management has no power to control, e.g. rent, raw material costs, power costs.

Figure 9.2   Cost Accounting: a Summary

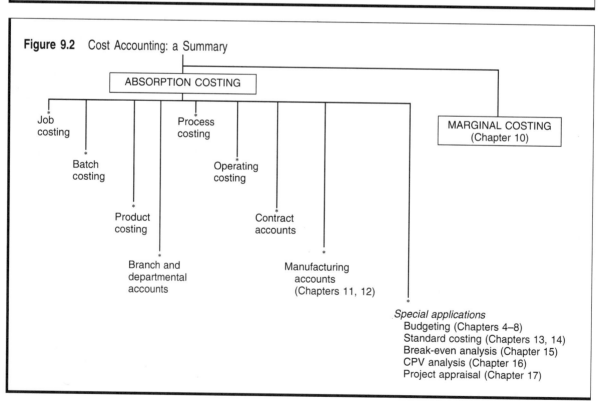

9.3 ABSORPTION COSTING – GENERAL NATURE

Costing methods can be broadly divided into (i) absorption costing and (ii) marginal costing. The purpose of *absorption costing* is to identify all costs of production, fixed and variable. In simple costing statements, costs are 'absorbed' into the total cost of a product on the basis of an appropriate cost unit – for example, in the case of soft-drinks manufacturers, a typical cost unit is *per can produced*. Because all costs are absorbed (i.e. included), this approach is sometimes known as *total absorption costing*. This should be contrasted with marginal costing which picks out just a few of the costs (described in Chapter 10).

Although the basic costing principles are similar in all cases, absorption costing methods are modified to suit the particular form of production or service being undertaken. Examples of absorption costing include:

- *Product costing*
  In product costing, the cost centres (see Figure 9.1) are the particular products concerned.
- *Job costing*
  The purpose of job costing is to establish the profit or loss on individual 'jobs'. It is suitable where the work undertaken by the firm varies considerably in size and cost, such as in general engineering and electrical contracting work. The basis is the identification of direct expenses such as labour and materials for the job concerned, to which is added an element for overheads based on an appropriate overhead recovery rate.
- *Contract costing*
  Contract costing is very similar to job costing, but is very often 'site-based'. It has special problems such as the most suitable form of overhead recovery rates for the capital equipment which is often involved, the treatment of interim profits, and the question of interim profits on long-term contracts.
- *Batch costing*
  Batch costing is suitable where quantities of identical articles are produced as a complete batch, after which production is re-organised and another complete batch is produced. There tends not to be an 'on-going' process. Costs can vary considerably between different batches of the same product, and therefore the 'batch' becomes a convenient cost centre to which the overhead recovery is related. Batch costing is common in clothing, footwear and in engineering work such as the manufacture of standard components.

- *Operating costing*
  Operating costing is usually applied where an on-going service rather than an identifiable product is being offered. Costs then have to be related to a costing unit suitable to the industry or service involved. Examples include patient/days for hospitals and passenger/miles for transport undertakings.
- *Process costing*
  Process costing is usually applied in situations where there is an on-going sequence of several processes in the production of the commodity concerned. It is common in brewing, paint production, paper making, and food processing. It involves averaging the total costs of each process over the entire production, and charging the output cost of a particular process as the raw material input to the next process.

  A particular problem which arises is the valuation of *work in progress*. This is dealt with on page 109.
- *Standard costing*
  Standard costing is primarily concerned with comparing actual costs with a pre-determined (i.e. budgeted) 'standard' and noting the differences, known as *variances*. The technique is dealt with more fully in Chapters 13 and 14.

9.4   PRESENTATION OF COSTING DATA

Costing data may be presented:

- *In conventional style* within the structure of double-entry accounting. Manufacturing accounts are an example.
- *In statement form* with or without assumptions and projections and non-financial data. These statements may include calculations partly or wholly outside the normal structure of accounts, such as in calculations of costs per unit of production, break-even analysis, budgeting and capital investment appraisals.
- *In diagrammatic, pictorial or graphical form*, which can often bring the 'message' home more dramatically than by more formal methods. Graphs, bar charts and pie charts are commonly used in accounting work, particularly when it is desired to communicate information to non-accountants.

Costing statements provide considerable scope for ingenuity and imagination. These must, however, be exercised with discretion. All statements should have a proper heading. There must be consideration of what data is – and is *not* – to be included. The 'plan' of the table needs careful thought as regards what information is to be represented horizontally and what vertically; what size and style of type is to be used; whether colour should be employed. Columns should be clearly headed, and the units shown if necessary (e.g. '000' or £m). Consideration should be given to what degree of 'rounding' is acceptable. Horizontal lines should be restricted to those absolutely necessary. If relevant, the sources of data included in the table should be stated. A very simple costing statement is shown in Example 9.1.

EXAMPLE 9.1   *Quencho-Fresh is small company producing two types of canned drink – Popkola, selling at £0.20 per can and Superkola selling at £0.50 per can. During last month a total of 77 100 cans were produced and sold, giving a sales revenue of £17 850. Rent of premises amounted to £2750, ingredients and materials £5500, wages £2000, electricity (power, lighting, heating) £2500, depreciation £1000 and administrative costs £1000.*

REQUIRED: *A suitable cost statement with percentage columns showing (i) total cost and profit and (ii) average costs and profit per can is required.*

SOLUTION:

Quencho-Fresh: Cost Statement, Month Ended ... 19–

Cans sold (no):	77 100	
	£	%
Sales revenue	17 850	100.0
Costs:		
Ingredients	5 500	30.8
Wages	2 000	11.2
Electricity	2 500	14.0
Depreciation	1 000	5.6
Rent	2 750	15.4
Administrative	1 000	5.6
Total	14 750	82.6
Profit	3 100	17.4
Average cost per can	0.19	
Average profit per can	0.04	

In this example, the average cost and the profit 'per can produced' are derived from the original data. This becomes the *cost unit*. From the statement, management can see that at this level of output the average cost per can is £0.19, and an average of profit of £0.04 per can is being made, giving a profit on sales ratio of 17.4%.

Now suppose that Quencho-Fresh produced two separate products. Although the average costs, and the profits per can, have some value, the statement would be much more informative if it were to give a 'breakdown' of revenue and costs for each product with costs apportioned between the two. There is usually no difficulty in apportioning direct costs (such as materials, power and wages) as the actual amounts directed to each product can usually be identified. A decision has to be made, however, on the best bases on which to split the other costs. Examples include respective floor areas, outputs, and working hours.

Quencho–Fresh's costs, when apportioned, could appear as in the following modified statement. Note the changed picture which is given of the firm's operation, and the obvious questions which it raises for management.

Quencho–Fresh: Cost Statement, Month Ended . . . 19–

	Total		Popkola		Superkola	
Cans sold (no):	77 100		69 000		8100	
	£	%	£	%	£	%
Sales revenue	17 850	100.0	13 800	100.0	4 050	100.0
Costs:						
Ingredients	5 500	30.8	4 125	29.9	1 375	40.0
Wages	2 000	11.2	1 500	10.9	500	12.3
Electricity	2 500	14.0	1 875	13.6	625	15.4
Depreciation	1 000	5.6	650	4.7	350	8.6
Rent	2 750	15.4	2 500	18.1	250	6.2
Administrative	1 000	5.6	600	4.3	400	9.9
Total	14 750	82.6	11 250	76.8	4 150	102.5
Profit (loss)	3 100	17.4	2 550	23.2	(100)	(2.5)
Average per can						
cost	0.19		0.163		0.512	
profit (loss)	0.04		0.037		0.012	

It is obvious from this more detailed statement that, taking the apportionment of costs as stated, only Popkola is producing a profit – Superkola in fact is being manufactured at a loss. The first reaction is that since Superkola appears to be selling at a loss, should the price be increased? This may, or may not, be possible. Secondly, is the apportionment of costs 'fair'? If Popkola took a larger share of the fixed charges, Superkola could be shown as running at a profit (though the profit on Popkola would be correspondingly decreased). Thirdly, the production of Superkola could be abandoned – but what would this really achieve? What, for example, would be the saving (if any) on rent of premises? And on general administrative costs?. Depreciation may reduce slightly, but not necessarily proportionally, and only the power element of the electricity cost will reduce significantly. In other words, Superkola is absorbing a significant proportion of the fixed costs which Popkola will have to bear if production of the 'loss-making' Superkola is abandoned. If the spare productive capacity is turned over to Popkola, there is no certainty that the increased quantities could be sold.

TASK 9.1   Assume Quencho-Fresh abandons production of the 'loss-maker'. This results in a complete saving of Superkola's ingredients and wages cost. Electricity costs reduce to £1700, depreciation to £750 and administrative costs to £900. Rent remains the same. The sales and unit price of Popkola also remain as before. Prepare a cost statement for the production of Popkola alone. What conclusions are you able to draw?

9.5 OVERHEAD ABSORPTION RATE

It is easy, in the simple theoretical situation, to identify the direct costs of manufacturing a product and to add on a given figure for overheads. In the practical situation, it is often difficult to decide what the figure for overheads should be. This is because the actual figure will not be known until some while later, and because different 'jobs' often demand the use of resources (e.g. labour, materials and machine-time) in different proportions and it is through these that overheads are usually 'recovered'.

The task also becomes more difficult if the nature of individual jobs or contracts vary throughout the year.

The initial problem – that of not knowing the actual overheads for the year until some time afterwards – is overcome by using an *assumed* or estimated figure for total overheads expected to be incurred during the year. This is usually the budgeted figure. This is then divided between the direct-cost centres (or processes through which the product will pass) on some agreed basis – such as floor area occupied or workers employed.

Each of the cost centres concerned will then add on to the direct costs of every 'job' it undertakes an element to cover the overheads allocated to it. The overhead charge added to the direct costs for any particular job is based on the *overhead absorption rate (OAR)* – sometimes known as the *overhead recovery rate*. This is obtained by taking

> (a)   the total overheads allocated to the centre and dividing it by
> (b)   the *total productive capacity* of the centre.

The 'total productive capacity' represents the total work the centre is excpected to perform during the year and is usually measured in labour hours or machine hours.

EXAMPLE 9.2

A firm producing high-quality dresses has budgeted total overheads for the current year of £900 000 allocated to the three production departments as follows: cutting department £100 000, machining department £500 000 and finishing department £300 000. The total productive capacity of the departments are: cutting department 16 000 machine hours, machining department 40 000 machine hours, finishing department 60 000 direct-labour hours.

REQUIRED:

(a)   The overhead absorption rate for each department.

(b)   The overhead to be added to the direct costs of each department in respect of the production of Job ECO16 – a particular batch of dresses which required 10 machine-hours work in the cutting department, 50 machine-hours work in the machining department and 20 direct labour-hours work in the finishing department.

SOLUTION:

(a)   Overhead absorption rate:

Department:	Cutting	Machining	Finishing
Total overhead	£100 000	£500 000	£300 000
Productive capacity	16 000 machine-hours	40 000 machine-hours	60 000 direct-labour hours
OAR (Overhead productive capacity)	£6.25 per machine hour	£12.5 per machine hour	£5 per direct-labour hour

(b)   Overheads to be recovered in respect of job ECO16:

		£
Cutting department:	10 machine-hours × £6.25 =	62.50
Machining department:	50 machine-hours × £12.50 =	625.00
Finishing department:	20 direct-labour hours × £5 =	100.00
Total overhead to be recovered:		787.50

TASK 9.2   The productive capacity of a production department for the current year has been estimated at:

Total output of units	6000
Direct labour-hours	12 000
Machine-hours	19 200

The overhead cost allocated to the department was budgeted at £12 000

(1)   Calculate an overhead absorption rate on *each* of the following bases:

    (a)   Direct labour hours
    (b)   Machine hours
    (c)   Units of output.

(2)   Using each of the above overhead absorption rates in turn, calculate the cost of producing a single unit which requires 4 hours of direct labour at £2 an hour, takes two hours of machine time at £5 per hour and uses materials costing £6.

PRACTICAL ASSIGNMENTS: [1]   A firm produces three products, and the following information is available referring to the last financial year:

Product	X	Y	Z
Units produced (000)	20	30	40
Sales revenue (£m)	40	30	20
Number of employees (00)	15	20	25
Wage costs (£000)	18	22	21
Factory operating hours	1500	1800	1200

REQUIRED:
A statement, with reasons, of the bases on which each of the following costs be apportioned:

1. Salesmen's commissions
2. Lighting
3. Wages
4. Depreciation of machinery
5. Power
6. Interest charges
7. Materials handling
8. Accident insurance
9. General costs
10. Insurance of plant charges
11. Management salaries
12. Heating

2 A factory produces three products coded X, Y, and Z. The estimated factory costs for next month are:

	TOTAL £000	X £000	Y £000	Z £000
Direct materials	360	120	90	150
Direct labour	650	200	300	150
Direct expenses	160	70	50	40
Factory indirect expenses	500			
Factory lighting, heating	140			
Indirect materials	80			
Establishment overheads:				
General admin	300			
General selling	210			
General distribution	150			
Anticipated production (units)	18	5	10	3

Product X occupies half the factory floor; the remainder is divided equally between Y and Z.

Indirect factory expenses should be apportioned to the products in the ratio of their respective labour costs. Lighting and heating should be apportioned in the ratio of the floor area occupied and the indirect materials in the ratio of the respective prime costs. Establishment overheads should be apportioned on the basis of the respective costs of production. *All apportionments should be rounded £000 as in the above table.*

REQUIRED:
(a) A statement showing the structure of anticipated costs for next month and the selling price per unit if
   (i) a 40% return on costs is required,
   (ii) a 20% return on selling price is required.
(b) A revised costing statement for the products X and Z, assuming that it has been decided to suspend production of Y. Any assumptions made should be noted

3 Spectro Lens Ltd is a producer of binoculars and similar equipment. The company expects to sell 20 000 of its *Popular M* type telescope at a unit selling price of £30 during the forthcoming year. Fixed costs are expected to be £110 000 and salesmen's commissions will be 10% of sales. Basic materials are expected to cost £160 000, direct wages £70 000 and variable overheads £44 000.

A well-known retail chain has approached the company with a proposal to purchase 8000 of the telescopes which would be marketed under their own brand name but are not willing to pay more than £20 per telescope.

Spectro Lens Ltd has the productive capacity to undertake the order in addition to their normal production.

The marketing director of Spectro Lens Ltd is apprehensive of the effect the retail chain's sales may have on the company's own sales. He is of the opinion that, provided there is an advertising back-up costing approximately £8000, a 10% reduction in selling price could result in the company selling the whole of the increased production itself.

REQUIRED:

A report to the management of Spectro Lens Ltd, with appropriate costings, advising the directors which course of action should be taken. Your report should note any non-accounting considerations which should be borne in mind.

4 Dolan Ltd has for many years marketed basic building materials in the UK and has recently been attempting to expand into Europe. It also introduced, two years ago, a range of house decoration products which it markets and distributes alongside the building materials The following data refers to the last three years of operation:

(£m)	Building materials			Decoration materials		
Year:	1	2	3	1	2	3
Sales	19	18	17	–	6	8
Cost of sales	8	10	11	–	5	6
Overheads	6	4	3	–	3	4
Profit	5	4	3	–	(2)	(2)

It has been suggested to the directors that, because of the persisting losses on the decoration materials, that side of the operation should be closed down.

REQUIRED:

A report to the directors interpreting the above figures and stating whether you agree with the suggestion to close down the decoration materials operation. Point out the value of adequate costing information for management purposes and describe, with reasons, what additional information which would be helpful in coming to a final decision.

5 Crane Ltd produces three products, coded A, B and C. During the year ended 31 December last, the company produced 50 000, 60 000 and 40 000 units respectively of the three products. The direct materials costs were A £80 000, B £70 000 and C £75 000. The direct labour costs were £2 per unit in the case of products A and B, and £3.375 per unit in the case of C. The variable overheads attributable to the products were A £20 000, B £28 000 and C £32 000. The gross profit mark-up on cost was 25% in the case of

products A and C, and 20% in the case of product B. The fixed manufacturing overhead for the year was £80 000. Fixed selling and administrative costs amounted to £70 000 whilst payments for rent and rates were £50 000.

The cost and management accountant has decided to allocate fixed manufacturing overhead in proportion to direct labour costs, fixed selling and administrative costs in proportion to the number of units produced and rent and rates in proportion to the total variable costs.

REQUIRED:
(a) A full cost statement showing total profit together with the profit attributable to, and the unit cost of, each product.
(b) A statement of other relevant bases on which the allocation of each of the overheads could have been based.

6 Woodcrafts Ltd manufacture high-quality carved wooden sculptures for sale through country craft and souvenir shops. Jobs pass through two cost centres – shaping and polishing. Overheads are absorbed on the basis of machine-hours in the shaping department and on direct labour-hours in the polishing department. Budgeted data for the year in question is:

department	Shaping department	Polishing
Direct-labour cost (£000)	75	120
Factory overhead (£000)	162	150
Direct labour (000 hours)	30	60
Machine time (000 hours)	20	–

The following data relates to job number EOTW6:

	Shaping department	Polishing department
Direct materials (£)	248	122
Direct labour (hours)	6	12
Machine time (hours)	2	–

Administration overheads are absorbed at 20% on factory cost.

REQUIRED:
(a) A calculation of the overhead absorption rates for the two departments.
(b) A cost statement for job EOTW6

7 Two firms are engaged in manufacturing engineering products. Both have total overhead costs of £750 000 which are allocated as follows:

Department	Firm A (%)	Firm B (%)
Moulding	35	30
Machining	35	45
Polishing and finishing	30	25

The productive capacity of both firms is as follows:

Moulding department	15 000 machine-hours
Machining department	25 000 machine-hours
Polishing and finishing department	12 000 direct-labour hours

REQUIRED:
(a) A calculation of the overhead absorption rate for each department of both Firm A and Firm B.
(b) The overhead (OH) cost of each firm for a unit which requires 10 machine-hours to mould, 25 machine-hours to machine and 12 direct-labour hours to finish.

8 Azinger Ltd is a small engineering company with two production departments – the machine shop and the assembly shop. The budgeted figures for the current year are:

Product:	A	B	C
Production units	35 000	25 000	20 000
Unit material cost (£)	20	15	18
Unit production times:			
Machine shop (machine-hours)	6	8	2
Assembly department (labour-hours)	5	10	3

Factory overheads of £1 250 000 have been allocated to the machine shop, and of £850 000 to the assembly shop.

REQUIRED:
A calculation of
(i) The overhead absorption rate per machine-hour for the machine shop
(ii) The overhead absorption rate per labour-hour for the assembly shop.
(iii) The production cost of one unit each of products A, B and C.

9 Gaines, Cropper and Walls, practising accountants, estimate their annual overheads to be:

	£
Office rent	3500
Rates	2000
Wages	8000
Stationery	800
Heat and light	900
Motor expenses	2000
General expenses	1800

Each partner works 46 weeks per year. The working week consists of 42 hours of which 35 hours is spent working on the books of their clients.

REQUIRED:
(a) A calculation of the overhead absorption rate per partner-hour.
(b) Chris Gaines has suggested that each partner receives a salary of £25 000 p.a. If this suggestion is implemented, how much will the partners need to charge per hour to cover overheads and salaries?
(c) If all the partners worked the full working week on their clients' books, calculate how much extra salary the partners could be paid using the combined rate for overheads and salaries.

10 MARGINAL COSTING

Think about this . . . *Addo Ltd is a manufacturer of pocket calculators. John Smith is an entrepreneur who wishes to enter the market and who has yet to secure his first order. Both Addo Ltd and Smith are approached by a large distributor who asks for a quote for a significant quantity of calculators'.*

(a) Precisely why could Addo Ltd probably quote a lower price than Smith?
(b) Are there any circumstances in which Addo

(i) would not be able to quote, and
(ii) may not wish to quote,

a price lower than Smith's?

10.1 THE NATURE OF MARGINAL COSTING

The purpose of marginal costing is to identify the *additional* income and costs resulting from a increase in production. It is, therefore, not concerned with fixed costs or with general overheads, but only with the variable costs resulting from the increase in production.

EXAMPLE 10.1 Suppose that Quencho-Fresh Ltd (see Chapter 9) is asked to produce 1000 cans of Popkola as a 'special one-off order' in addition to the normal sales. What is the *cheapest* price possible at which this could be done?

Assuming that ingredients, wages and electricity vary directly with output and that depreciation, rent and administrative charges remain fixed, the additional cost of meeting the special order would simply amount to the proportionate increase in the variable costs, i.e. a total of £108.696 (or £0.108696 a can). This means that if the price offered exceeds £0.11 per can (assuming £0.01 to be the smallest unit of currency), the firm will be increasing its overall profit.

The surplus of marginal income over marginal cost is known as the *contribution*, i.e. it is a 'contribution' to general expenses, thus increasing the total profit (or reducing the loss). Marginal costing concepts form the basis of a number of further techniques, such as break-even analysis (see Chapter 15) and cost-profit-volume (CPV) theory (see Chapter 16).

Marginal costing is of considerable importance in management decision making. It is, first, a guide to the 'true costs' relating to a given increase in production. Secondly, it indicates the minimum price which must be asked in competitive tendering (see the example of the special order to Quencho-Fresh on page 101) and it provides a clear guide whether an order should be accepted or not. The importance of the marginal concept is shown in the following Example 10.2. Compare, carefully, the 'changed situations' with the basic situation.

EXAMPLE 10.2   Basic situation

A small firm produces jam under the trade name *Real Fruit Jams* which it markets at 55p per jar. Its production run per week is 100 000 jars but it occasionally has difficulty in maintaining sales at this level because of competition from big manufacturers, and this is a constant worry. At the above production level, the weekly fixed costs amount to £30 000 and the direct variables (i.e. marginal costs) to 15p per jar, i.e. a total of £15 000. There are no other costs.

From this data, it will be seen that:

(a)   *Total weekly costs*: fixed costs of £30 000 and variable costs £15 000, i.e. a total of £45 000.
(b)   *Average cost per jar*: at this level of production is £45 000 divided by 100 000, i.e. £0.45 per jar.
(c)   *Marginal cost per jar*: 15p (£0.15) per jar.
(d)   *The variable cost per jar*: £15 000 divided by 100 000, i.e. 15p.
(e)   *Total income*, if all jars are sold: 100 000 × 55p = £55 000.
(f)   *Profit* = £(55 000 − 45 000) = £10 000.

Changed situation 1

The firm is approached by a supermarket chain which wishes to place an order for 50 000 jars per week which it intends to market under its own, quite distinct, brand name. The maximum price the supermarket is willing to pay is 30p per jar (i.e. less than the present average cost per jar). The firm can cope with this order as well as maintain its existing output. The variables remain at 15p per jar. If the order is accepted, the calculations become:

(a)   *Total production costs*: £30 000 + £(0.15 × 150 000) = £52 500
(b)   *Average cost per jar*: £52 000 divided by 150 000 = 35p.
(c)   *Total income*: £(0.55 × 100 000) + £(0.30 × 50 000) = £70 000.
(d)   *Profit*: £(70 000 −52 500) = £17 500 (i.e. an increase of £7500 on the basic situation.

COMMENT: Although the price offered by the supermarket chain is still below the average cost of production, acceptance of the order will increase total profits. This is because the price offered by the supermarket is above the marginal cost, the fixed costs having already been covered by the original production run.

   The acceptance of the contract could lead to further orders. However, the firm would have to consider whether the supermarket sales would undermine the sale of jam under the original name as this could materially alter the situation.

Changed situation 2
The supermarket later approaches the firm and offers to purchase the entire production run (150 000 jars per week) over a five-year period provided the firm ceases to manufacture under its own trade name. The price offered by the supermarket remains at 30p per jar. Should the firm accept?

COMMENT: Under this arrangement, total costs would remain at £52 500. Total income would become £(150 000 × 0.30) = £45 000 . This means a loss of £7800. The order should therefore be refused. Although the price offered is above the marginal cost, the production run now has to cover fixed cost and this cannot be achieved at (a) this level of production, and (b) the lower price.

Changed situation 3
The firm is also approached by an independent wholesaler who offers to purchase 32 250 jars of the jam per week without prejudice to the firm's production under its own brand name. The price offered is 42p per jar.

Total production costs: £30 000 + (15p × 132 250) = £49 837.50.
Total income: £(100 000 × 0.55) + £(32 250 × 0.42) = £ 68 545.
Profit: £(68 545 − 49 837.50) = 18 707.5.

COMMENT: The firm should accept.

TASK 10.1   If the firm has not the productive capacity to meet both the initial offer of the supermarket and the offer of the wholesaler, which of the two should it accept?

10.2 LIMITATIONS OF MARGINAL COSTING

The following limitations of marginal costing should be remembered:

- Overheads have to be covered somewhere. A firm cannot price all of its production on a marginal cost basis.

- The extra productive capacity for an additional order may not be available.
- Fixed costs may not, in fact, remain fixed. An extra order may mean building a new factory or taking on extra managerial staff – i.e. introducing a 'step variable'.
- Offering a product to one customer on a marginal cost basis may undermine the main market and lead to 'market segmentation'.
- The time factor may be significant. Accepting an order on a marginal cost basis may mean committing resources for a lengthy period This could result in the firm having to refuse a full cost order.
- Successful marginal costing depends on being able to *identify* and *classify* costs accurately. This information may not, in fact, be available.

10.3 STOCK VALUATION AND MARGINAL COSTING

Some manufacturing firms value closing stocks on a marginal rather than a total cost basis – this means that only the variables are taken into account in the valuation, the entire overheads being written off to the current period. The effect of this is to produce a lower valuation for the closing stock – consequently reducing the current profit. However, note that the closing stock of the one period is the opening stock of the next succeeding period. The effect of a lower valuation, therefore, is also to increase profit in that succeeding period. In other words, valuing stock on a marginal basis has the effect of 'shifting' a portion of the profit from the one year to the next. This is prudent where high risk industries are concerned.

PRACTICAL ASSIGNMENTS

1   Framework Ltd produces a single product which, during the last two years, has sold at £130 per unit. The variable costs per unit have been direct labour £30, direct materials £45, variable overheads £15. The fixed costs of the company vary with level of production. During the last two years, they were as follows:

Output level in units	£
0–15 000	360 000
15 001–30 000	440 000
30 001–40 000	500 000

During the first of the two years, 21 000 units were produced and 20 000 sold. In the second of the two years, 18 000 units were produced and 19 000 sold.

Stocks are valued on a first-in, first-out (FIFO) basis. The stock at the beginning of the first year was 2000 units valued, on a cost per unit basis, as follows:

	£
Labour	27
Material	40
Variable overhead	13
Fixed overhead	18

REQUIRED:
(a) TWO sets of profit statements for each of the two years using (i) absorption (total) costing and (ii) marginal costing principles.
(b) A statement summarising the advantages and disadvantages of valuing opening and closing stocks on a marginal costing basis.

2 Kenway Ltd is a small company which produces a standard component used in the electronic industry. In the year to 31 March last, it produced and sold 40 000 of the components. Its costs were: wages £600 000; rent £100 000; electricity £80 000; business rates £40 000; materials £140 000; depreciation of machinery £60 000; insurances £10 000; general administrative overheads £15 000. Selling price is determined by allowing a gross mark-up of 40% on cost.

REQUIRED:
(a) A statement showing (i) the total cost of production, (ii) the absorption unit cost per component produced, (iii) the total gross and net profits, (iv) the unit gross and net profits.
(b) A calculation of the lowest price which could be quoted for the production of an additional 5000 components whilst retaining the same profit margins.
(c) A calculation of the difference in the unit price if production had been planned on a basis of 30 000 components instead of 36 000.

3 Cumbria Upholstery is a small firm which manufactures a particular type of office chair. Its projections for the forthcoming year indicate that it could sell 12 000 chairs at a unit price £35 and that its cost levels would be:

	£	
Direct labour	68 000	
Supervisory labour	12 000	
Materials	154 000	
Rent	24 000	
Machine running costs	8000	
Machinery depreciation	7500	
Selling and distribution	48 000	(20% of which is variable)
Administration	24 000	

The firm has some spare capacity and it could possibly increase sales to 15 000 by reducing the price to £32. It could, however, increase price to £38, but this would be likely to reduce demand to 10 000 chairs.

REQUIRED:
A report to the owner, backed by an appropriate costing statement, summarising the three options. Your report should include a statement of additional factors which might have to be taken into account before a decision is made.

4 Achison, Brown & Co produce a variety of products for the haulage industry, including a tachodisk for use by long-distance lorry drivers. Over the last two years, production was reduced from 21 000 units in the earlier year to 18 000 in the second, whilst sales fell from 20 000 units to 19 000. The following data was standard for both years.

	£
Unit selling price	26
Variables: direct labour	6
direct materials	9
variable overheads	3

The allocation of fixed costs vary with the level of production, i.e £72 000 for production up to 15 000 units, £87 000 for production up to 30 000 units and £100 000 for production beyond that level.

Stock is valued a FIFO basis. 6000 disks were in stock at the beginning of the review period, valued as follows:

	£
Unit variables: labour	5
material	8
variable overheads	2
Unit fixed overhead allocation	4

REQUIRED:
(a) A suitable cost statement for the two-year period. The statement should show, for each year, profits and costs using, in each case,
   (i)   absorption (total) costing
   (ii) marginal (variable) costing
   as a basis for the valuation of stock.
(b) A comment on the implications of basing stock valuation on marginal costs as opposed to total costs.

11 MANUFACTURING ACCOUNTS – 1: GENERAL PRINCIPLES

Think about this . . . *The item* purchases *in a retailer's trading account represents the cost price of 'ready made' goods. However, the manufacturer's selling price (i.e. the retailer's cost – or purchase – price) includes a wide range of different costs. How many different items of cost can you think of which go into the manufacturer's selling price (i.e. the retailer's 'Purchases' price)? Can you see a basis for dividing those costs into two distinct groups?*

11.1 GENERAL NATURE OF MANUFACTURING ACCOUNTS

Costing data and calculations may be presented in statement form independent of the conventional accounts. In certain cases, however, the data can be integrated into the conventional double-entry system. One of the most common examples of this is in *manufacturing accounts.*

The purpose of manufacturing accounts is to ascertain the actual cost of manufacturing the goods, and they take the form of an additional final account prepared immediately before the trading account. This means that a manufacturer's final accounts consist of:

1. A manufacturing account
   which summarises the cost of goods produced.
2. A trading account
   in which the cost of goods produced replaces purchases. The opening and closing stock figures for finished goods are included as usual.
3. A profit and loss account
   in which the normal expenses are usually sub-grouped into (i) administrative, (ii) selling, and (iii) distributive costs.
4. A balance sheet
   with separate closing stock figures being given for raw materials, work-in-progress and finished goods.

11.2   STRUCTURE OF MANUFACTURING ACCOUNTS

Manufacturing costs consist of such items as the direct cost of raw materials, factory-floor wages and power for the machines. In addition, there are indirect factory overheads such as supervisory salaries, general lighting, heating, factory rent, and depreciation of machines and factory buildings. A sharp distinction is drawn in manufacturing accounts between the direct (or 'prime') costs and factory overheads. Each is listed as a separate sub-total on the debit side of the manufacturing account. The total of direct and indirect expenses then has to be adjusted for any variation in the stocks of work-in-progress.

Prime Costs

Prime costs are those which vary directly with output and consist of:

(a) cost of raw materials used (opening stock + net purchases – closing stock of raw materials)
(b) direct labour
(c) direct power
(d) any other directly variable manufacturing costs.

Factory Overheads

Factory overheads commonly consist of:

(a) indirect labour (such as supervisors' wages)
(b) factory lighting and heating
(c) factory rent, rates and insurance
(d) plant repairs
(e) depreciation of plant, machinery and factory buildings.

In the practical situation, there are other costs (e.g. insurance of premises and management salaries) to be apportioned (i.e. split), partly to manufacturing (and which therefore appear in the manufacturing account), and partly to general overheads in the profit and loss account. Directors' salaries are sometimes dealt with in this way. The items concerned, and the basis on which they are to be apportioned, will usually be a matter of known policy within the organisation concerned. In assignment work the apportionment will be stated in the question.

The close connection between manufacturing accounts and the principles of costing (see Chapters 9 and 10) should now be obvious.

Work-in-Progress

Work-in-progress refers to the value of goods on which the manufacturing process has been commenced but not completed, Variations in work-in-progress are allowed for by subtracting its closing valuation from the opening. This is usually brought into account immediately after the factory overheads.

The prime costs and the factory overheads (adjusted for variation in work-in-progress) give the *factory cost of goods produced* – which is then carried down to the trading account and added to the opening stock of finished goods. In other words, it takes the place of purchases as found in a retailer's trading account.

Work-in-progress is usually valued on the basis of factory cost of production (i.e. the valuation includes an allowance for the factory overheads). If it has been valued on the basis of prime costs only, it should appear immediately after the prime cost calculation. It may also be valued on the basis of marginal costs – i.e. of all variables including any overheads which are regarded as variable.

If the closing stock of work-in-progress is greater than the opening stock, then a negative figure will result which must be deducted from the other costs. The net figure is normally shown in brackets.

EXAMPLE 11.1 *A conventional manufacturing account is set out as follows:*

Raw materials, opening stock	260 000	Trading account:	
purchases	960 000	Cost of goods produced	1 678 500
	1 210 000		
closing stock	320 000		
Cost of raw materials used	890 000		
Direct labour	560 000		
Factory power	126 000		
Prime cost	1 576 000		
Factory overheads:			
Supervisors' salaries	48 000		
Depreciation machinery	12 000		
Factory lighting, heating	30 500		
Factory insurances	12 000		
	1 678 500		1 678 500

TASK 11.1   Manufacturing accounts are often shown as statements in vertical format rather than as 'T' accounts. This requires careful planning in the use of columns and sub-totals.

REQUIRED: Re-write the above account in vertical statement form.

11.3   TRADING AND PROFIT AND LOSS ACCOUNTS

The trading account normally follows the conventional form with cost of goods produced replacing purchases (though an alternative procedure is discussed in Chapter 12). In the profit and loss account, the expenses are usually sub-grouped into

(a) administrative costs;
(b) selling costs   } these may be grouped under one heading if
(c) distributive costs } insufficient detail is given to separate them

11.4   COSTING COMPLICATIONS

In practice, a number of complications can arise. The principal ones are:

1. *The large number and range of costs involved.* This leads to considerably greater administrative and organisational problems in tracking, classifying and recording the items concerned.
2. *The different cost patterns involved.* Some costs are direct variables, some semi-variables, and some are fixed.
3. *Apportionment of costs.* Some costs have to be split between manufacturing and trading, or between one product and another. Bases often chosen include:

    (a) floor area occupied
    (b) operating hours
    (c) manufacturing costs or volume
    (d) sales volume or value
    (e) capital employed
    (f) labour costs.

Failing any other basis, costs may be apportioned on an agreed but arbitrary basis – such as one-third to manufacturing, two-thirds to profit and loss.

EXAMPLE 11.2　The following balances were extracted from the books of A. Producer at 31 December 19–5

	£
Stocks at 1 January 19–5:	
raw materials	324 000
work-in-progress (see (a) below)	396 000
finished goods	464 580
Stocks at 31 December 19–5:	
raw materials	243 000
work-in-progress (see (a) below)	123 000
finished goods	428 850
Wages and salaries:	
direct manufacturing wages	456 900
work manager's salary	159 600
office salaries	232 310
salesmen's salaries and commissions	242 200
directors' emoluments (see (b) below)	600 000
Electricity:	
factory power	183 360
factory lighting and heating	63 990
office lighting and heating	19 500
warehouse lighting and heating	16 500
Depreciation for the year:	
machinery	360 000
buildings (see (c) below)	60 000
salesmen's cars	100 000
distribution lorries	80 000
Purchases of raw materials	1 116 500
Sales	7 506 000
Carriage-in	1560
Warehouse rent and rates	600 000
Office rates	25 000
Factory rates	40 000
General distribution expenses	1 100 000
Advertising expenses	753 940
General office expenses	554 680
Carriage-out	7000
Returns-out	1500
Returns-in	800

Additional information:

(a) Work-in-progress has been valued at factory cost of production.
(b) Directors' emoluments should be apportioned equally between manufacturing and administration.

(c)   Three-quarters of depreciation charge for buildings refers to the factory; one-quarter to the office.

REQUIRED: The manufacturing, trading and P&L accounts for the year.

SOLUTION: Manufacturing, Trading and Profit and Loss Account for year ended 31 December 19–5

	£	£	£			£
Raw materials:				Factory cost of production		3 079 410
Opening stock		324 000				
Purchases	1 116 500					
Carriage-in	1560					
Returns-out	(1500)					
Net purchases		1 116 560				
			1 440 560			
Closing stock			(243 000)			
Raw materials used			1 197 560			
Direct labour			456 900			
Factory power			183 360			
PRIME COST			1 837 820			
Factory overheads:						
Depreciation:						
machinery		360 000				
buildings		45 000				
Work manager's salary		159 600				
Lighting, heating		63 990				
Rates		40 000				
Directors emoluments		300 000	968 590			
Work-in-progress:						
Opening stock		396 000				
Closing stock		(123 000)	273 000			
			3 079 410			3 079 410
Finished goods:				Sales	7 506 000	
Opening stock		464 580		Returns-in	(800)	7 505 200
Factory cost of production		3 079 410				
Closing stock		(428 850)				
Cost of sales			3 115 140			
Gross profit	c/d	390 060				
			7 505 200			7 505 200

		Gross profit	b/d 4 390 060

Administrative:		
Office salaries	232 310	
Lighting, heating	19 500	
Rates	25 000	
Directors' emoluments	300 000	
Depreciation, buildings	15 000	
General	554 680	1 146 490

Selling:		
Salesmen: salaries, commission	242 200	
Depreciation: cars	100 000	
Advertising	753 940	1 096 140

Distribution:		
Lighting, heating	16 500	
Depreciation: lorries	80 000	
Rent and rates	600 000	
Carriage-out	7000	
General	1 100 000	1 803 500
Net profit		343 930
		4 390 060

		4 390 060

Extract from balance sheet
Closing stocks:

Raw materials	243 000	
Work-in-progress	123 000	
Finished goods	428 850	794 850

TASK 11.2   (a)   Classify each of the following costs taken from the accounts of the Fettes Engineering Co Ltd under one of the following headings:

(i)	direct costs	(iii)	selling and distribution
(ii)	manufacturing overhead	(iv)	adminstration and finance

	£		£
Office rent	8000	Advertising	20 000
Depreciation, salesmen's cars	12 000	General manager's salary	25 000
Office cleaning	6000	Office expenses	9000
Rent and rates, factory	16 000	Machinery depreciation	15 000
Office wages and salaries	35 000	Manufacturing wages	145 000
Machinery repairs	7000	Delivery costs	3500
Lighting, office	4000	Storekeeper's wages	8000
Factory salaries	42 000	Loan interest	5000
Audit fees	2000	Factory power	26 000

	£		£
Materials consumed	200 000	Lighting, factory	8000
Salesmen's salaries	35 000	Marketing manager's salary	18 000
Marketing consultant's fees	12 000		

(b)   From the above data, calculate
    (i)   prime cost
    (ii)   cost of production
    (iii)   total cost.

PRACTICAL ASSIGNMENTS

[1]   Synchro Ltd manufactures car components and its accounting year ends on 31 March. The following data was available on 30 March last:

Stocks: Opening	£
Raw materials	350 000
Work-in-progress	135 000
Finished goods	496 000
Closing	
Raw materials	264 000
Work-in-progress	145 000
Finished goods	315 000

Sales	8 300 000
Purchases of raw materials	1 988 000
Insurance	75 500
Direct power	289 000
Factory lighting and heating	78 200
Office lighting and heating	34 500
Factory wages	2 750 000
Factory supervisors' salaries	560 000
Returns out	95 000
Office salaries	382 900
Carriage-in	12 500
Returns-in	105 000

The machinery of the company cost £350 000 against which a depreciation provision of £240 000 had been built up by the beginning of the year in question. The company's policy is to depreciate machinery at 25% p.a. on a diminishing balance method, and to allocate insurance to the factory and to the office in the ratio of two-fifths and three-fifths respectively.

REQUIRED:
A manufacturing and trading account for the year under review showing clearly the cost of materials used, the prime cost, the cost of manufactured goods produced, and the gross trading profit or loss.

2 Martyn Thorpe is the owner of a small manufacturing business producing christmas novelties. The following balances were taken from his books on 30 June 1994:

		£
Stocks at 1 July 1993:	raw materials	5600
	work-in-progress	4800
	finished goods	6500
Stocks at 30 June 1994:	raw materials	6300
	work-in-progress	5200
	finished goods	5100
Purchases of raw materials		63 500
Sales of finished goods		300 000
Carriage on sales		1000
Carriage on raw materials		1250
Depreciation of factory equipment		3600
Depreciation of delivery vehicle		2000
Direct wages		20 000
Factory rent and rates		7600
Office rent and rates		2800
Selling and marketing expenses		17 000

REQUIRED:
(a) Thorpe's manufacturing account for the year, showing clearly the cost of materials used, the prime cost and the production cost of goods manufactured.
(b) Thorpe's trading account for the same period.

3 Ranger Enterprise Ltd was formed on 1 April 19-8 in order to exploit a franchise granted by National Television PLC for the manufacture and sale of toy armoured cars featured in a popular TV series.

Fixed manufacturing costs for the first full year of operation to 31 March 19-9 amounted to £44 000 and general administrative expenses to £70 000. Variable selling expenses of 50p per toy were incurred. The cost of raw materials was £5 per car and, at the end of the year, the stock of raw materials in hand was valued at £2500 and the work-in-progress at £1700. Direct labour was costed at £4 per toy and variable overheads at £5. A franchise licence fee of £1 per toy produced was payable to National Television PLC.

A total of 28 000 toys were produced of which 22 000 were sold at £25 each. Depreciation of plant and machinery was reckoned at £12 000.

There was no work-in-progress at the year-end.

On inspection, it was found that 500 of the finished toys on hand at the end of the year had been incorrectly finished in the paint-shop. These would be placed on the market at £5 each.

REQUIRED:

(a) A manufacturing, trading and profit and loss account for the year, with stock being valued on the basis of factory cost of production.

(b) A comment on the effect, both short-term and long-term, that valuation of closing stock on the basis of prime cost would have.

4 The following data was extracted from the records of Global International and refer to the year ended 31 December, 19-8

	£m
Authorised capital:	
200 million ordinary shares of 50p	100
150 million 8% preference shares of £1	150
Issued capital:	
40 million 8% preference shares of £1	40
120 million ordinary shares of 50p	60
Loan capital:	
10% debenture stock redeemable 2020	400
General administrative expenses	80
Selling expenses	94
Carriage-in	10
Carriage-out	20
Returns-in	14
Returns-out	6
Sales	1904
Administrative salaries	88
Debenture interest paid to 30 June 19–8	20
Distribution expenses	50
Purchases of raw materials	440
Machinery at cost	260
Delivery vans at cost	80
Direct manufacturing wages	500
Factory power	120
Factory indirect expenses	240
Rents (paid to 30 June 19-9)	210
Balances at bank and in hand	84
Debtors	68
Trade creditors	98
Depreciation provisions: machinery	104
delivery vans	48

Stocks (£m) at:	1 Jan 19–8	31 Dec 19–8
Opening stocks, raw materials	120	136
Work-in-progress	66	78
Finished goods	96	124

Note:

(i) Rent is apportioned between the factory and the office in the ratio of three-fifths and two-fifths respectively.

(ii) Debts amounting to £760 000 in respect of general administrative expenses have accrued.

(iii) Depreciation on delivery vans is allowed at 25% diminishing balance and on machinery at 10% straight-line.

(iv) Provision should be made for the preference dividend and for a dividend of 10% on the ordinary shares. There had been no issue of preference shares or of debentures during the course of the year.

REQUIRED:

(a) The company's manufacturing, trading and profit and loss account for the year ended 31 December 19-8, and a balance sheet as at that date.

(b) A comment on the company's profitability and liquidity position as disclosed by the data.

5 The following balances were taken from the books of the Highrise Manufacturing Co at 31 December 19-5:

	£
Stocks at 1 January 19-5:	
Raw materials	17 000
Work-in-progress	10 000
Finished goods	12 000
Stocks at 31 December 19-5:	
Raw materials	13 000
Work-in-progress	13 960
Finished goods	16 000
Carriage on raw materials	560
Carriage on sales	900
Manufacturing wages	41 000
Purchase of raw materials	60 000
Returns inwards	4000
Office rent and rates	1820
Sales	196 000
General expenses	9000
Discount allowed	800
Discount received	1120
Depreciation, factory machinery	1800
Factory expenses	16 000
Selling expenses	18 000
Office salaries	10 600

REQUIRED:

A manufacturing, trading and profit and loss account for the year ended 31 December 19-5.

6 From the following data, draw up the manufacturing, trading and profit and loss accounts of Omega Manufacturing Ltd for the year to 31 August 19-5:

Stocks at 1 September 19-4: raw materials £108 000; work-in-progress £130 200; finished goods £150 486.

Stocks at 31 August 19-5: raw materials £80 100; work-in-progress £140 100; finished goods £140 286.

Wages: direct wages £152 230; work manager's salary £45 320; office salaries £159 114; warehouse staff wages 50 420; directors' emoluments £280 000; salesmen's commissions £82 124

Electricity: factory power £68 112, factory lighting £29 133, office lighting £15 200

Depreciation: machinery £120 000, buildings £20 000.

Other: purchases of raw materials £386 500; sales £1 646 840; carriage-in £5120; carriage-out £4120; advertising £40 000.

Notes:

(i) Directors' emoluments should be apportioned half to manufacturing account and half to P&L.

(ii) Three-quarters of the depreciation charge for buildings relates to the factory, one-quarter to the office block.

7 Judith has been unemployed since leaving full-time education but she believes that she 'could make a go' of designing and producing dresses and selling them direct to local retailers.

Preliminary enquiries with samples among local retailers indicate marked interest. Sales could amount to 600 dresses a year provided the price is right, and that the product is up to sample. Other enquiries reveal the following possible costs:

(i) Premises could be obtained in an enterprise development estate at a cost of £1000 a year inclusive of rent and rates.

(ii) The necessary equipment is likely to cost £8850 and to have a working life of five years.

(iii) The costs of materials for the production of 600 dresses is likely to be in the region of £15 000. Reasonable credit terms will be available from the suppliers.

(iv) Wage costs for assistants will be limited to £6000 a year.

(v) Transportation costs are estimated at £5000 for the year. Two-fifths of this will relate to collecting materials from suppliers; three-fifths to transporting the finished dresses to retailers.

(vi) The estimate for electricity costs is £1200 for the year. Four-fifths of this will be incurred by the workshop, the balance to the office section

REQUIRED:
(a) Judith has asked you
    (i)   to advise her on the significance for her business of the various types of costs involved;
    (ii)   to calculate her selling price per dress assuming that she requires a net profit of 30% on cost;
    (iii) to prepare a draft of the projected final accounts for her first year of operation, assuming that she sells 600 dresses as expected; a note should be added explaining the significance of each section of the accounts.
(b) If Judith found that her dresses proved popular and that production could possibly increased to 800 dresses in the full year, what advice would you give her regarding pricing and production policy?

12 MANUFACTURING ACCOUNTS – 2: FURTHER APPLICATIONS

Think about this . . . *The cost of purchases in a retailer's trading account will normally include one further element than those listed in the manufacturing accounts set out in Chapter 11. What is it?*

12.1 MANUFACTURING PROFIT

The form of the manufacturing account set out in Chapter 11 summarises the *costs of manufacturing only* It does not show any *profit* which might be attributable to the manufacturing activity as such. Consider a manufacturer who makes and sells a standard component (say nuts and bolts) which could alternatively be purchased from elsewhere. If the manufacturer is able to make the nuts and bolts cheaper than they can be purchased elsewhere, then he is making a profit on manufacturing them for himself. If he then makes an additional profit by selling them, he is also making a profit on trading.

12.2 MANUFACTURING ACCOUNTS – ALTERNATIVE FORMAT

By modifying the format of manufacturing accounts, it is possible to separate the profit (or loss) on manufacture from the profit (or loss) on trading. Instead of transferring the *cost of goods produced* from the manufacturing account to the trading account as shown in Example 11.1 on p. 109, the actual or assumed market value of the goods is transferred (and added to opening stock of finished goods in the normal way). The market value is obtained by taking either:

(a) the price at which the goods produced could have been bought on the open market; or

(b) an assumed price (such as manufacturing cost plus a given percentage). Although this gives a fictitious manufacturing profit, it enables a more realistic view to be taken of the efficiency of the trading activity – provided, of course, that the assumed manufacturing profit was itself realistic. This assumed price is known by various terms, e.g. 'manufacturing transfer price', 'warehouse price'.

The balance remaining on manufacturing account after crediting it with the market value of goods produced represents either a manufacturing profit (credit balance) or a manufacturing loss (debit balance) and this is transferred directly to P&L. The subsequent balance of the trading account then represents the profit or trading loss.

EXAMPLE 12.1   A manufacturer produces and markets a standard chemical preparation under a trade name. From the following data construct a manufacturing, trading and profit and loss accounts in both the conventional and the alternative formats.

		£
Raw materials:	opening stock	110 000
	closing stock	130 000
Finished goods:	opening stock	120 000
	closing stock	92 000
Work-in-progress:	opening balance	56 000
	closing balance	58 000
Purchases of materials		160 000
Direct manufacturing costs		60 000
Factory overheads		42 000
Sales		400 000
Administrative, selling and distribution		84 000

The trade price of the goods manufactured during the period was £200 000.

REQUIRED: The manufacturing, trading and profit and loss accounts in conventional and in alternative format.

CONVENTIONAL FORMAT
Manufacturing account for the period ending:

Raw materials		£		£
Opening stock		110 000	Factory cost of production	240 000
Purchases		160 000		
Closing stock		(130 000)		
		140 000		
Direct manufacturing costs		60 000		
Prime cost		200 000		
Factory overheads		42 000		
		242 000		
Work-in progress:				
Opening balance	56 000			
Closing balance	58 000	(2000)		
		240 000		240 000

Trading account for the period ending:

Finished goods:			Sales	400 000
Opening stock		120 000		
Factory cost of production		240 000		
Closing stock		(92 000)		
Cost of sales		268 000		
Gross profit	c/d	138 000		
		400 000		400 000

Profit & loss account for the period ending:

Administrative, selling			Gross profit	b/d 138 000
and distribution		84 000		
Net profit		48 000		
		400 000		400 000

ALTERNATIVE FORMAT
Manufacturing account for the period ending:

Raw materials				
Opening stock		110 000	Trade price of production	c/d 200 000
Purchases		160 000	Loss on manufacturing,	
Closing stock		(130 000)	c/d to P&L	40 000
		140 000		
Direct manufacturing costs		60 000		
Prime cost		200 000		
Factory overheads		42 000		
		242 000		
Work-in-progress:				
Opening balance		56 000		
Closing balance 58 000		(2000)		
		240 000		240 000

Trading account for the period ended:

Finished goods:		Sales	400 000
Opening stock	120 000		
Trade price of production	200 000		
Closing stock	(92 000)		
Cost of sales	228 000		
Profit on trading	172 000		
	400 000		400 000

Profit & loss account for the period ended:

Manufacturing loss	b/d 40 000	Trading profit	b/d 172 000
Administrative, selling			
distribution	84 000		
Net profit	48 000		
	172 000		172 000

12.3   MANUFACTURING LOSS – SIGNIFICANCE

The alternative format set out in Example 12.1 shows up a situation not immediately apparent from the conventional format – namely one where a particularly successful operation (i.e. the trading activity) is covering up a possibly inefficient operation (i.e. the manufacturing activity). There may, however, be good reasons why a manufacturer might wish to continue with the manufacturing operation despite an apparent loss on it. These include:

- The need to have control over supplies, standards and quality.
- The manufacturing loss may be only of a temporary nature.
- The manufacturing operation may be absorbing a considerable amount of overheads which would otherwise have to be absorbed by the trading function. The loss may therefore be more apparent than real.
- Social reasons, such as maintenance of employment levels or avoidance of the loss of goodwill if the factory is closed.

12.4   OTHER CALCULATIONS

In costing, the data required for a particular statement or account is not always immediately available. This means that it has to be calculated indirectly from such information as is available. It is impossible to lay down formulae or procedures to cover every possible situation which may arise. Flexible thinking is therefore required. It is necessary:

(a) to decide what specific data is needed (but is not given) for the statement required; then
(b) whether – and in what way – that required data can be calculated from the (information which is available or which, in the practical situation, can be obtained.

Often, the required data can be calculated accurately. If, however, the calculation is no more than an *estimate* of the required item, or if assumptions have had to be made, then a full explanatory note should be attached to the account or statement.

EXAMPLE 12.2   A forecasted trading account is required by Andrews & Co for the forthcoming year. The data available includes:

(i)   Opening stock £4m
(ii)   Budgeted sales for forthcoming year £55m
(iii)   Rate of turnover – to be no more than 10.

The firm wishes to know

(a)   what their level of purchases will have to be, and
(b)   their closing stock,
        in order to sustain the above requirements.

SOLUTION: The clue to this problem lies in understanding – and being able to *apply* – the formula for calculating the rate of turnover, and in appreciating that purchases will have to match the sales at cost plus the closing stock *less* the opening stock.

$$\text{Sales at cost} \quad = \frac{£55m \times 100}{110} \quad = £50m$$

$$\text{Rate of turnover} \quad = \frac{\text{Sales at cost}}{\text{Average stock}} \quad = 10$$

$$= \frac{£50m}{\dfrac{(£4m + £xm)}{2}} \quad = 10 \text{ (where x = closing stock)}$$

$$\therefore \quad £50m \ = 10 \, \frac{(£4m + £xm)}{2} \quad = £20m + £5xm$$

$$\therefore \quad £50m \quad - £20m \ = £5xm$$
$$x \quad = £6m \ = \text{closing stock}$$
$$\text{Purchases} = \text{cost of sales} + \text{closing stock} - \text{opening stock}$$
$$= £m \ (50 + 6 - 4) = £52m$$

TASK 12.1   The direct wage payments made by a firm producing three products was found to be £362 500. The following data is available:

Product	Production time per unit (mins)	Direct wage rate per hour (£)	Units produced
A	15	5	10 000
B	30	8	20 000
C	90	6	30 000

The direct wage cost is to be apportioned to the three products on the basis of the above data.

PRACTICAL ASSIGNMENTS: 1   The following data was extracted from the records of George Flambo on 31 December Year 1. George, a pharmaceutical chemist, had commenced business on 1 January previous as a manufacturer of two chemical products with the trade names aphondrine and nephrex.

	£
Sales for the year	560 000
Raw materials: purchased during year	225 000
(in stock at end of year	45 000
Wages: direct labour	150 000
Overheads: factory variables	21 000
factory fixed	50 000
selling and distribution variables	36 000
administrative fixed	45 000

Additional information:

	£
(a) Depreciation to be allowed: plant and machinery	27 000
delivery vehicles	13 000

(b)   30 000 bags of nephrex were produced. All were sold at £10 per bag. 45 000 bags of aphondrine were produced, half of which remained in stock at the end of the year. The other half was sold through the trade for a variety of prices throughout the year.

(c)   The production of nephrex uses twice the quantity of raw materials used in the production of aphondrine

(d)   Factory variables and the depreciation of plant and machinery are to be allocated to the products in the ratio of the output produced each year. Fixed factory costs are split equally between the two products.

(e) Aphondrine requires 20 minutes per bag direct labour. Nephrex needs 30 minutes direct labour. Labour is charged at £5 per hour.

(f) Closing stock is valued on the factory cost of production of the product concerned.

(g) A manufacturing profit of 20% (based on factory cost of goods produced) is to be assumed.

(h) Administrative, selling and distribution overheads, and the depreciation of delivery vehicles, are to be allocated to the products in the ratio of their sales during the year.

(i) There was no work-in-progress at the end of the year.

REQUIRED:

(a) A manufacturing, trading and profit and loss account for the year showing the costs and revenues of the two products separately.

(b) A statement explaining the advantages and disadvantages of transferring goods to the trading account at cost plus a percentage.

2 A. Manufacturer produces a standard component which he markets under a trade name. The following data refers to his affairs for the last year:

	£
Raw materials	
opening stock	110 000
closing stock	130 000
Finished goods	
opening stock	120 000
closing stock	92 000
Work-in-progress	
opening stock	15 000
closing stock	13 000
Purchase of raw materials	158 000
Direct manufacturing costs	60 000
Factory overheads	40 000
Sales	400 000
Administrative costs	30 000
Selling costs	25 000
Distribution costs	29 000

(The trade price of the goods manufacturer during the period was £200 000.)

REQUIRED:

(a) A manufacturing, trading and profit and loss account for the year, showing clearly the profit or loss on manufacturing distinct from that on trading. In the light of the position shown up by the accounts, what action do you think A. Manufacturer should be considering?

(b) What other considerations do you consider should be borne in mind before a final decision is made?

3 H.H. Products commenced business on 1 January Year 1 and the following balances were extracted from the books at 31 December following:

	£	£
Sales	1 090 000	
Purchases of raw materials	560 000	
Rent	30 000	
Royalties to patent holder of product, payable on units manufactured	24 000	
Transport costs on purchase of raw materials	4000	
Transport costs on sales	3000	
Wages of workshop staff	250 000	
Returns	2 000	8000
Distribution and selling expenses	40 000	
Supervisory staff wages	48 000	
Administrative costs	70 000	
Factory running expenses	30 000	
Plant and machinery purchased	280 000	
Motor vehicle purchased	20 000	
Factory power	15 000	

Take into account that:
(i) Rent is to be apportioned on the basis of two-thirds factory, one-third office.
(ii) There are accrued distribution costs of £10 000.
(iii) Provisions for depreciation are to be created on the basis of plant and machinery at 20% straight line, and motor vehicles 25% diminishing balance.
(iv) Closing stocks: raw materials £80 000
                      work-in-progress £15 000
                      finished goods 4000 units out of a total production of 25 000 units

REQUIRED:
(a) A manufacturing, trading and profit and loss account for the year ended 31 December Year 1.
(b) A statement explaining the basis on which you have calculated the value of the closing stock of finished goods. State any other bases upon which closing stock could have been valued.
(c) The firm is considering a second, related, product. Explain the advantages in having, and the difficulties involved in obtaining, separate cost figures for each of the two products.

4 Memphis Ltd manufacture components. At 31 March 19-9, the following balances appeared in their ledger:

			£
Ordinary share capital:	1 100 000 share of £1		1 100 000
Stocks at 1 April, 19-8:	raw materials		22 000
	work-in-progress		32 000
	finished goods		40 180
Wages:	direct manufacturing		406 160
	factory supervisors		26 650
	general office		20 400
	warehouse		36 600
Electricity:	direct factory power		190 000
	heating and lighting		18 000
Purchase of raw materials			512 000
Carriage-out			1972
Plant and machinery			160 000
Premises			1 240 000
Returns inwards			840
Office equipment			30 000
Rates			12 000
Administrative expenses			3600
Debtors			28 000
Creditors			24 000
Cash in hand			7324
Sales			1 600 580
Bank overdraft			63 146

Additional information:

1.	Stocks at 31 March 19–9:	raw materials	34 000
		work-in-progress	36 000
		finished goods	36 080

2.   Assets are given at net value. Depreciation should be ignored for the purposes of this assignment.

REQUIRED:

(a)   The manufacturing, trading and profit and loss account of Memphis Ltd for the year to 31 March 19-9, and a balance sheet as at that date. Heating, lighting and rates should be apportioned one-half to the factory, one-third to the warehouse and one-sixth to the office.

(b)   An explanation why it is important in manufacturing to distinguish between variable and fixed expenses. What are the shortcomings of making such a distinction?

5   The following summarised information refers to the affairs of Chemi-Con Ltd which produces and markets a standard chemical preparation under a trade name for the year ended 30 September last:

	£			£
Prime costs	50 000	Stocks of finished		
		goods:	opening	15 000
Factory overheads	10 000		closing	23 000
Sundry office costs	20 000	Sales		90 000

The same product could alternatively have been purchased on the open market at a trade price of £49 000

REQUIRED:
(a) (i) A manufacturing, trading and profit and loss account in the conventional manner, carrying the cost of goods manufactured to the trading account.
    (ii) *On the basis only* of the information disclosed in these accounts, a statement of whether or not the profit appears to be satisfactory.
(b) (i) A revised manufacturing and trading account showing the profit or loss on manufacturing separately from that on the trading operation.
    (ii) A comment on the situation now revealed.
(c) Under what circumstances, and for what reasons, might a manufacturing firm decide to continue to produce its own product even though it could be bought more cheaply on the open market?

6 The OK Engineering Co has been offered as a fixed price contract to manufacture 100 000 standard components at a price of £5 per component. The company accountant has produced the following information relating to the possible costs of the operation:

	£
Raw materials required	198 750
Power	18 750
Heating and lighting	8300
Carriage in	4950
General and factory expenses	2750
Direct labour	50 000
Maintenance labour	19 750
Factory rent and rates	15 000
Depreciation of machinery	17 500
Other indirect factory costs (non-variable)	8600

At the same time, the company received an enquiry for 50 000 of the components in respect of which only £3.50 per component could be charged.

It is the policy of the company to accept only work which will yield a profit on manufacturing of at least 22.5% of the contract price.

The major trade union of the firm is pressing for a major pay award which could increase direct labour costs by as much as 60%.

REQUIRED:

An accounting statement summarising the proposals and their implications, together with a recommendation (with reasons) whether or not the company should accept only the first contract, only the second, or both the first and the second. Include a calculation of the profit/contract price percentage in each case.

You may assume that the company has the capacity to undertake all three contracts if this is wished.

7 The Malvern Engineering Co Ltd produce, among other products, two types of boiler component – the Malvern Standard and the Malvern Super. During the year to 31 December last, the following apportioned costs were allocated to the production section concerned:

	Standard (£)	Super (£)
Stocks of materials: opening	21 000	31 000
closing	22 800	32 600
Purchases of materials	35 645	88 400
Wage costs: direct labour	46 800	62 100
maintenance staff	1500	2200
Factory rent and rates	3500	5800
Number of boilers produced during the year	22 000	85 000

There was no work-in-progress either at the beginning or the end of the year.

REQUIRED:

(a)   A manufacturing account with analysis columns for the two products showing distinctly the prime cost and the factory cost of production of each.

(b)   (i)   A calculation of what would have had to be the minimum selling price of the boilers in order to give a return of 20% on the factory cost of production.

(ii)   Assuming that the prices you have just calculated were in fact charged, prepare an analysed trading account assuming that, at the end of the year, there were 10 000 Malvern Standard and 15 000 Malvern Super boiler components in stock.

13 STANDARD COSTING AND VARIANCE ANALYSIS – 1: MATERIALS AND LABOUR VARIANCES

Think about this . . . *What factors account for the cost of raw materials used in a particular job? If the total cost is less than had been anticipated, is this necessarily a 'good thing'?*

13.1 NATURE AND PURPOSE OF STANDARD COSTING

Standard costing links budgeting with costing. It identifies the basic major elements of cost – i.e. the principal direct and indirect costs – together with sales and compares the actual expenditure (or income) in respect of them with a previously-determined 'control' or *standard* figure.

As in budgeting, the variance is noted and, if significant, investigated. Unlike budgeting, standard costing is primarily concerned with controls centred on individual 'jobs' rather than on annual totals. Also, each of the costs concerned are made up of two separate elements. Since each can vary independently of the other, both have to be checked. An example is the total cost of materials used in a particular job. This is made up of (i) the quantity of material used (including any wastage), and (ii) the 'unit price' of the material.

EXAMPLE 13.1   A firm has found, in the past, that a particular job normally uses 5000 kg of material at a cost of £5 per kg. These have been agreed as the 'standards' for that type of job. In a particular instance, the material cost only £4 per kg, but the job used 5500kg.

This means:

> Total standard (i.e. anticipated) cost: 5000 kg × £5 = £25 000
> Actual cost: 5500 kg × £4 = £22 000
> Net variance (favourable): £3000.

Note, however: Two distinct factors have varied. One is the quantity (5500kg instead of the expected 5000kg – an adverse variance); the other is the unit price (£4 per kg instead of £5 – a favourable variance). There are, therefore, three variances to be considered, namely those arising from:

(a)   the quantity or volume of units used;
(b)   the price per unit of the materials used;
(c)   the net cost of the two combined.

TASK 13.1   Discuss, in a group, the different factors which could have led to the variances identified in Example 13.1. To what extent is it in fact true to say that the variances are *entirely* independent?

13.2 SETTING THE STANDARDS

The first step in setting up a standard cost system is to 'fix the standards' against which the individual variances will be calculated. The factors usually considered are:

- Previous records such as the number of hours' work particular jobs have taken, the quantity of materials used, and current price levels.
- Allowances for foreseeable problems such as material wastage, labour rest periods, holidays, normal rates of sickness.
- Known or anticipated changes which will affect cost levels. Examples (include inflation and general price levels, purchasing policy (e.g. whether a change in supplier is proposed, in quantities to be ordered, or in trade terms), possible wage increases, whether technological development is likely to affect efficiency levels, anticipated level of output (this will directly affect any fixed cost element included within the standard), and general market conditions.

A number of difficulties and problems can arise in the setting of standards. There is, *first*, the initial difficulty of setting a realistic standard, particularly if inadequate data is available on which to base it. *Secondly*, badly set standards can, *if they are too low*, cover up inefficiencies. *If they are too high*, they can undermine morale and motivation.

Thirdly, difficulties can often arise in distinguishing between 'cause and effect' since a particular variance may be either the cause of, or the effect of, another variance. For example, the use of cheap raw materials (resulting in a favourable variance) may well result in a poor standard product, greater wastage of materials, increased machine breakdown and wastage of labour.

Fourthly, fluctuations in variances may well be due to causes external to, and outside the control of, the firm.

Finally, the apparent precision of the variance calculations (see Chapter 14) may suggest a level of accuracy not justified by the circumstances. It is important that the variance figures should be taken only as a guide, not as an exact measure.

The process of standard costing provides useful data on which to base future production planning, pricing policies and other management decisions. The standards, once they have been satisfactorily established, also provide a framework of objectives for the staff to aim at, though it may well be necessary for standards to be modified from time to time in the light of experience and changing circumstances.

13.3 THE PRINCIPAL VARIANCES

After the standards have been established, the actual costs have to be compared with their respective standards and the variances – summarised in Figure 13.1 (on the following page) – calculated. Note how each principal cost element is always affected by two completely independent factors (volume and unit price), each of which influences the final net variance.

13.4 CALCULATION OF DIRECT MATERIALS VARIANCES

After the standards have been set and jobs completed, it is necessary to calculate the variance by comparing the standards against the 'outcomes' – i.e. the actual costs incurred. If the variances are significant (see pp. 61–3), then investigation is required. This

---

Figure 13.1   The Principal Variances

(A)   DIRECT COST VARIANCES
   1.   Materials
      (a)   materials usage variance
      (b)   materials price variance
      (c)   materials net variance
   2.   Labour
      (a)   labour efficiency variance
      (b)   wage rate variance
      (c)   labour net variance
(B)   Indirect cost variances
   3.   Variable Overheads
      (a)   variable overhead efficiency variance
      (b)   variable overhead budget variance
      (c)   variable overhead net variance
   4.   Fixed Overhead Variance
      (a)   fixed overhead volume variance
      (b)   fixed overhead budget variance
      (c)   fixed overhead net variance
(C)   Sales Variances
      (a)   sales volume variance
      (b)   sales price variance
      (c)   sales net variance

Note: In Figure 13.1, the variance marked (a) in each case refers to the 'volume' aspect, and the one marked (b) refers to the unit 'price' aspect, or their respective equivalents.

---

encourages a 'management by exception' approach, the advantage of which is to concentrate attention on problem areas.

This chapter will consider the calculation of variances associated with materials and labour; Chapter 14 will consider sales variances and those connected with overheads.

Materials Usage Variance

This variance measures the difference in the *quantity* of materials actually used and the standard:

(a)   the difference between the standard and the actual quantities used, and
(b)   multiplying that difference by the unit price.

EXAMPLE 13.2   Firm A expected to use 500 tonnes of aggregate at a cost of £20 per tonne in a building project. In the event, the firm used 600 tonnes.

SOLUTION: $(500 - 600) \times £20 = £2000$ (adverse).

Note:
1. In this example, it is assumed that there was no variance between the standard price and the unit price. The complication which this causes is dealt with in Illustration 13.4 below.
2. It is convenient to deduct the *actual* from the *standard*. This means that a positive answer indicates a favourable variance. A negative answer indicates an adverse variance.

Materials Price Variance

This variance measures the difference between the *cost* of materials used and the standard.

EXAMPLE 13.3   Firm B expected to use 500 tonnes of aggregate per mile at a cost of £20 per tonne in a building project. It actually used 500 tonnes as estimated, but at a cost of only £15 per tonne.

SOLUTION: £(20 − 15) × 500 = £2500 (favourable).

Note: The illustration assumed no variation in the quantity used.

Materials Net Variance

The net variance is, basically, the sum of the usage and price variances. However, a complication can arise if the actual and the standard varies in the case of *both* price and quantity. This can, in certain circumstances, lead to 'double counting' when the two variances are added. This is overcome by following convention:

1. When calculating the materials *usage* variance, multiply the 'usage' difference by the **STANDARD** price.

2. When calculating the materials *price* variance, multiply the 'price' difference by the **ACTUAL** of the quantity used.

The rule can be remembered by the phrase:
Quantity **S**urveyors have **P**ersonal **A**ssistants
[i.e. *multiply Quantity by Standard and Price by Actual*]

EXAMPLE 13.4   Firm C expected to use 500 tonnes of aggregate in a building project a road at a cost of £20 per tonne. Its actual use was 600 tonnes at a cost of £15 per tonne.

SOLUTION: Materials usage variance: £(500 – 600) × 20 = £2000 (adverse).
Materials price variance: £(20 – 15) × 600 = £3000 (favourable).
Materials net variance = £1000 (favourable)

Note: The two variances, when combined. give the net variance. The accuracy of the figure can be checked by comparing the total standard cost with the total actual cost, i.e.

		£
Total standard cost:	500 tonnes at £20 per tonne =	10 000
Total actual cost:	600 tonnes at £15 per tonne =	9000
Favourable net variance:		1000

Interpretation of Materials Variance

Considerable care must be taken in interpreting any variance. The first question is whether the standard was a reasonable one in the first place. Obviously, if it was carelessly fixed or has not been up-dated in line with current price levels or conditions, then a variance will occur. *Materials usage variances*, may result from such factors as:

- the use of inferior materials;
- errors in calculating waste;
- poor workmanship or machinery;
- pilfering, or deliberate or careless waste by workers;
- the introduction of improved methods.

Materials price variances may arise from:

- fluctuations in market price
- purchasing on more, or less, favourable terms than anticipated;
- inefficient purchasing;
- failure to take advantage of discount terms.

The possible 'diseconomy' of cheap prices should be remembered. It is always possible to achieve a favourable price variance by purchasing sub-standard materials, but this could have highly adverse effects upon usage variances, and even wage rate variances (through the time wasted on having to re-work reject products). There could also be repercussions on the reputation of the firm and its products.

13.5 CALCULATION OF DIRECT LABOUR VARIANCES

The net direct labour variance is calculated from the labour efficiency variance and the wage rate variance. These are equivalent to the 'quantity' aspect and the 'price' aspect of materials variances respectively, and the same principles apply.

Labour Efficiency Variance

This variance measures the difference between the standard and the actual hours of work of a particular job (the 'quantity' aspect). If standard hours *and* the standard wage rate differ from the actual, the same problem regarding double counting arises which was described in connection with materials variances. The same convention is followed in order to overcome the difficulty and therefore the formula used is:

(standard hours *less* actual hours) × *STANDARD* wage rate.
(Note how this follows the 'QS – PA' rule)

An example is given in Example 13.5 below.

Wage Rate Variance

This variance measures the difference between the standard and the actual wage payments (the 'price' aspect). Following the convention, the formula used is:

(standard wage rate *less* actual wage rate) × *ACTUAL* hours
(Note how this again follows the 'QS – PA' rule)

Labour Net Variance

The labour net variance is the sum of the labour efficiency and the wage rate variances.

EXAMPLE 13.5   A firm expects a particular process will require 400 hours of labour at a wage rate of £5 per hour. In the event, it takes 500 hours and, because of the need to undertake much of the work on an over-time basis, the wage cost is £6 per hour.

SOLUTION: Labour efficiency variance: £(400 – 500) × 5 = £500 (adverse).
Wage rate variance: £(5 – 6) × 500 = £500 (adverse).
Net labour variance: 1000 (adverse).

Note:

1.   Since the component variances are both adverse, they are added in order to obtain the net variance.
2.   Remember: 'Quantity' variation multiplied by the *standard* of the price. 'Price' variation multiplied by the *actual* of the quantity.

Interpretation of Labour Variances

Labour efficiency variances may arise from:

- use of unsuitable labour;
- use of unsuitable machinery;
- mechanical breakdown;
- production delays;
- delays in the delivery of raw materials;
- poor quality raw materials;
- bad management organisation of the work flow;
- psychological attitudes – efficiency is notoriously low the day after holidays, and the afternoon before the weekend.

Labour wage rates are often agreed nationally or with trade unions, and as such are out of the control of the individual firm. However, variances may arise from:

- an unanticipated wage rate rise;
- a variation in the grade of labour used – such as where older workers who are paid on an age-related scale have been employed instead of younger people or where the work has been undertaken by a more highly qualified person than is necessary, and payment is made according to the qualification; this could happen, for example, where an organisation has a 'no redundancy' agreement.
- the employment of staff at overtime rates, when the standard assumed normal rates.

13.6 SOME WORKED EXAMPLES OF VARIANCE CALCULATION

1.   Calculate the materials variances where the standard for a job was 120 yards of material at £7 a yard, but the actual proved to be 110 yards £5 per yard.

SOLUTION: Materials usage variance: $(120 - 110) \times £7$ $= £70$ (favourable).
Materials price variance: $£(7 - 5) \times 110$ $= £220$ (favourable).
Materials net variance: $= £290$ (favourable).

2. Calculate the labour variances for a process which normally requires 700 hours of labour at a wage cost of £10 an hour, but which in fact took 650 hours at a wage cost of 12 per hour.

SOLUTION: Labour efficiency variance: $(700 - 650) \times £10$ $= £500$ (favourable).
Wage rate variance: $£(10 - 12) \times 650$ $= £1300$ (adverse).
Labour net variance $= £800$ (adverse).

PRACTICAL ASSIGNMENTS

1 Explain the main objectives of a standard costing system and discuss the principal factors which should be taken into account when setting standards.

2 Sailcraft Ltd is a small firm manufacturing boats for use on local lakes. A budget for December estimated that 100 tonnes of steel at £180 per tonne would be used and 240 cubic metres of timber at £300 per cubic metre. The actual usage was 110 tonnes of steel purchased at £170 per tonne, and 260 cubic metres of timber purchased at £320 per cubic metre.

The budget also anticipated that 800 hours of semi-skilled labour at £7 per hour would be required together with 1600 hours of unskilled labour at £5 per hour. In the event, 840 hours of semi-skilled labour were used at £7.60 per hour and 1500 hours of unskilled labour at £5.20 per hour.

REQUIRED:
(a) A calculation of the standard and the actual cost of production for the month. Demonstrate that it is equal to the total of
   (i) the materials price and usage variances *(the variances for steel and timber should be calculated independently and then added)*
   (ii) the direct wage and labour efficiency variances *(the variances for direct skilled and direct unskilled should be calculated independently and then added)*
(b) Comment on the materials price variance and the labour efficiency variances.

---

14 STANDARD COSTING AND VARIANCE ANALYSIS – 2: SALES AND OVERHEAD VARIANCES

Think about this . . . *If material or wage costs exceed the standard figures, they are treated as adverse variances. In this chapter, we shall see that if the sales figures exceeds the standard, it is a favourable variance. Is this a contradiction of the general rule, or is there a logical reason underlying it?*

Chapter 13 considered the direct variances. The same general principles apply to the sales and the overhead (indirect) variances which are dealt with in this chapter.

14.1 SALES VARIANCES

The sales variances follow the normal pattern and consist of the sales volume variance, the sales price variance and the sales net variance. As with the cost variances, the volume and the price variances can vary independently of each other, and for different reasons. There tends, however, to be a closer connection between them than with costs and variations in either one usually cause – or are the result of – variations in the other.

The procedure for calculating sales variances is the same as for direct cost variances (see Chapter 13) except that income is being dealt with and not expenditure. This means that:

A *FAVOURABLE* variance is one in which the standard *is less than* the actual.
An *ADVERSE* variance is one which the standard *is greater than* the actual

The same rule is applied as in the other variances, i.e. the 'quantity' variation is multiplied by the *standard* of the price, and the 'price' variation is multiplied by the *actual* of the quantity. However, in order that the arithmetic sign (+ or −) should indicate whether the variance in favourable or adverse, the standard should be deducted from the actual (*not* the actual from the standard as in the case of the cost variances).

EXAMPLE 14.1   A firm's target sales budget for a particular period was 20 000 units at £10 per unit. The sales actually achieved were 15 000 units at £12 per unit.

SOLUTION: *Sales volume variance: (15 000 – 20 000) × £10 = £50 000 (adverse)*
Sales price variance: £(12 – 10) × 15 000   = £30 000 (favourable)
Sales net variance: = £20 000 (adverse)

Interpretation of Sales Variances

Sale volume variances may be affected by:

- changes in the demand pattern;
- breakdowns or failures in the distribution channels;
- incompetent sales staff;
- ineffective advertising;
- effect of technical developments
- government and other reports – and even by unfounded rumour;
- the emergence of rival products or substitutes;
- changing levels of tax or import duties;
- general social or economic prosperity or depression.

Sales price variances may be affected by:

- the efficiency of the sales team in negotiating terms;
- necessary revision in prices due to rival or substitute products;
- deliberate policies of the firm e.g. to clear old stocks or to counter increased cost levels.

14.2 OVERHEAD VARIANCES

Preliminary Calculations

Overhead variances are difficult because overheads are usually expressed as the total sum spent (or to be spent), not as a rate per hour. This is because there is no direct *unit of input* with which overheads are directly linked. However, in order to obtain a measure for monitoring purposes, the total sum expended on overheads has to be related to an input unit with which it has an indirect connection. The one usually chosen is direct labour hours. Unfortunately this has a further complication in that labour hours only have meaning as a measure of input if considered in conjunction with units of output: obviously, 500 hours of labour producing 3000 units is less effective than 500 hours of labour producing 6000 units.

The problem is tackled by calculating beforehand:

(a) *the standard variable overhead rate* by dividing budgeted variable overheads by budgeted hours
(b) *the standard fixed overhead rate* by dividing budgeted fixed overhead costs by budgeted hours
(c) the standard hours for the work actually completed – i.e. by dividing actual units produced by budgeted units and multiplying by budgeted hours.

The variances are then calculated on the basis of the formulae set out in Figure 14.1. Notice how these follow the same basic principles described for the direct cost variances.

Figure 14.1   Summary of Sales and Overhead Variances

SALES:
Volume variance:
(actual sales volume – standard sales volume) × standard unit selling price.
Price variance:
(actual unit selling price – standard unit selling price) × actual sales volume.

OVERHEADS:
Variable overhead efficiency variance:
(standard hours – actual hours) × standard variable overhead rate
Variable overhead budget (spending) variance:
(standard variable overhead rate × actual hours) – actual variable overhead cost.
Fixed overhead volume variance:
(budgeted hours – standard hours) × standard fixed overhead rate.
Fixed overhead budget variance:
(budgeted fixed overhead cost – actual fixed overhead cost)

EXAMPLE 14.2   A firm's production plans anticipated 200 hours direct labour producing 800 units, a variable overhead cost of £600, and fixed overhead cost £4000.
Its actual production was 400 hours direct labour producing 1200 units, a variable overhead cost of £1000, and fixed overhead costs of £3500.

Initial calculations

1. Standard variable overhead rate:

    $$\frac{£600 \text{ (budgeted variable overheads)}}{200 \text{ (standard hours)}} = £3 \text{ per standard labour hour}$$

2. Standard fixed overhead rate:

    $$\frac{£4000 \text{ (budgeted fixed overheads)}}{200 \text{ (standard hours)}} = £20 \text{ per labour hour}$$

3. Standard hours for work actually completed:

    $$\frac{1200 \text{ (actual units produced)}}{800 \text{ (budgeted units)}} \times 1200 \text{ (budgeted hours)} = 300 \text{ hours}$$

These figures are then used in the calculation of the overhead variances as follows:

Variable overhead efficiency variance:

   ([standard hours for work completed *less* actual hours for work completed] multiplied by standard variable overhead rate)

   $= (300 - 400) \times £3 = £300$ (adverse)

Variable overhead budget variance:

   ([actual hours for work completed multiplied by standard variable] *less* actual variable overhead cost)

   $= £(400 \times 3) - 1000 = £200$ (favourable)

Fixed overhead volume variance:

   ([budgeted standard hours *less* standard hours for work completed] multiplied by standard fixed overhead rate)

   $= (200 - 300) \times £20 = £2000$ (adverse)

Fixed overhead budget variance:

   (budgeted fixed overhead costs less actual fixed overhead costs) $=$ $£(4000 - 3500) = £500$ (favourable)

Interpretation of Overhead Variances

In order to identify the causes of overhead variances, it is necessary to examine the component parts of the variance and establish which has caused the departure from the anticipated norm. Some of the component elements, such as indirect materials, are controllable items and variations in these may warrant further enquiry on the shop floor or in the purchasing office. Others, such as depreciation, are matters of accounting policy and procedure.

Usually, the variances are caused by changes in the *level of activity* – namely, that the volume of activity is either greater than, or lower than, that originally planned.

The actual numeric result is, in itself, relatively meaningless and should be taken as a pointer rather than a measure. Accurate forecasting of overhead costs is extremely difficult and, in practice, a certain degree of variance should be expected

14.3 VARIANCE REPORTING

It is pointless to maintain a standard costing system, with calculation of the variances, unless appropriate action is taken where this should be necessary. This means that there should be proper systems for:

(a) reporting variances to those responsible for taking action;
(b) identifying those variances which are significant and which warrant investigation.

It is normal for the costing department of an organisation to circulate on a regular basis a statement of the variances over a stated period. This is known as a *variance report*. The structure, form and layout of these reports varies considerably from one organisation to the next. The problems raised by the variance report, and their implications, are usually discussed at the regular meetings of the organisation's management team.

PRACTICAL ASSIGNMENTS:

[1] Metalprod Ltd assemble a specialised valve for the engineering industry. The valve is manufactured from two basic sub-components which are manufactured by, and purchased from, other companies. The company has a standard cost system and the following data refers to production and sales for last month:

REQUIRED:

	Budget for month	Actual for month
Materials:		
Sub-component A	100 units at £135 per unit	110 units at £125 per unit
Sub-component B	200 units at £225 per unit	290 units at £230 per unit

Labour:

Direct skilled	800 hours at £8 per hour	850 hours at £8.50 per hour
Direct unskilled	1600 hours at £5 per hour	1650 hours at £5.50 per hour
	2400	2500

Sales:	800 valves at £180 each	1000 valves at £170 each
Overheads:		
Variable	£9000	£10 500
Fixed	£6000	£5500

(a) A calculation of the standard and the actual profit or loss for the month. There were no stocks of materials in hand, nor any work-in-progress, at either the beginning of the month or the end of the month. All valves produced were sold

(b) A calculation of the variances and a report outlining their significance.

2 Delta Agricultural Products Ltd manufactures artificial fertiliser which has to pass through two separate processes – process A and process B. The following data was drawn up in February last and refers to anticipated levels of activity for process A for March last:

Output	24 000 bags
Raw materials required	12 000 kilos at £5 per kilo
Direct labour	144 000 hours at £4 per hour

In the event, the company experienced sharply rising costs and a downturn in demand with the result that only 18 000 bags were produced. The cost of the raw materials actually consumed at standard prices was £50 000, but £55 000 was actually paid for it. Direct labour hours amounted to 124 000 for which the wage bill proved to be £558 000.

   It was subsequently calculated that the variances in respect of process B were:

Labour efficiency variance	£1500 (favourable)
Labour wage rate variance	Nil

REQUIRED:

(a) Cost statements in respect of process A for the month based on:
   (i)   The anticipated levels of production and costs.
   (ii) The anticipated levels of production and costs flexed to the actual production.
   (iii) The actual level of production and costs.

The budgets should include computations of the data which will be required for the calculation of materials and labour variances.

(b)   Calculations of the materials usage and price variances, and of the labour efficiency and wage rate variances, based upon:
(i)   the original budget
(ii)   the flexed budget.

(c)   A comment why the variances based upon the flexed budget are a better guide to management than those based upon the original budget.

(d)   A brief explanation of possible reasons for the variances in respect of process B.

REVISION QUESTIONS: PART III

In questions 1–10, answer:
A if only the assertion (the first part of the question) is correct
B if only the response (the second part of the question) is correct
C if both the assertion and the response are correct statements, but the response is NOT a correct explanation of the assertion
D if both the assertion and the response are correct statements and the response IS a correct explanation of the assertion
E if neither the assertion or the response are correct

1 | The net variation in opening and closing valuations of work-in-progress is shown in the manufacturing account | *because* | the variation affects the cost of goods produced.

2 | Factory overheads do not include factory power | *because* | factory power is part of the electricity charged to the P&L account.

3 | Salesmen's commissions are reckoned as part of prime cost | *because* | they are a variable expense.

4 | The price at which goods produced could be bought is sometimes charged to manufacturing account | *because* | this distinguishes profit on manufacturing from profit on trading.

5 | Machinery depreciation provision is charged to the P&L account | *because* | it is normal to charge general overheads to P&L

6 | Marginal cost will be lower than average cost if average cost is falling | *because* | rising average cost means an increasing marginal cost

7 | In calculating variance, the 'volume' element is multiplied by the standard of the other, and the 'price' element by the actual of the other | *because* | this eliminates the risk of 'double counting'.

8 | A nil net variance does not necessarily mean efficient production | *because* | standards may have been badly set in the first place.

9 | Marginal cost does not include fixed costs | *because* | fixed costs are not included in average total cost.

10 | A favourable materials price variance is not necessarily desirable | *because* | it may have been achieved through buying sub-standard materials.

In questions 11–25, note the option which best answers the question.

11 | The primary purpose of manufacturing accounts is to calculate the
(a) prime cost
(b) factory cost of production
(c) profit on manufacturing
(d) factory overheads.

12 | Factory overheads include
(a) work-in-progress
(b) direct manufacturing wages

(c) carriage on purchases of raw materials
(d) supervisors' salaries

13 Cost of raw materials consumed is part of
(a) prime cost
(b) work-in-progress
(c) factory overheads
(d) general overheads.

14 The closing value of work-in-progress appears in the
(a) trading account and balance sheet
(b) manufacturing account and trading account
(c) manufacturing account and balance sheet
(d) P&L account and balance sheet.

15 In addition to allowing for variations in work-in-progress, the cost of goods manufactured is calculated by adding
(a) materials used and direct expenses, and deducting factory overheads
(b) prime cost, direct expenses and factory overheads
(c) prime cost and factory overheads, and deducting direct expenses
(d) materials used, direct expenses and factory overheads.

16 Depreciation of factory buildings is treated as
(a) an indirect overhead in the P&L account
(b) a factory indirect cost in the manufacturing account
(c) a direct factory cost in the manufacturing account
(d) a general overhead in the P&L account.

17 Factory overheads do not include
(a) factory lighting
(b) foremen's wages
(c) machinery depreciation
(d) cost of raw materials used.

18 For balance sheet purposes, closing stock of finished goods should be valued at the lower of
(a) net realisable value or factory cost of production
(b) prime cost or market value
(c) net realisable value or selling price
(d) marginal cost of production or net realisable value.

19 Which of the following is least likely to be a controllable cost?
(a) wages
(b) advertising
(c) postage and packing
(d) factory insurance.

20 Wages of factory cleaners employed temporarily in cleaning the warehouse should be charged to
(a) direct factory expenses
(b) manufacturing overheads
(c) distribution costs
(d) administrative charges.

21 Overhead apportionment means
(a) dividing overheads on the basis of the benefits received by each cost centre
(b) an arbitrary division of overheads between cost centres
(c) a charge for the use of the overhead facility by the cost centre
(d) a hire charge to the cost centre for the use of the overhead facility centre.

22 Marginal cost is not an acceptable basis for the valuation of closing stock for
(a) short-term decision making
(b) cost control purposes
(c) balance sheet listings
(d) management accounting procedures.

23 The standards set for a production run were 1800 kg of material at a price of £2 per kg. The out-turn figures were 1200 kg at £3 per kg. The net materials variance was
(a) £2400 (adverse)
(b) £3000 (favourable)
(c) nil
(d) £1800 (favourable).

24 The standards for a job were fixed at 60 hours at a wage cost of £5 per hour. The job actually took 70 hours at a wage cost of £6 per hour. The labour efficiency variance and the wage cost variance were, respectively,
(a) £50 (adverse); £70 (adverse)
(b) £60 (adverse); £60 (adverse)
(c) £700 (adverse); £5 (adverse)
(d) £10 (adverse); £10 (adverse).

25 A firm's expenses for the production of 100 units of a product were raw materials £1000, administrative costs £850, direct manufacturing expenses £3000, factory overheads £1500, selling and distribution costs £650, royalty to patent owner for each unit produced 10% of factory cost of production. The marginal cost of the last unit produced was:

(a) £6050
(b) £75.50
(c) £55
(d) £60.50.

In questions 26–30, answer:
A if responses a, b and c are all correct
B if responses a and b only are correct
C if responses b and c only are correct
D if response a only is correct
E if response b only is correct
F if response c only is correct

26 Standard costing involves
(a) determining desirable levels for price and performance before the production begins
(b) comparing pre-determined levels of price and performance with the actual levels

(c) adjusting price and performance to the pre-set standards.

27 A favourable materials usage variance indicates that the use of materials was
(a) greater than anticipated
(b) less than the standard
(c) the same as the standard

28 The labour net variance includes the
(a) variable overhead variance
(b) labour efficiency variance
(c) wage rate variance.

29 Factory overheads includes
(a) salesmen's commissions
(b) foremen's wages
(c) machine operatives' wages.

30 A firm's current assets at a given date includes
(a) the value of the work-in-progress
(b) the stock of finished goods
(c) the amount of raw materials in hand.

The calculations for the answers to questions 31–35 should be based on the following selected accounting data of Wartoys Ltd for the year ended 31 December 19–. Wartoys Ltd is primarily a manufacturing company, but purchases some products ready made.

(£000)
Stocks at 1 January: raw materials 300; work-in-progress 80; finished goods 450.
Stocks at 31 December: raw materials 140; work-in-progress 100; finished goods 390
Wages: manufacturing 900; factory indirect 260; administrative 180.
Electricity: direct power 100; factory light and heating 120; office lighting and heating 80.
Depreciation: machinery 200; delivery vehicles 120; office equipment 49.
Rent and rates: factory 240; office 130.
Maintenance: factory 20; warehouse 30.
Purchases: raw materials 900; finished goods 300.
Goods manufactured are transferred to the warehouse at prime cost plus 60%

31 Calculate the cost of raw materials used.

32 What was the prime cost of the goods produced?

33 What did factory overheads amount to?

34 State the factory cost of production during the period.

35 What was the assumed manufacturing profit or loss?

MAJOR ASSIGNMENT: PART III

INTRODUCTION

You are employed as a trainee accountant in the firm of Berry and Galway which acts for many different types of clients. You are provided with financial details concerning two of the clients. You should study the information carefully because part of your training programme requires you to prepare working papers on selected clients.

Client 1: Mick Wright

Mick Wright is a self-employed antique restorer who specialises in the restoration of furniture and paintings. The following is a breakdown of his actual costs and sales for the year ended 31 December last.

		£
Turnover		30 000
Materials:	opening stock	500
	closing stock	200
Direct labour costs for restoration		15 000
Business rate		2000
Wages of part-time staff		2500
Heat, light and electricity		1200
Telephone bill		500
General expenses		1500
Insurance		800
Depreciation of fixtures		100
Materials purchases		6000

Although he has a full work-book, Mick is very concerned about his business because he fears that he is not making any money. Mick believes that his job-costing may be at fault.

Mick quotes the following job as an example. Phil Woodcock, the captain of the local golf club, asked him to restore a picture belonging to the club. Mick estimated, at the time, that the job would take 8 hours at a labour cost of £4.50 per hour and that he would use four boxes of materials at £3.25 per box. Mick therefore quoted Phil a price of £65 for the job.

The job, however, took 10 hours to complete. The price of materials had been increased to £4 per box, but he managed to complete the job using only 3.5 boxes.

Mick's had decided that, for this particular job, he would add a mark-up of 32% on his labour and material costs in order to arrive at the price. It was his practice to vary the mark-up according to the job and the customer.

Client 2: Bari and Khan

Bari and Khan is a profitable partnership concerned with the manufacture of sportswear. The following data is available for the year to 31 December last:

	£
Sales: 26 000 dozen at £50 per dozen	
Materials: opening stock	15 000
closing stock	23 000
Finished goods: opening stock 4000 dozen at £38 per dozen	
closing stock 2350 dozen	
Purchases of materials	530 000
Direct labour	300 000
Production salaries and indirect labour	98 000
Factory indirect expenses	58 000
Salesmen salaries and commission	65 000
Selling and marketing expenses	26 000
Distribution costs	19 000
Staff salaries (administration)	22 000
Office and administration expenses	7250

The firm manufactured 24 450 dozen sports shirts during the period.
The overheads had been analysed by the accountant as follows:

> Factory indirect: variable four-fifths; fixed one-fifth.
> Salesmen's salaries and commission: variable three-fifths; fixed two-fifths.
> All other overheads should be regarded as fixed.

Bari and Khan had budgeted to use 50 000 boxes of material at £11 per box, and 70 000 direct labour hours at £4.50 per hour. Their actual was 43 500 boxes at £12 per box and 73 350 labour hours at £4.09 per hour. They had budgeted to manufacture 25 000 dozen shirts during the period.

REQUIRED: The senior partner, Carol Walker, has asked you for the following information. She requires this information because both clients have made appointments with her to review their financial position.

1. *Client 1 – Mick Wright*
   (a) Prepare a profit statement for the year ended 31 December last.
   (b) A note outlining how Mick might be advised how to improve his job costing. Illustrate your note with references to the Phil Woodcock job. Explain why his present policy is not good business practice.
2. *Client 2 – Bari and Khan*
   (a) Produce a statement showing the value of closing stock of finished goods using both marginal cost and total cost bases. Which method should be used in the final accounts, and why?

    (b) Prepare a draft manufacturing, trading and profit and loss account for the year ended 31 December last.

    (c) Prepare a variance report for the following:
  (i)   material price
  (ii) material usage
  (iii) labour usage
  (iv) labour efficiency

Explain why the variances might have occurred.

PART IV FINANCIAL TECHNIQUES AND DECISION MAKING

TOPIC OVERVIEW

Effective decision making is dependent upon the accuracy and suitability of the 'feed' information. Various techniques have been developed which enable us to review the mass of data coming forward and to pin-point – and *assess* – those aspects of crucial importance to the problem under review.

Chapter 15 is concerned with the importance of the 'break-even' point which is the minimum level of production at which it is usually feasible for firms to operate. Alternative ways of calculation are considered together with further applications and complications. Chapter 16 takes the argument further by examining more closely the relationships between costs, volume of production and profit.

Chapter 17 is concerned with appraising and comparing the return on capital investment – investment, that is, in 'capital projects' such as new factories, railways, dams and generating stations. In situations where – over a number of years – there is a different pattern of investment and returns on each of the options available, the appraisal can be particularly difficult. Chapter 17 discusses specific techniques that have been developed to help resolve such problems.

15 BREAK-EVEN ANALYSIS

Think about this . . . *Assume that you about to set up a small manufacturing firm. What factors would you bear in mind when deciding the minimum level of production at which you could operate?*

15.1 THE BREAK-EVEN POINT AND ITS SIGNIFICANCE

Definition

> The *break-even point* is the number of units which must be produced and sold in order to cover the costs of production.

Significance

- If sales do not reach the break-even point, losses will be incurred.
- If sales exceed the break-even point, then a profit is made.
- At the break-even point, there is neither profit nor loss.

Every firm has fixed costs. These are usually heavy and have to be incurred before any production takes place. Each item then produced incurs a variable cost. The selling price of each unit is designed to cover its variable cost and to make a 'contribution' towards meeting the fixed costs. When the contribution equals the fixed costs, the break-even point has been reached. Thereafter, the contribution from additional units will make up the profit.

The main value of calculating the break-even point is that it identifies the *minimum level of production and of sales* which is necessary in order to avoid a loss. In addition, it indicates the extent to which production can be reduced without making a loss (see *margin of safety* on pp. 157–9). The technique can also be used for

155

forecasting profits at different levels of production, particularly if a graphical approach is adopted. In addition, it permits the comparison of alternative policies.

15.2 CALCULATING THE BREAK-EVEN POINT

It is important in production planning to know the number of units which must be produced in order to 'break-even'. This can be calculated arithmetically or graphically.

Arithmetic Calculation

Since the break-even point is that at which the contribution (i.e. income *less* the variable costs) is sufficient to meet the fixed costs, it can be calculated by the formula:

$$\frac{\text{fixed costs}}{\text{unit selling price} - \text{unit variable}}$$

EXAMPLE 15.1   A firm produces shoes which sell at £50 a pair. The firm has fixed monthly overheads of £25 000 and each pair of shoes then costs £35 to produce. How many pairs of shoes does the firm have to sell in order to break even?

SOLUTION: Applying the above formula, we obtain:

$$\frac{25000}{50-35} = 1\ 666.6\text{r}$$

Although the arithmetic answer is 1666.6r pairs per month, when deciding break-even points, common sense must be used. Is it reasonable to talk of producing and selling 0.6r of a pair of shoes? Is anyone likely to buy 0.6 of a pair? We can only realistically think in terms of complete pairs of shoes. The answer, therefore, must be that the break-even point is at 1667 pairs, since 1666 pairs would yield a loss.

Calculation of Sales Revenue at the Break-even Point

Sales revenue at the break-even point is given by multiplying the break-even production (or the formula which gives the break-even production, provided this results in a discrete figure) by the unit selling price. Thus, in the case of the shoes, the break-even point has been reached when the monthly sales revenue reaches

$$1667 \times £50 = £83\ 350$$

TASK 15.1   A company manufactures a standard garden summer-house. During the last financial year, it produced and sold a total of 900 summer-houses which were sold at £350 each. Fixed costs of £60 000 were incurred, and the variable costs amounted to £200 per unit.

REQUIRED: Calculate   (a)   the total sales revenue on the operation;
(b)   the profit;
(c)   the break-even point in terms of
    (i)   units produced   (ii)   sales revenue.

In the forthcoming financial year, it is expected that both fixed and variable costs will rise by 10% but that output and sales can be maintained at the original level.
    Calculate the percentage by which selling price will have to be increased in order to break-even at the same unit level of production

---

Calculation by Graph

A break-even graph maps the costs and income on the y (vertical) axis against the number of units produced on the x (horizontal) axis. This is shown in Fig 15.1 (on following page), which is based on the data in Example 15.1 above. Note the fixed costs, which are constant for all levels of production. The variable costs at each level of production are added to the fixed costs to give the total costs of production at each level. The income from sales is graphed starting from zero for nil production.
    The break-even point is at the intersection of the income curve with the total cost curve. Note how, on the graph, this agrees with the arithmetic calculation in Example 15.1. The distance between the income curve and the total cost curve at any other point represents the loss or the profit for that particular level of production.
    The *actual level of production* can also be marked on the graph. If this is beyond the break-even point (i.e. if profits are being made), the distance between the break-even production and the actual level of production is known as the *margin of safety*. As well as being shown diagrammatically on the graph, the margin of safety may be expressed in terms of:

(a)   units (actual production *less* units necessary to break-even);
(b)   net revenue (actual sales revenue *less* revenue at break-even);
(c)   percentage (fixed costs as a percentage of sales revenue).

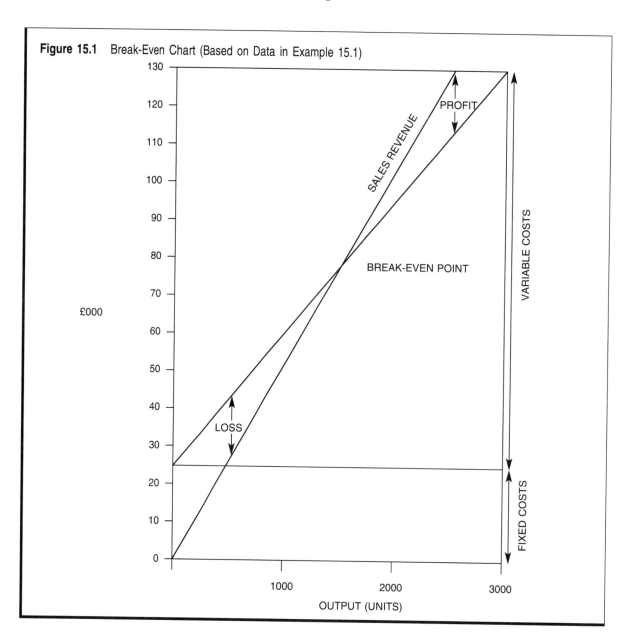

Figure 15.1   Break-Even Chart (Based on Data in Example 15.1)

An advantage of the graphical approach is that it is possible to map quickly a number of possible options on the same graph (see Task 15.3). A disadvantage, however, is that it is difficult to obtain the same accuracy as by arithmetic calculation.

TASK·15.2   Market research indicated that a company would be likely to sell up to 80 000 units of a product at a unit price of £30. Fixed costs would be £300 000 and variable costs would be £20 per unit. It was decided to produce 60 000 units.

Construct a break-even graph for the planned production. Identify the break-even point in terms of unit output and sales revenue, the profit or loss on the production run, and the margin of safety (if any).

Check the break-even point and your calculation of profit or loss arithmetically. Express the margin of safety in each of the three ways listed in the text.

15.3 VARIATIONS IN THE METHODS

Contribution Break-Even Graphs

The unit contribution is the difference between the unit selling price and the unit variable. Taking the data in Example 15.1, the unit contribution was:

$$£(50 - 35) = £15$$

Total contribution at any given level of production is given by the difference between total sales revenue and the total variable costs at that point. Taking again the data in Example 15.1, the contribution at the break-even point of 1667 pairs of shoes is:

$$£(1667 \times 50) - £(1667 \times 35)$$

$$= £(83\ 350 - 58\ 345)$$

$$= £25\ 005$$

Note: The contribution is normally equal to fixed costs at break-even point. The fixed costs in the case of shoes amounted to £25 000. The slightly higher figure for the contribution calculated above is as a result of the practical requirement of taking 1667 pairs of shoes (and not 1666.6 pairs) as the break-even point.

The conventional break-even graph can be re-drawn to show the contribution at each level of output. In order to show this, the variable costs are marked on the graph first: the fixed cost is then shown as an addition to the variable cost. The income from sales is marked in as before. This is shown in Figure 15.2.

The distance between the variable cost curve and the income curve represents the contribution at each level of production. Note how the total contribution increases as production expands (corresponding to the progressively reducing loss shown on the graph in Figure 15.1). At the break-even point, the contribution can be seen to equal fixed costs.

Figure 15.2   Contribution Break-Even Graph (Based on Data in Example 15.1)

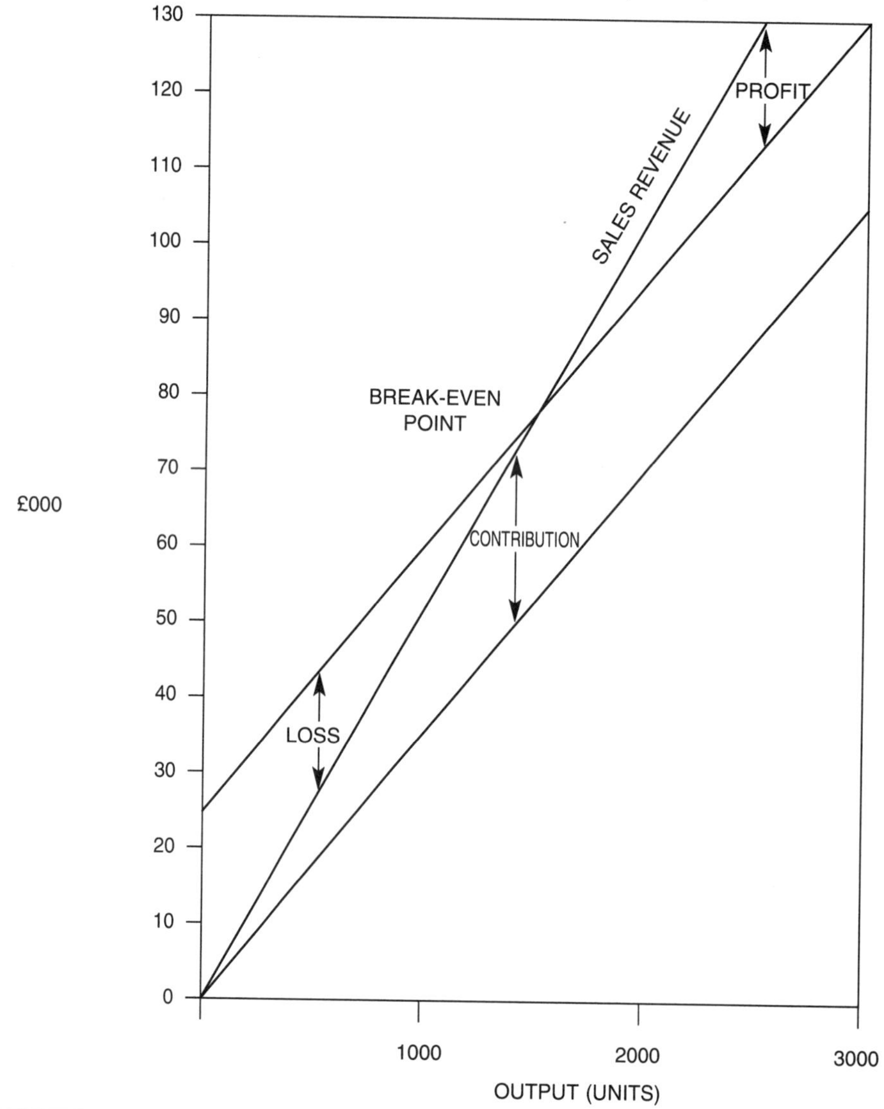

The total contribution continues to increase after the break-even point, and this of course corresponds to the increasing profit margin on the graph in Figure 15.1.

TASK 15.3   Calculate the unit contribution, the contribution at break-even point, and the contribution on total actual production for each of the products described in Tasks

15.1 and 15.2. (The answers can be obtained by graphing the data.) Comment on the relationship between the contributions and the profit.

The contribution concept is important for small businesses as well as large, although the owner may well be unaware that he is using it. A small retail shop, for example, will have to meet all its fixed charges (such as rent, rates, lighting, insurance) whether or not any sales are made, as well as the cost of any goods which cannot be returned to the suppliers. If few sales are being made, the contribution towards the fixed costs will be small and losses will be likely. The owner will then be concerned with selling what he can, even if it means reducing the mark-up on the goods, in the hope of increasing turnover – and also the contribution.

Scale of Production

Batch production

Where batch production is concerned, the break-even point can be discussed in terms of batches. If, for example, the shoes in Example 15.1 could only be produced in batches of 300, then 6 batches (1800 shoes) would have to be produced as obviously five batches (1500) shoes would not produce sufficient income. The calculation may be made directly by substituting batch cost data for the unit data. Fixed costs remain the same at £25 000, the batch income would be (300 × £50) = £15 000, and the batch variable would be (300 × £35) = £10 500. The calculation would therefore be:

$$\frac{25000}{15000 - 10500} = 5.55, \text{ i.e. 6 batches.}$$

'Total output' data

Data may be given only for total output levels. The information can be reduced to unit cost level, or alternatively calculated directly by the following formula:

$$\frac{\text{fixed costs} \times \text{level of output}}{\text{total sales revenue} - \text{total variables}}$$

(This has the effect of multiplying both lines of the equation by the level of output.)

As an example, suppose the data relating to the shoes had been given as:

Anticipated output 8000 pairs; Fixed costs £5000; Total variables £56 000; Total sales revenue £80 000.

The calculation then becomes:

$$\frac{5000 \times 8000}{80\,000 - 56\,000} = 1\,666.6r, \text{ i.e. } 1\,667 \text{ pairs, as before.}$$

This method can often be employed when the data given makes reduction to unit costs and income inconvenient or impossible.

TASK 15.4   A review of last year's production indicated that the 500 units produced sold for a total of £1.2m. Total variable costs amounted to £100 000 and fixed costs were £950 000.

Calculate, *from the above information only*, the break-even point in terms of (i) units produced and (ii) sales revenue.

Assuming that each unit was sold at the same price, calculate the unit price and unit variable, and check your-break-even calculation.

15.4 CRITICISMS OF BREAK-EVEN ANALYSIS

It is vital, in the practical situation, to be as aware of the shortcomings of a particular technique as it is to know how to use the technique itself. The principal criticisms of break-even analysis are:

1. The specific nature of the calculations suggest a greater level of precision accuracy than may actually exist in the practical situation.
2. 'Linear' relationships are normally assumed, particularly for projected levels of output, i.e. that fixed costs remain permanently fixed, and that variable costs increase proportionately (as shown by a straight line on the graph). Neither of these assumptions is necessarily true.
3. A clear and finite distinction is assumed between fixed and variable costs. This is not always the case in the practical situation.
4. Break-even analysis tends to assume that costs can be accurately predicted for the future, and for different levels of output. This, again, is seldom the case in practice.
5. It is assumed that the entire output will be sold.

Break-even calculations must, therefore be approached with some caution. As with so many of these techniques. it should be looked upon as a guide, not as a conclusive answer.

15.5 BREAK-EVEN IN A MULTI-PRODUCT SITUATION

A more complex problem arises where several products with differing cost structures are being produced at the same time, or where a differential pricing policy (i.e. different prices to different customers for the same product) is being operated. It is, of course, easy to calculate the break- even point on each of the products independently, but if:

(a) the contribution of each is different, and
(b) they are being produced in various quantities simultaneously

the break-even point – as measured in terms of *total* revenue and *total* costs – will not be the sum of the two individual break-even points. For example, assume the total fixed cost of two products being manufactured together is £200 000. The contribution of product A is £100 per unit and of product B £10 per unit; it is obvious that the break-even point will be reached much more quickly (in terms of units produced) if production is concentrated in product A rather than product B.

If the order in which production takes place is not known, then it can only be assumed that the manufacture of each product is spread evenly throughout the year. The break-even point on total production can then be found by applying the basic formula to the total revenue, and the total costs, for the period concerned.

EXAMPLE 15.2   The following data to the production of two different types of aircraft which have been sold to both home and foreign governments:

	Aircraft A	Aircraft B
Number of aircraft produced	100	200
	£m	£m
Total variables	1 600	1000
Fixed cost	120	16
Total sales revenue	1800	1200

REQUIRED: 1. The break-even points in the production of each individual aircraft and the sales revenue associated with each of these points.
2. Assuming that production and sales of both aircraft were evenly spaced throughout the period, the break-even point for the firm's complete production and the sales revenue at that point.

3. A statement of the danger which may arise if the firm relies on the figures in 2 above, and the assumption proves not to be true.

SOLUTION   1. *Break-even point on production of the individual aircraft*

	Aircraft A		Aircraft B

Aircraft 'A' $\dfrac{120m \times 100}{1800m - 1600m}$ Aircraft 'B' $\dfrac{16m \times 200}{1200m - 1000m}$

= 60 aircraft   = 16 aircraft

Revenue at individual break-even points
Aircraft 'A' 60 × £18m = £1080m Aircraft 'B' 16 × £6m = £96m

2. *Break-even on total production*
(assuming production and sales evenly spaced throughout the period)

$$\frac{136m \times 300}{3000m - 2600m}$$

= 102 aircraft

Revenue at this break-even point
Since production and sales are evenly spaced for both aircraft throughout the period, it means that production of aircraft A to aircraft B must be in the ratio of 100:200 (i.e. for every one of the A type, two of the B type would be manufactured and sold). The 102 aircraft at the break-even point must therefore consist of 34 A and 68 B type aircraft. Consequently, sales revenue would be:

(34 × £18m) + (68 x £6m) = £1 020m

3. *Danger in the assumption*
The above calculations show that, although a greater *number* of aircraft have to be produced in 2 above in order to reach the break-even point than is necessary in 1 above, the sales revenue required is in fact less. This is, in fact, because of the ratio in the production of the two aircraft, i.e. fewer A type aircraft being produced compared with B type aircraft.

Sales revenue at break-even point, therefore, depends upon the 'product-mix'. If the assumption made in 2 above is not valid, then the sales revenue at break-even point will be other than the figure calculated.

PRACTICAL
ASSIGNMENTS

1 A firm producing cigarette lighters decides to introduce a new model. Fixed costs are expected to be £30 000 per month and variable expenses £2.40 per lighter. Market research indicates that if the lighters are sold at £6 each, a minimum of 9000 and a maximum of 10 000 could be sold each month.

Additional research shows that with a suitable 'twist' in the advertising campaign, the lighters could be sold for £10 each but that monthly sales at this price would not exceed 4000 lighters.

REQUIRED:
(a) A graph of the above information and calculate the minimum production to cover costs at each possible price (i.e. the break-even points). Check the answers arithmetically.
(b) A statement of the advice you would give to the firm regarding its pricing policy.
(c) What advice would you give to the firm if, due to a shortage of raw materials, the maximum production run the company could consider was 5000 lighters?

2 Agri-Products Ltd produce a major component for agricultural tractors. The following was originally forecast for the next financial year:

Sales: units	20 000
	£
Sales revenue	3 000 000
Direct materials	600 000
Direct labour	1 000 000
Other manufacturing costs: variable	560 000
: fixed	200 000
Administrative, selling and distribution: variable	140 000
: fixed	100 000

Subsequent developments have made it desirable to revise the forecast, taking into account:

(i) As a result of inflation, anticipated fixed costs should be increased by 10% and variables (other than wages) by 15%.
(ii) A wage award is pending and it is possible that direct wages will increase by 12%.
(iii) The market research department state that sales of 20 000 units can only be maintained if price increases are limited to 5%.

REQUIRED:
(a) A revised forecast based on the information above showing total contribution and anticipated profit or loss.
(b) The break-even points under both the original forecast and the revised forecast.
(c) Advice to the management on the steps which could be taken to improve the forecasted profit, and the likelihood of restoring it to the level of the forecast.

3 Imbibe Ltd's managers are considering introducing a new product. It is reckoned that, in its first two years, it will absorb fixed costs of £500 000 of

£580 000 respectively. This will include development costs of £900 000 which will be written off in equal instalments over three years. Other data available:

	Year 1	Year 2
Sales (units)	3500	7000
	£	£
Unit selling price	600	700
Unit costs: material	210	250
wages	115	130
variable overheads	175	225

Market research reports indicate that, in the third year of production, costs are likely to remain as in the second year, but a drop in unit price of £20 could increase demand by 1000 units.

REQUIRED:
(a)   A calculation of (i) the break-even points, and (ii) the profit or loss for each of the first two years of production.
(b)   A comment on the policy that management should follow.

4   Gemini Ltd was formed to manufacture and market a new type of security lock. It is proposed to charge £9 for each lock plus VAT. Fixed factory overheads for the first year have been estimated at £210 000 and fixed administrative and marketing overheads at £190 000. Unit costs are expected to be £2 for materials, £3.50 for labour and 50p for variable overheads. It is planned to produce 200 000 units during the first year.

REQUIRED (1):
(a)   A calculation of the break-even point.
(b)   A break-even graph showing the margin of safety.

Market research suggests that a sales drive in the second year could increase annual demand to 300 000 locks. The necessary advertising would cost an additional £50 000. Direct costs could be expected to increase by 10% and fixed costs, other than advertising, by 5%.

REQUIRED (2):
(c)   A report to management arguing whether the additional sales drive should be undertaken or not.
(d)   A statement explaining the effects that an increase of 2% in the rate of VAT might have.

5   Bond and Robinson are manufacturers, packers and wholesalers of office supplies and equipment. The partners are considering introducing a new line of copier paper to be packaged in boxes containing 100 individually-wrapped reams. It is proposed to sell the paper at £250 per box. Fixed overheads, including selling and distribution costs, are likely to be £20 000. Variable costs in pence per ream are estimated at:

| Labour | 30 | Paper | 60 |
| Packaging | 40 | Indirect variables | 15 |

REQUIRED:
(a) A calculation of the number of boxes necessary to break-even.
(b) A contribution break-even graph.
(c) A statement of the sales necessary if a profit of £30 000 is to be achieved on the line.
(d) A statement explaining the shortcomings of break-even analysis.

6 Disco-green Ltd has pioneered the development of cheap pre-recorded disks of pop music which self-destruct after being played for the sixth time. It is expected that there will be a considerable demand from parents, once the advantages of the product are fully appreciated. In its first three years of operation, the company expects to produce and sell 30 000, 50 000 and 60 000 disks respectively, and it expects to sell these at an average price of £10 per disk.

The present cost of raw materials amounts to £3 per disk and it is expected that this will increase by 5% in the second year and by 6% in the third year. Direct labour during the first year will cost £1 per disk. Wage awards have already been agreed which will increase this by 3% in each of the two subsequent years. Variable overhead costs for the first year are £0.50 per disk, but these are expected to increase substantially over the next two years. An increase of 30% per annum should be allowed.

Fixed costs for the first year have been estimated at £100 000. This includes research and development costs of £90 000 which are being written off in equal instalments over three years. The pure fixed cost element is likely to increase by 20% per annum.

REQUIRED:
A suitable accounting statement showing the break-even points, and the projected profits, for each of the three years.

7 Simon Deller manufactures and sells golf clubs, specialising in metal-headed woods. He has produced the following forecast financial information for the next twelve months.

	£
Sales	750 000
Direct costs: materials	150 000
labour	250 000
Manufacturing overheads: variable	140 000
fixed	50 000
Sales and administrative overheads: variables	35 000
fixed	25 000

Simon has based the above forecast on the sale of 15 000 metal clubs. After taking advice from his business partner Helen Moody, he decided that the original forecast should be reviewed to take account of the following:

(i)   All fixed costs should be decreased by 5%.
(ii) The assembly workers on the production line had now settled for a new wage deal which would include a 4% rise for direct labour plus a bonus of £2.50 for each club sold.
(iii) On reflection, Simon has come to the conclusion that unit sales of 15 000 clubs can only be achieved if any price increases are limited to 5% on each club.
(iv) All other variables will have to be increased by 10%.

REQUIRED:
(a) A calculation of the number of clubs necessary to break-even under the original estimate.
(b) A calculation of the number necessary to break-even under the revised estimate.
(c) A revised income statement showing the total contribution and the total profit.
(d) A summary of what other actions Simon could take to increase his profits.

8 Carpenter and Joiner make garden furniture. They currently produce 5000 garden seats subject to fixed costs of £20 000 and variable costs of £320 000. The unit selling price is £80.

REQUIRED:
A calculation of the selling price which would have to be charged if the present break-even point was to be maintained following an increase in variable costs of 8% and an increase in fixed costs of £2500.

9 Williams & Co produce quality pottery for the export market. The following forecast data has been produced concerning a certain type of jug:

Sales: 20 000 jugs at a unit price of £40
Maximum output: 25 000 jugs
Fixed costs for the period: £110 000
Unit variable costs: direct labour £20; direct material £7; variable overheads £5.

REQUIRED 1:
(a) A calculation of the break-even point in units and turnover.
(b) The number of units which must be sold to make a profit of £30 000.
(c) If the firm sold its maximum output, a calculation of the total contribution and the total profit.

16 COST–VOLUME–PROFIT ANALYSIS

Think about this . . . *Consider the graph in Figure 16.1.*

Figure 16.1 Profit-Volume Graph (Based on Data in Example 15.1)

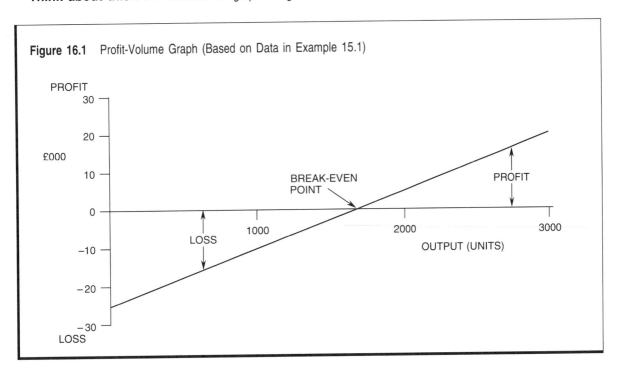

1. What do you think it represents?
2. In what ways does it differ from the graphs shown in Figures 15.1 and 15.2?
3. From the graph in Figure 16.1, can you identify the amount of the fixed costs?
4. At what point does the break-even point occur?
5. Can you calculate the total of the variables at the break even point?

16.1 PROFIT-VOLUME GRAPHS

The distinction between fixed and variable costs is fundamental to an understanding of manufacturing accounts, to marginal costing, break-even studies, flexible budgeting, forecasting and contribution analysis. The distinction is also an essential element in studies relating volume of production to profit. This area is known as cost–volume–profit (CVP) analysis.

Figure 16.1 is a profit–volume graph in respect of the production of shoes described in Example 15.1. In many ways, this graph is similar to the break-even charts discussed in Chapter 15 but it shows the data in a different way.

TASK 16.1 Abida Ltd makes a single product. Its maximum level of output is 15 000 units with fixed costs of £72 000. Unit selling price is £25 and unit variable is £13.

REQUIRED: Prepare a profit–volume graph to illustrate the above data.

The primary purpose of profit–volume graphs is to highlight the relationship between sales revenue (though output can be substituted on the x axis) and profit (or loss). It therefore enables the profit at different levels of sales to be read much more easily. The graph does not, however, identify the distinction between fixed and variable costs though it is possible to calculate them. In order to do this, three important relationships must be remembered:

1. At the break-even point, there is neither profit nor loss.
   Therefore, on a profit–volume graph, the break-even point can be identified as the point at which the curve cuts the x (horizontal) axis – a point which corresponds to the calculated break-even point in Example 15.1
2. At the nil production level, there are no variable costs.
   The loss at this point therefore represents the total of fixed costs, i.e. £25 000. Having identified the fixed costs, we can therefore say that the variable costs equal total revenue less fixed costs: £(83 350 – 25 000), i.e. £58 350.
3. Since there is no profit or loss at break-even, the revenue at this point must represent the total of fixed and variable costs only.

TASK 16.2 Jaconda Ltd is a small manufacturing company producing a specialist component for the motor trade. The unit variable costs for a particular period will be direct labour £8, direct material £5 and variable overhead £2. The allocated fixed costs amount to £50 000. The maximum level of output during the period will be 20 000 units and the unit selling price £20.

REQUIRED: (A)   Draw a break-even graph in respect of the above data.

The company is considering increasing the selling price of the product by 20% and improving the quality of the component. This will increase the unit direct labour cost by £2 and the unit material cost by £1. All other costs are expected to remain the same.

REQUIRED: (B)   Construct a profit–volume graph in respect of the new proposal.

As with break-even graphs, profit–volume graphs can be used to compare quickly and easily data relating to different products, or to alternative courses of action.

TASK 16.3   Construct a profit–volume graph from the following data relating to three products produced by a particular firm.

PRODUCT	A	B	C
Maximum output (000 units)	12	12	12
Apportioned fixed costs (£000)	72	60	50
Unit variable cost (£)	32	17	55
Unit selling price (£)	40	32	65

Identify the break-even point in each case.

16.2 CONTRIBUTION/SALES (C/S) RATIO

The contribution/sales (C/S) ratio is the ratio between the contribution and the sales revenue. This ratio remains constant for any level of production provided sales revenue and variables are linear. This means that, given data for one level of activity, it is possible to calculate data for other levels.

We have already seen that the contribution is the unit selling price *less* the unit variable, this being the 'contribution' which each unit makes towards (i) the fixed costs and then (ii) the profit. In the case of the shoes in Example 15.1, the unit price was £50 of which £35 was taken up by covering the variable costs. This meant that the contribution was £15 per unit.

Assuming that both sales revenue and variable costs are, in fact, linear, then the ratio between the two will remain constant for any level of production (i.e. at 70% of revenue in the case of the shoes). This enables profit to be predicted for any level of production without having to calculate the change in the variables.

As a simple example, suppose a firm's sales are £35 000 and variable costs £24 500, the contribution will be £10 500 – in other words, variable costs are 70% of sales revenue, and contribution 30%. If the firm's sales are increased to £60 000, then the management could expect the variable cost to rise to £42 000 (i.e. still 70% of sales) and the contribution to £18 000 (still 30% of sales).

EXAMPLE 16.1 A firm sells three products coded A, B and C. The following information refers to the last financial year:

Product	A £m	B £m	C £m
Sales revenue	4.5	3.6	4.2
Direct variables	3.375	2.52	3.36
Fixed costs were £2.1m			

Market research indicates that sales in the current year will rise to £9m for product A, £4.5m for product B and £6.3m for product C. Unit sales revenue and unit variables will remain as last year, but fixed costs are expected to rise to £2.5m.

REQUIRED: Net profit for the past year, and the anticipated net profit for the coming year.

SOLUTION:

Past year:		A	B	C
Sales revenue	(£m)	4.5	3.6	4.2
Direct variables	(£m)	3.375	2.52	3.36
Contribution	(£m)	1.125	1.08	0.84
C/S ratio	(%)	25	30	20
Total contribution	(£m)	3.045		
Fixed costs	(£m)	2.1		
Net profit	(£m)	0.945		

Next year:		A	B	C
Sales revenue	(£m)	9.0	4.5	6.3
(C/S ratio – calculated above)		*(25%)*	*(30%)*	*(20%)*
Contribution	(£m)	2.25	1.35	1.26
Total contribution	(£m)	4.86		
Anticipated fixed costs	(£m)	2.50		
Anticipated profit	(£m)	2.36		

TASK 16.4 The total sales revenue in respect of a particular product is £20 000 and the total variable cost is £12 000.

REQUIRED: (a) Calculate the contribution-sales ratio.
(b) Calculate the actual increase or decrease in the contribution if sales revenue had been (i) £25 000, (ii) £18 000, (iii) £32 000.

16.3 PRODUCT-MIX CALCULATIONS

Contribution analysis can be used to determine the most profitable 'mix' of a number of different products given a limitation in one resource item (known as the 'key factor'). The procedure is to:

1. Calculate the contribution in respect of each product.
2. Calculate the contribution per unit of the key factor.
3. Plan production on the basis of 2 above, giving priority to products with the highest contribution per unit of the key factor, noting the amount of the key factor being consumed at each stage.

EXAMPLE 16.2 A firm estimates a maximum demand of 5000 units for each of its products coded A, B, C and D. The relevant costing data is as follows:

	A	B	C	D
Unit selling price (£)	40	60	80	72
Labour input: hours per unit	3	2	7	5
: cost at £4 hour	12	8	28	20
Materials: consumption, kg per unit	6	18	10	12
: cost at £2 per kg)	12	36	20	24

REQUIRED: The best 'product mix' in each of the following two separate situations:

(a) if the maximum amount of labour available is 41 000 hours;
(b) if the maximum amount of materials which can be obtained is 110 000 kg.

SOLUTION: (a) Labour as key factor (£):

	A	B	C	D
Unit selling price	40	60	80	72
Total unit variables (labour + materials)	24	44	48	4
Contributions per unit	16	16	32	28

Labour hours required		3	2	7	5
Contributions per labour hour		5.3	8	4.57	5.6
Priority for production		3	1	4	2

PRODUCTION PLAN

	Units demanded	Use of key factor (units)	Cumulative use of key factor	Contribution (£)
Product B 5000		$(5000 \times 2) = 10000$	10000	$5000 \times 16 = 80\,000$
D 5000		$(5000 \times 5) = 25000$	35000	$5000 \times 28 = 140\,000$
A 2000		$(2000 \times 3) = 6000$	41000	$2000 \times 16 = \underline{32\,000}$
				$\underline{\underline{252\,000}}$

Note: No production of C

(b) Materials as the key factor (£)

	A	B	C	D
Contribution per unit (see above)	16	16	32	28
Materials needed	6	18	10	12
Materials per unit	2.6	0.8	3.2	2.3
Priority for production	2	4	1	3

PRODUCTION PLAN

	Units demanded	Use of key factor (units)	Cumulative use of key factor	Contribution (£)
Product C 5000		$5000 \times 10 = 50000$	50000	$5000 \times 32 = 160\,000$
A 5000		$5000 \times 6 = 30000$	80000	$5000 \times 16 = 80\,000$
D 2500		$2500 \times 12 = 30000$	110000	$2500 \times 28 = \underline{70\,000}$
				$\underline{\underline{310\,000}}$

Note: No production of B

Note that when labour was the key factor, there was no production of product C. When materials were taken as the key factor, there was no production of product B. It must be appreciated that the calculations are only concerned with the theoretical maximisation of profit. There may well be other factors which a prudent businessman would consider, e.g.:

1. Product C (i.e. the one not produced) may be an essential component of the other three which may be useless without it. The manufacturer may not wish to be so dependent on an outside supplier.
2. Consideration may have to be given to long-term customer relations and market-share.

TASK 16.5   A firm makes three products, the unit costs (£) of which are:

PRODUCT	A	B	C
Direct materials	50	30	40
Direct labour	20	28	10

Fixed costs are estimated at £700 000.
The anticipated demand for the products are:

Product A: 7000 units at £100 each.
Product B: 11 000 units at £90 each.
Product C: 9000 units at £85 each.

The firm discovers that there is a 25% shortfall in the amount of material available.

REQUIRED: Calculate the production programme which will maximise profit.

16.4 'MAKE OR BUY' DECISIONS

Firms often have the option of buying components on the open
market instead of manufacturing them for themselves. The decision
whether 'to make or buy' depends upon the circumstances in which
the firm is placed at the time.

'Make or Buy' Decisions when the Firm has Idle Capacity

The decision in these circumstances will depend solely on a
comparison of the marginal cost of manufacture with actual cost of
purchasing.

EXAMPLE 16.3   A firm currently manufactures 50 000 units of product 'Alpha' at a fixed
cost of £800 000 and a unit variable of £10. Unit selling price is £50. The
profit on manufacture is therefore £1 200 000.
   The firm receives an additional order for 10 000 units of component
'Beta' which can be produced at a unit variable of £8.50 and for which a sale
price of £14 per unit is offered. Surplus capacity exists at the factory and no
additional fixed costs will be incurred. Alternatively, the component can be
'bought in' at £12 per unit.
   Should the firm 'make or buy'?

SOLUTION: Since fixed costs are already covered by the main product, the contribution to profit arising from manufacturing the additional order is

$$10\,000 \times £(14 - 8.50) = £55\,000$$

This is obviously more than the contribution which would arise from 'buying out' which would be

$$10\,000 \times £(14 - 12) = £20\,000$$

'Make or Buy' Decisions When the Firm Does Not Have Idle Capacity

A more complicated position arises when the additional production requires a cut-back in current production. In this situation, the true cost of manufacture is the marginal cost of producing the component *plus* the reduction in contribution on the production which is sacrificed. It is this which has to be compared with the price of 'buying out'.

EXAMPLE 16.4 Facts as in Example 16.3 except that in order to produce 10 000 of the components, machines would have to be used which would otherwise produce 1000 units of product 'Alpha' (unit marginal cost £10, unit selling price £50). Should the firm 'make or buy'?

SOLUTION:

	£
Cost of producing 10 000 units of component Beta (£8.50 × 10 000) =	85 000
Reduction of contribution of product Alpha (£[50 – 10] × 1000) =	40 000
	125 000
Less: cost of 'buying out' (£12 × 10 000)	120 000
GAIN BY BUYING OUT	5000

'Make or Buy' Decisions when Additional Fixed Assets would be Required

In this situation, the cost of the additional fixed assets must be added to the variable cost in order to find the net increase in contribution.

EXAMPLE 16.5 Facts as for Example 16.3 except that the production of the additional components would require increasing the fixed-asset investment from £800 000 to £900 000.

SOLUTION:

	'MAKE' SITUATION	£
	Cost of additional fixed assets	100 000
	Additional variable cost	85 000
		185 000
	Sale price	140 000
	Reduction in contribution	
	(i.e. loss on additional production)	45 000

'BUY' SITUATION

As seen in Example 16.3, 'buying out' would result in an additional contribution 10 000 × £(14 − 12), i.e. £20 000.

In this situation, it would therefore be preferable for the firm to 'buy out'. Note that the example does not allow for any residual value of the additional fixed assets.

Other Considerations

A number of further factors must be taken into account when making a 'make or buy' decision. If investment has to be made in additional fixed costs, these may permit additional work to be undertaken at a later date, or may have some scrap value, which will affect the calculation. In addition, there may be cash-flow complications. Cash flow is of crucial importance to firms, and an injection of a large amount of working capital into additional fixed assets may cause short-term problems. Against this, however, is the cash inflow which would result from the sale of the additional production. The time factor between the cash outflow and the subsequent inflow could be an important consideration. A further problem may arise from the need to recruit – and then possibly dispense with – skilled labour to undertake the additional production.

If the decision is made to 'buy out', the reliability of the supplier has to be considered. Problems will obviously arise if a firm enters into a contract to supply goods relying on external suppliers who then fail to do so or if deliveries are delayed. 'Buying out' may also mean the loss of a certain degree of quality control (some firms, e.g. Marks and Spencers) have overcome this by purchasing the complete production of a supplier; this gives them much greater opportunity to insist on their own very high standards of quality.

PRACTICAL ASSIGNMENTS

[1] Blix PLC is a major manufacturing company which produces a certain component for one of their products. The unit costs (£) attributable to the component are:

Direct labour   5
Direct materials   10
Variable overheads   7

Some 60 000 of the components are produced each year and the fixed cost allocation is £840 000. The component can be purchased on the open market at a unit price of £31.

REQUIRED:
A summary of arguments whether the firm should continue to produce the component, or whether it should buy on the open market.

2 Alex Ltd is a small company with limited resources. It currently 'buys in' 40 000 units of a component at price of £24 each. Investigation reveals that the company could manufacture the component at the following unit costs (£):

Direct labour   5
Direct materials   8
Variable overhead   6

This would mean, however, taking up machine-time at present allocated to the manufacture of the main product which would result in a reduction in output of 4000 units of that product. The main product has a marginal unit cost of £240 and a unit selling price of £320.

REQUIRED:
A report stating whether the company should continue to 'buy out' or should manufacture the component itself.

3 A.P. Construction assemble bicycles from imported kits. Careful estimates made at the beginning of their last financial year (which ended on 31 December last) indicated that a sales revenue of £1 430 000 would be needed in order to break-even.

Their records for the year indicated that the actual sales revenue was £1 300 000 and that a gross profit of £182 000 was made. The firm had no opening or closing stock of kits, assembled cycles or of work-in-progress. Kits imported and assembled during the year had cost £546 000. Variable manufacturing costs were £78 000 and direct labour costs £364 000. The contribution was £260 000.

REQUIRED:
An operating statement for the year to 31 December last, showing the fixed costs for manufacturing, and the fixed costs and variable costs for administration, distribution and selling.

Guidelines
1. *Remember that direct costs vary directly with output (and in this case with sales since all stock was sold).*

2. *The contribution is a constant percentage of sales revenue.*
3. *The net profit at break-even point is nil.*

4 Byrne Ltd manufactures a single product. Estimated fixed costs for a particular production run are £65 000 and the unit variable is £25. The unit selling price is £35. The total production run will be 12 000 units.

REQUIRED:
(a) Complete the following table.

Output (000 units)	Fixed costs (£000)	Total variables (£000)	Total costs (£000)	Sales (£000)	Profit(loss) (£000)
0	65	–	65	–	(65)
1	65	25	90	35	(55)
2					
3					
4					
5					
6					
7					
8					
9					
10					
11					
12					

(b) Using the data provided by the table, draw
(i) a break-even graph
(ii) a profit–volume graph.
(c) Explain any important relationships which your graphs demonstrate between profit, volume, fixed costs and variable costs. Illustrate your answer with actual figures drawn from the data given.

5 (a) A product takes 36 hours to process on machine X. Its unit variable cost is £115 and its selling price is £220. A component part is at present purchased from a sub-contractor at a unit price of £12 but could be manufactured on machine X in 2.5 hours at a unit variable cost of £8.50. Machine X is already working at full capacity.

REQUIRED:
A statement explaining whether the firm should continue to purchase from the sub-contractor.

(b) A manufacturer of power generators, which has been operating at 75% of full capacity, has been considering using the spare capacity to produce smaller generators which are currently bought from a local supplier for £520 each. The necessary equipment and labour are already available. Direct material costs would amount to £130 per unit, and direct labour to £260 per unit. The plant overhead rate has been calculated at 150% of direct labour; of this, 60% is variable and 40% is fixed.

REQUIRED:
A statement, with reasons, whether the manufacturer should 'make or buy'. Explain any non-financial reasons which should also be taken into account.

6 The budgeted profit and loss statement of Murray Manufacturing for the year to 31 December next is:

PRODUCT:	A £000	B £000	C £000	TOTAL £000
Sales	192	432	240	864
Cost of sales				
Materials	72	72	48	192
Labour	48	96	48	192
Fixed overhead	72	72	48	192
Variable overhead	24	48	24	96
Profit (Loss)	(24)	144	72	192

The fixed costs have been apportioned between the products on the basis of floor area occupied. They remain constant irrespective of the number of products manufactured. It has been proposed that the manufacture of product A should be abandoned.

REQUIRED:
(a) An accounting statement showing the contribution made by each product.
(b) A comment, with reasons, stating whether or not you agree with the proposal to drop product A.

7 A firm's actual sales and production figures for January and February last were:

(£000)	January	February
Sales	200	300
Costs	150	212.5
Profit	50	87.5

Throughout both months, the unit variable cost was £25 and the fixed cost remained constant.

REQUIRED:
A calculation of the:

(a) contribution/sales ratio
(b) unit selling price
(c) fixed costs
(d) number of units required to break-even in each of the months
(e) sales volume required to achieve a profit of £150 000 in each of the months.

17 APPRAISAL OF CAPITAL PROJECTS

Think about this . . . *Which would you rather have – and why:*

(a) *£10 000 today*
(b) *£2100 a year for the next five years*
(c) *£14 500 in five years' time?*

17.1 THE IMPORTANCE OF THE TOPIC

Firms – and governments – always have more capital projects which they would like to undertake than they have money with which to finance them. This means that decisions have to be made. It is particularly important that the *right* decisions are made because:

- Large sums of money are usually involved.
- Once such projects are begun, they cannot usually be abandoned without considerable financial loss – nobody is interested in half a bridge.
- Such projects can influence the fortunes of a firm – or of a country – for many years.

This means that a careful assessment of the expected returns must be made in each of the uses to which the available funds could be put. In the practical situation, social as well as purely financial aspects have also to be considered.

17.2 METHODS OF APPRAISAL

Go back to the think about this section ... at the beginning of the chapter. Did you opt for:

(a) the cash sum immediately, or

(b) the flow of income over a number of years, or
(c) the greater cash sum at the end of the period?

Different people will choose differently, depending upon their needs and desires. So the question becomes:

Which of the options will meet YOUR needs best?

Similarly with large-scale capital projects. Before deciding in which project to invest, the question has to be asked:

What is wanted from the investment?

The firm, or the government, has to decide what sort of 'return' it wants from the investment. Will it be

(a) a quick return of a significant part of the investment,
(b) a steady flow of income over a number of years,
(c) the maximum possible return irrespective of when received?

It may also have to consider the timing of the receipts and payments, and whether changes in the value of money over that time are likely to affect the calculation.

   Once it has been decided what sort of return is wanted, the various investment options must be assessed to see which best meets that need. This process is known as *capital appraisal.*

   The principal techniques have been developed to assist in such appraisals are:.

1. Estimate of *overall profit.*
2. Calculation of the *average annual rate of return* on capital invested.
3. Identification of the *pay back* point.
4. Application of *discounted cash flow* (DCF) techniques.

DCF procedures include a number of techniques, including estimates of

(a) net present value (NPV), and
(b) internal rate of return (IRR).

It must be emphasised that these methods assess only the *financial* aspects of the investment : other factors – e.g. whether sufficient capital is obtainable, whether the necessary technical and servicing facilities are available, and what environmental and social implications there might be – may also have to be taken into account before final decisions are made.

Each of the techniques assess the project *from a different point of view*. The different approaches will be explained by reference to the situation described in Example 17.1.

EXAMPLE 17.1   A multi-national oil exploration company is considering developing one of three possible sites. The investment required and the anticipated returns are summarised below:

INVESTMENT COSTS ($m)			
	SITE A	*SITE B*	*SITE C*
Investment cost (start of year 1)	112	150	180
Additional investment cost (end of year 2)	–	54	–

RETURNS ($m)									
	SITE A			*SITE B*			*SITE C*		
YEAR	Net cash income	Deprec- iation *Cum.*	Net profit (loss)	Net cash income	Deprec- iation *Cum.*	Net profit (loss)	Net cash income	Deprec- iation *Cum.*	Net profit (loss)
1.	18		28 (10)	14		34 (20)	20		36 (16)
2.	20	(38)	28 (8)	20	(34) 34	(14)	25	(45) 36	(11)
3.	42	(80)	28 14	50	(84) 34	16	42	(87) 36	6
4.	40	(120)	28 12	80	(164) 34	46	70	(157) 36	34
5.				100	(264) 34	66	133	(290) 36	97
6.			8	60	(324) 34	26 120			110

Notes:

(i)   *Net cash income* is the cash income less cash expenses arising from normal operations.
(ii)   The column marked *Cum.* represents the cumulative net cash income to date.
(iii)   Taxation is ignored in this Example.
(iv)   The amounts in brackets represent the cumulative net cash income year by year.
(v)   It should be assumed that all returns are received at the end of the year.
(vi)   The cost of capital to the company is 12% (see Figure 17.1).
(vii)   The American dollar ($) is the 'international currency' of the oil industry.

Overall Profit

The *purpose* of this approach is simply to compare the total profits from projects over the whole period of the operation. The *method* consists simply of deducting total costs from total income. Examination of the net 'profit' columns in Example 17.1 shows that the total profit for each site is:

$$\textit{Site A } \$8m \qquad \textit{Site B } \$120m \qquad \textit{Site C } \$110m$$

On the basis of this assessment, therefore, site B would be chosen as the preferred option.

This method has the advantage of being easy to calculate and to understand. It does not, however, relate profit to the amount which had to be invested in the first place, nor does it make any allowance for the 'timing' of the receipts (notice that the net cash income in respect of both of the other sites is higher in the each of the first three years than it is for site B).

Average Annual Rate of Return on Capital Invested

The shortcomings of the overall profit approach are *partly* overcome by calculating the average annual rate of return, which relates profit to the amount of capital which has had to be invested. It also eliminates the effect of yearly fluctuations in profit. The procedure is to calculate the average annual profits (i.e. total profit divided by the number of years concerned) and to express it as a percentage of the original investment. This can be done by taking either

$$\frac{100 \times (\text{average profits})}{\text{total investment}} \quad \textit{or, alternatively,} \quad \frac{100 \times \text{total profit}}{\text{total investment} \times \text{years}}$$

Applied to the situation in Example 17.1, we obtain:

$$\text{Site A } \frac{100 \times 8}{112 \times 4} = 1.8\% \qquad \text{Site B } \frac{100 \times 120}{204 \times 6} = 9.8\%$$

$$\text{Site C } \frac{100 \times 110}{180 \times 5} = 12.2\%$$

It will be seen that, *on the basis of this assessment*, site C becomes the preferred option.

This method has the advantage of being fairly easy to understand and to calculate. Again, however, no significance is given to the timing of receipts. Also, disagreements can arise over the precise definition of 'capital invested'.

TASK 17.1 Company A has a capital invested of £25m and company B £40m. Their trading profits over the past five years have been:

	Company A £m	Company B £m
Year 1	2	3
2	4	5
3	3	6
4	5	3
5	2	3

CALCULATE: For each of the two companies:

(a)   The total profit over the five-year period.

(b)   The average annual rate of return on capital invested over the same period.

Comment on your results.

Pay Back

Some organisations find themselves in a position where a speedy cash return of the amount invested is a more important consideration than the total profits which might ultimately be realised. This may be because there are heavy development costs which have to be paid off quickly, or because there are other projects which can be undertaken once the capital is available. The pay back method of capital appraisal therefore measures how quickly the original investment will be recouped. This is based on the actual cash income to the firm before deduction of any 'notional' (non-cash) expenses such as depreciation. Any *actual* payments in respect of tax must be deducted from the receipts, but not any provisions for tax on current profits. The net cash income accumulated year by year. When the amount of the original investment, the 'pay back' position has been reached.

   The calculation of the pay back position for each of the sites in Example 17.1 is:

$$\text{Site A 3 years plus } \frac{32}{40} \text{ of year 4} = 3.8 \text{ years}$$

Note:

It is necessary to add $32m to the net cash income accumulated at the end of year 3 to obtain the pay back needed (the amount of the original investment). The $32m is then taken as a proportion of the total cash income for year 4 (£40m). If the question required the answer in months, weeks or days, the fraction should be multiplied by 12, 52 or 365 respectively.

Site B 4 years plus $\dfrac{40}{100}$ of year 5 = 4.4 years

Site C 4 years plus $\dfrac{23}{133}$ of year 5 = 4.17 years

On the basis of *this* assessment, site A becomes the preferred option.

The pay back procedure has obvious limitations. No account is taken of the timing of the receipts. Also, undue importance is placed on the 'pay back' point as such. A particular project may have a much greater cash return in, say, the first year than other projects although the 'pay back' point as such is not reached as quickly (note, for example, that site C has a larger cash return in the first two years than either of the other two options although it is the last to reach the actual pay back position). This could be important if *immediate* cash flow is a problem.

In addition, it is often important to have a regular cash flow over an extended period, but the approach takes no account of the longer-term cash flows. No account is taken of profitability and seasonal fluctuations in demand (and therefore of cash receipts) may affect interpolation. It is customary, when calculating the point *during* a year when the pay back point will be reached, to assume that income is received (and costs incurred) at a steady rate throughout the period.

TASK 17.2 Andrew is considering undertaking a franchise operation. Three possibilities interest him, each of which will require an initial investment by himself of £60 000. The anticipated net cash inflows from each are:

	Franchise A £000	Franchise B £000	Franchise C £000
Year 1	18	14	5
2	20	16	8
3	23	20	15
4	24	28	30
5	25	33	45
6	18	34	53

CALCULATE:

The pay back point in each case. What other considerations might Andrew take into account before arriving at a decision?

Discounted Cash Flow (DCF) Methods

None of the capital appraisal methods discussed above allow for the *time* at which income is received – or costs incurred. For example, if the ruling rate of interest today is 10%, it could be argued that £1000 today is worth the same as £1100 in a year's time, and as £1331 in three years' time. The purpose of the DCF methods is to reduce all flows of income and expenditure to a common base – namely, their value as at today's date – a process known as *discounting* the cash flow. There are two main DCF methods.

Net present value (NPV)

The NPV method of appraisal

(a) Takes the 'net cash income' for each year (i.e. the operating income less the actual operating expenses excluding notional expenses such as depreciation) discounted to their *'present day values'* (PDVs), and

(b) Deducts from them the PDVs of the original investment (investments made at the beginning of a project will not need to be discounted since the sums will already at PDV).

This gives the *net present value* (NPV) of the project.

The calculation shows which, of several projects, will ultimately yield the highest return 'in real terms'. It also indicates whether a particular project is likely to yield at least a minimum rate of return.

The procedure for discounting amounts to their present day value involves multiplying the amount concerned by factors obtained from accounting tables (see Figure 17.1). (In accounting assignments and examinations, the factors are usually given in the question.)

Each sum of money to be discounted to its present-day value should be multiplied by the appropriate factor given in the following table. This is found by reference to the 'cost of capital' (i.e. the rate %) in the horizontal column, and the number of years over which the discounting is to take place in the vertical column.

The factor allows for the *cost of capital* of the firm – a figure assumed to be the percentage rate of return which the firm could obtain by investing its money in 'the next best alternative' (or at the minimum rate of return expected). If the final NPV of the project is nil (i.e. the PDV of the investment and cash returns balance), then the investment will just be worth while *at the cost of capital on which it based*. A positive balance will represent the surplus which will be obtained by investment in the project; a negative balance will represent the deficit.

Figure 17.1 Net Present Value Table

Years   Interest rates

Years	1	2	3	4	5	6	7	8	9	10
1	0.9901	0.9804	0.9709	0.9615	0.9524	0.9434	0.9346	0.9259	0.9174	0.9091
2	0.9803	0.9612	0.9426	0.9426	0.9070	0.8900	0.8734	0.8573	0.8417	0.8264
3	0.9706	0.9423	0.9151	0.8890	0.8638	0.8396	0.8163	0.7938	0.7722	0.7513
4	0.9610	0.9238	0.8885	0.8548	0.8227	0.7921	0.7629	0.7350	0.7084	0.6830
5	0.9515	0.9057	0.8626	0.8219	0.7835	0.7473	0.7139	0.6806	0.6499	0.6209
6	0.9420	0.8880	0.8375	0.7903	0.7462	0.7050	0.6663	0.6302	0.5963	0.5645
7	0.9327	0.8706	0.8131	0.7599	0.7107	0.6651	0.6227	0.5835	0.5470	0.5132
8	0.9235	0.8535	0.7894	0.7307	0.6768	0.6274	0.5820	0.5403	0.5019	0.4665
9	0.9143	0.8368	0.7664	0.7026	0.6446	0.5919	0.5439	0.5002	0.4804	0.4241
10	0.9053	0.8203	0.7441	0.6756	0.6139	0.5584	0.5083	0.4632	0.4224	0.3855

Years   Interest rates

Years	11	12	13	14	15	16	17	18	19	20
1	0.9009	0.8929	0.8850	0.8772	0.8696	0.8621	0.8547	0.8475	0.8403	0.8333
2	0.8116	0.7972	0.7831	0.7695	0.7561	0.7432	0.7305	0.7182	0.7062	0.6944
3	0.7312	0.7118	0.6931	0.6750	0.6575	0.6407	0.6244	0.6086	0.5934	0.5787
4	0.6587	0.6355	0.6133	0.5921	0.5718	0.5523	0.5337	0.5158	0.4987	0.4823
5	0.5935	0.5674	0.5428	0.5194	0.4972	0.4761	0.4561	0.4371	0.4190	0.4019
6	0.5346	0.5066	0.4803	0.4556	0.4323	0.4104	0.3898	0.3704	0.35621	0.3349
7	0.4817	0.4523	0.4251	0.3996	0.3759	0.3538	0.3332	0.3139	0.2959	0.2791
8	0.4339	0.4039	0.3762	0.3506	0.3269	0.3050	0.2848	0.2660	0.2487	0.2326
9	0.3909	0.3606	0.3329	0.3075	0.2843	0.2630	0.2434	0.2255	0.2090	0.1938
10	0.3522	0.3220	0.2946	0.2697	0.2472	0.2267	0.2080	0.1911	0.1756	0.1615

Years   Interest rates

Years	21	22	23	24	25	26	27	28	29	30
1	0.8264	0.8197	0.8130	0.8065	0.8000	0.7937	0.7874	0.7812	0.7752	0.7692
2	0.6830	0.6719	0.6610	0.6504	0.6400	0.6299	0.6200	0.6104	0.6009	0.5917
3	0.5645	0.5507	0.5374	0.5245	0.5120	0.4999	0.4882	0.4768	0.4659	0.4552
4	0.4665	0.4514	0.4369	0.4230	0.4096	0.3968	0.3844	0.3725	0.3611	0.3501
5	0.3855	0.3700	0.3552	0.3411	0.3277	0.3149	0.3027	0.2910	0.2799	0.2693
6	0.3186	0.3033	0.2888	0.2751	0.2621	0.2499	0.2383	0.2274	0.2170	0.2072
7	0.2633	0.2486	0.2348	0.2218	0.2097	0.1983	0.1877	0.1776	0.1682	0.1594
8	0.2176	0.2038	0.1909	0.1789	0.1678	0.1574	0.1478	0.1388	0.1304	0.1226
9	0.1799	0.1670	0.1552	0.1443	0.1342	0.1249	0.1164	0.1084	0.1011	0.0943
10	0.1486	0.1369	0.1262	0.1164	0.1074	0.0992	0.0916	0.0847	0.0784	0.0725

In Example 17.1, assume that the firm's 'cost of capital' is reckoned to be 12%. Reference to the accounting table extracts in Figure 17.1 will give the factors to be used for each year of the projects. The calculation of the respective NPVs therefore becomes:

	YEAR	FACTOR	SITE A $m NPV		SITE B $m NPV		SITE C $m NPV	
Investment* costs	(see below)	–	112	112	150	150	180	180
	2	0.7972	–	–	54	43.0488	–	–
			112	112	204	193.0488	180	180
Net cash income	1	0.8929	18	16.0722	14	12.5006	20	17.8580
	2	0.7972	20	15.944	20	15.944	25	19.93
	3	0.7118	42	29.8956	50	35.59	42	29.8956
	4	0.6355	40	25.42	80	50.84	70	44.485
	5	0.5674	–	–	100	56.74	133	75.4642
	6	0.5066	–	–	60	30.396	–	–
			120	87.3318	324	202.0106	290	187.6328
NPV of net cash income *less* investment				(24.6682)		8.9618		7.6328

* *Since the original investment is made at the START of the project, its present day value is the same as its actual value.*

Site B obviously has the highest NPV of the three projects, realising $8.9618m over that which would be obtained by investing the original amount at 12% – the given 'cost of capital'. It is interesting to note how the discounting has turned an apparent profit on site A into a loss in real terms. Before any conclusions are drawn, however, the following limitations of the method should be borne in mind:

- Over a period of time, interest rates may vary and the calculations may therefore be based on inaccurate assumptions.
- There is always a risk factor present to some degree at least, and this may be difficult to assess in real terms – a slightly less risky venture may be a more attractive investment than one which may happen to have a higher NPV.
- NPV calculations do not normally include a factor for inflation (though there is no reason why such a factor could not be built in. (Again, it may be difficult to predict over a long period of time.)
- The apparent 'precision' of the calculations may blind management to the unreliability of much of the data involved.
- It is usually assumed, for convenience, that the cash flow is either evenly spaced throughout the year, or arises at the end of the

year. This may not be the case in practice, leading to much more complicated calculations.
- The preferred option as shown by the NPV calculation may vary according to the rate of discount applied.

TASK 17.3   A company is considering undertaking a project which will require the investment of £200 000 initially and a further £150 000 at the end of the second year. The net cash inflows are expected to be:

Year	£000
1	100
2	180
3	110
4	60

The cost of capital to the company is 9%. Will the project be worth undertaking?

Internal rate of return (IRR)

The internal rate of return is also based on calculation of the NPV. Instead, however, of calculating the NPV for a given rate of discount, the rate of discount is calculated which will give a nil NPV – in other words, the IRR is the rate of discount at which the NPV of the net cash income equals the NPV of the investment.

If a given rate of discount gives a positive NPV (as in the case of sites B and C in Example 17.1), then the IRR will be higher. If, on the other hand, a given rate of discount results in a negative NPV (as in the case of site A), then the IRR will be lower.

One problem with the IRR is that it cannot be calculated directly. The usual way is by trial and error – that is, by calculating the NPV for an estimated rate of discount, and gradually refining it (by either increasing or decreasing it) until a rate is found which will have a nil NPV. An *approximate* value for the IRR can, however, be found by plotting the NPVs for two or more discount rates on a graph. The NPVs are plotted on the y (vertical) axis and the rates of discount on the x (horizontal) axis. The IRR will be at the point where the line cuts the discount axis. Unfortunately, the IRR line is slightly curved. This is the reason why the answer is only approximate: the error can be reduced by choosing two co-ordinates (one of which should give a positive NPV and one a negative) as close as possible to the IRR.

TASK 17.4   Finding IRR by graph

As a practical example, undertake the following:

1.   Construct a graph with values for NPV on the y axis ranging from +$30m to −$30m and rates of discount on the x axis ranging from zero to 25%.
2.   From the NPV data calculated on p. 000 for the oil company, plot the IRR curve for each of the three sites.
    Suggestion: Plot the NPV for 1% and 5% in connection with site A, and 10% and 20% in connection with sites B and C.
3.   From your graph, estimate the IRR (the point at which the curve cuts the x axis) in respect of each site. Check this by arithmetic calculation of the NPV. If the rate does not give a nil balance, repeat the calculation with other rates. See how close you can get to a nil balance

Remember − if a given rate gives a positive NPV, then the IRR will be greater; if it gives a negative NPV, then the IRR will be lower.

4.   What conclusions can you draw, particularly as regards site A?

What the IRR shows is the 'break-even point' – that is, the discount rate at which a particular project ceases to yield a surplus. In a sense, it measures the efficiency of the capital when invested in the particular project concerned (which is why the economist Keynes preferred to call it the *marginal efficiency of capital*). This means that if the cost of capital is greater than the IRR for a particular project, it will not be worth investing in it. However. if the IRR is below the IRR in respect of two or more projects, then the investment will be worthwhile and the usual NPV calculation (based upon the actual cost of capital) can be used to differentiate between them.

PRACTICAL ASSIGNMENTS

1   A firm has the opportunity to purchase the lease of an amusement arcade at a local holiday resort. The equipment would cost £180 000 and be subject to straight-line depreciation over four years. The cost of the lease would be £20 000 a year. Operating costs (other than equipment depreciation) are expected to be £70 000 in each of the first two years, increasing to £75 000 in the third year, and to £80 000 in the fourth year. Receipts are expected to be £175 000 in the first year, rising to £180 000 in the second, then falling to £175 000 and £170 000 in the third and fourth years respectively.

REQUIRED:
(a)   A calculation of the average annual rate of return which the firm could expect from the investment.
(b)   A calculation of the pay-back date. What criticisms would you have of this figure?

2   The following data refers to alternative investment options facing a firm which has a cost of capital of 10% (use the NPV table given Figure 17.1):

Proposal		A £	B £
Initial investment		100 000	125 000
Net cash inflows: end of year	1	118 750	43 750
	2	48 750	71 250
	3	9000	70 000
	4	6000	30 000

REQUIRED:
A calculation of the net present value of each option, and a recommendation which should be selected.

3 Moy Ltd is considering the purchase of a new machine for its factory. Enquiries have been made concerning three machines and the following information is presented to you:

	Machine A £	Machine B £	Machine C £
Cost	24 000	26 500	16 800
Estimated Net Cash Inflows			
Year 1	4000	8000	6000
2	6500	10 000	7000
3	10 000	9000	7000
4	9000	6500	6000
5	2000	3000	6000
6	1500	1000	5000

Additional information:
(i)   Machines A and B will have no scrap value at the end of the sixth year.
(ii) Machine C has a three-year working life only and the operation would be continued by a similar machine which would be purchased for £18 000. None of the machines have any scrap value except that a possibility exists for trading-in machine A at the end of four years subject to a trade-in allowance of £4000.
(iii) The firm's current cost of capital is 12%. All net cash inflows arise at the end of the relevant year.

REQUIRED:
An evaluation of the purchase of each separate machine by the:
(i)   pay back technique
(ii) overall profit
(iii) average annual rate of return
(iv) net present value technique

together with a report for the directors of Moy Ltd indicating, with reasons, which machine should be purchased.

4 Haven PLC is considering purchasing one of two businesses in order to expand its industrial empire. The options are:

(a) Able Ltd
Estimated cost of the take-over bid: £2.15 million.
Production: 100 000 units per annum.
     Sales: 80% of output will be sold under an existing fixed-price contract which has a further four years to run at £15 per unit. The remainder of the production will be sold on the open market at the following anticipated selling prices:

Year	1	2	3	4
Selling price (£ per unit)	14	14	15	16

Operating costs: £750 000 over each of the next two years; £800 000 over each of the two subsequent years.
Depreciation and other provisions: £60 000 per year.

Cain Ltd
Estimated cost of the take-over bid: £3.5 million.
Production: 200 000 units per annum.
Sales: A fixed-price contract already exists covering the next four years under which the entire product will be taken at a unit price of £13 for the next two years, £14 for the third year and £15 in the fourth year.
Operating costs: £1.2 million in the first year, £1.3 million in the second, £1.5 million in the third and £1.7 million in the fourth.
     Depreciation and other provisions: £90 000 per year.
     Haven PLC's cost of capital should be taken as 12%, and it all receipts and payments should be assumed to take effect as at the year-end.

REQUIRED:
(a)   A forecast budget of profit or loss, and of net cash flow, over the next four years for both Cain Ltd and Able Ltd.
(b)   An evaluation, using appropriate capital appraisal techniques, of the two businesses and a recommendation, with reasons, as to which business appears to be the better investment.
(c)   A note explaining the limitations of the techniques which you have used and a statement of any further information you think will be needed before a final decision is taken.

5 The directors of Pendennis Pyrotechnics Ltd have recently decided that the company must be re-organised and rationalised if it is to survive the increasing level of competition it is having to face. The directors have

decided that present machinery must be scrapped (nil scrap value) and a new configuration of equipment purchased. Three options exist:

Configuration:	A	B	C
Purchase cost (£m)	20	18	31
Estimates net cash inflows (£m):			
Year 1	6	6	6
2	7	6	10
3	8	7	12
4	8	9	12

Each configuration is expected to have a working life of four years.

The rationalisation will enable the labour-force to be reduced by 50 workers at the end of the first year and 60 workers at the end of the second. The average salary of a worker is £12 000. In recent meetings, the unions involved have agreed to the proposals provided there is:

(i)   a payment of six months' salary at the end of the year concerned, and
(ii) a lump-sum payment of £3000

to each of the workers made redundant. The net cash flows listed above have not included any allowance for the cash savings on salaries.

The company's cost of capital should be taken as 10% and all receipts and payments (other than the purchase cost of the configurations) take effect as at the end of each year.

REQUIRED:
A report to the directors advising them which option should be chosen. Your report should be based upon appropriate capital appraisal calculations, but should also include comments on any other considerations which the management should bear in mind before coming to a decision.

6   Bill Murphy, chairman of the Redhill City Football Club (RCFC), is currently considering a player deal in which he will acquire Bob Shearer from one of RCFC's principal rivals, the Wanderers United Football Club (WULFC). The deal involves a cash payment of £1 500 000 plus Howard Jones, a regular first team full-back with RCFC who is currently receiving a salary of £45 000 a year. Bob Shearer is a top-rated defender and would be be Howard Jones' replacement.

Bob Shearer, aged 27, already has five international caps and has an estimated playing life in first-class football of five years. At the end of that time, the club could expect to sell him for at least £200 000. His recruitment to the team would be a popular move among supporters and it is expected that gate receipts would show a marked climb.

Howard Jones is the older of the two men at age 30. Although he, too, can look forward to another five years 'at the top', his age would then mean his playing career was virtually over and he would be placed on the free transfer list. RCFC has recently received a cash offer of £200 000 for Howard Jones from a new club in the south.

The accountant of RCFC has produced the following forecast data should the deal be accepted:

Year	Bob's salary (£000)	Extra gate receipts receipts(£000)	Extra expenses (£000) (e.g. bonus payments)
1	180	900	90
2	210	900	90
3	240	600	60
4	240	300	30
5	210	150	30

The club's current cost of capital is 10%.

REQUIRED:
A report for the club's board of directors stating whether, on the basis of the information given, RCFC should buy Bob Shearer. The report should also discuss the other factors which should be considered before a decision is made.

7 A small publishing company has recently had two manuscripts of merit submitted to it. It can, however, only consider one since it does not have sufficient capital to finance both.

Project Medico
This is a medical text written by a relatively unknown surgeon describing a new technique in transplantation surgery. Sales are likely to be low in the first two years until the technique has become accepted medical practice. They are then expected to increase markedly but it is anticipated that the book will not have a life of more than five years as, by that time, much more advanced techniques will have been developed.

Because of the need for expensive colour illustrations and the substantial binding necessary, initial production costs have been costed out at £20 000 and will be amortized on a straight line basis over the anticipated life of the book.

Market research indicates that the final net profits for each of the five years will be (£ooo) −1(loss); −1(loss); 15; 13; 2.

Project Best Seller (1)
This concerns a popular 'formula' novel of some merit by a relatively unknown author. It is thought that with the right sort of promotion, it could become a 'best-seller' very quickly. Sales are therefore likely to be high in the first year, but to follow the normal pattern of popular novels of falling very sharply thereafter. During year 5, it is expected that the author will have

completed a second novel, the sales of which will stimulate demand for the first one and justify a re-print; this is likely to happen again towards the end of year 8. There will be additional lump-sum royalties in later years from the sales of paper-back editions and from book-club sales.

The anticipated net annual profits over the ten-year life-span of the book are expected to be (£000) 7; 2; 1; Nil; 6; 6; 4; 5; 4; 1.

Initial costs will involve heavy expenditure on advertising and 'launch party' expenditure. Significant investment will be necessary to finance long print-runs and storage costs. These will amount to £20 000 and will be amortised on a straight line basis over the expected ten-year life of the book.

Project Best Seller (2)
Facts as for Best Seller (1), but the production development costs are payable £12 000 initially, and £8000 for the reprint and 'boost' promotion in year 5. The total development costs (£20 000) are to be amortised on a straight line basis over the whole life of the book, as in Project Best Seller (1).

REQUIRED:
An evaluation of the proposals, using appropriate capital appraisal techniques together with a report to management containing your recommendations. Note any further factors which management should take into account before coming to their decision.

Taxation should be ignored.

REVISION QUESTIONS: PART IV

In questions 1–10, state whether the statement is true (T) or false (F).

1 A break-even chart differs from a CVP graph in that a break-even chart maps fixed and variable expenses in relation to output, whilst a CVP graph shows profit or loss in relation to output.

2 Calculation of the net cash flow in DCF calculations involves making allowance for depreciation of assets.

3 A 'make-or-buy' decision involves comparison of the total cost of manufacturing a product compared with that of purchasing it on the open market.

4 If the value of an investment is equal to the cost of capital on which the calculation is based, the NPV is nil.

5 Discounted cash flow is a generic term covering a number of different but related techniques.

6 Cost–volume–profit graphs and break-even graphs show the same information but in different formats.

7 Capital appraisal techniques are particularly suitable in appraising options involving different patterns of investment and return over a period of years.

8 The financial factors in capital appraisal should be given priority over broader social factors.

9 The most profitable 'mix' in a multi-product situation depends upon the contribution in relation to the limiting (or 'key') factor involved.

10 The principal disadvantage of DCF techniques is that they do not relate receipts and costs to the time factor involved.

In questions 11–20, answer:
A if only the assertion (the first part of the question) is correct
B if only the response (the second part of the question) is correct
C if both the assertion and the response are correct statements, but the response is NOT a correct explanation of the assertion
D if both the assertion and the response are correct statements and the response IS a correct explanation of the assertion E if neither the assertion or the response are correct

11 It is important that financial techniques are thoroughly understood by accounting personnel

because effective decision making is dependent upon the accuracy and suitability of feed information.

12 Production managers should be well aware of the margin of safety

because the margin relates production options to profit.

13 There is nil profit at the break-even point

because the break-even point is, by definition, the point at which sales revenue equals fixed plus variable costs.

14 Break-even calculations in a multi-product situation are easier than in a single product one

because it is fair to assume that the different products are produced at a constant rate throughout the year.

15 A contribution break-even graph is helpful to production managers *because* the contribution at each level of production is shown in a way conventional break-even graphs do not.

16 'Make or buy' decisions involve comparing the total cost of manufacturing with the loss of contribution *because* the contribution is equal to manufacturing cost at the break-even point.

17 Break-even calculations must be interpreted with caution *because* of the limitations to which break-even analysis is subject.

18 It is important to appraise carefully capital investment projects *because* of the amounts of money invested, the time-period involved and the fact that, once started, there is usually no 'turning back' without loss.

19 The margin of safety indicates the extent to which production can be cut back without incurring loss *because* production below safety of margin means producing below the break-even point.

20 Break-even point may be lower in batch production than in unit production *because* every unit in the batch adds to the contribution if unit selling price is greater than unit variable.

In questions 21–30, note the option which best answers the question.

21 An increase in variables costs given constant fixed costs and selling price, will result in an
(a) increase in the break-even point and a decrease in the contribution
(b) decrease in the break-even point and an increase in the contribution
(c) decrease in both the break-even point and the contribution.
(d) increase in both the break-even point and the contribution.

22 The margin of safety is the
(a) difference between the break-even point and the fixed costs
(b) surplus of sales revenue over fixed costs
(c) extent to which the sales exceed the break-even point
(d) difference between contribution at actual production level compared with contribution at break-even point.

23 A rise in fixed costs can result in
(a) a decrease in the contribution
(b) an increase in the margin of safety
(c) an increase in the break-even point
(d) a decrease in sales revenue.

24 A firm has fixed costs of £50 000 and a unit variable of £80. The unit selling price is £100. The break-even point is reached when sales revenue amounts to
(a) £250 000
(b) £500
(c) £500 000
(d) £2500.

25 On a CVP graph, the break-even point is the point at which the revenue curve cuts the
(a) x axis
(b) y axis
(c) variable cost curve
(d) total cost curve.

26 A firm produces 100 000 units which sell at £6 each. Its fixed costs amount to £20 000 and its total variable costs to £100 000. Its break-even point is (or would be) at a production of
(a)   400 units
(b)   4000 units
(c)   40 000 units
(d)   400 000 units.

27 The best product-mix ratio is obtained by giving priority to products in order of
(a)   the least quantity of the key factor consumed
(b)   the greatest quantity of the key factor consumed
(c)   the lowest contribution made per unit of the key factor consumed
(d)   the highest contribution made per unit of the key factor consumed

28 A firm's sales revenue totals £25 million. Fixed costs amount to £8 million and profit to £5 million. The contribution/sales ratio (%) is
(a)   20   (b)   32
(c)   48   (d)   52.

29 A firm could manufacture for itself a component at present being purchased on the open market although this would mean restricting the output of one of its present products. It would be financially beneficial to the firm to manufacture the component for itself if the price on the open market is
(a)   less than the total cost of manufacturing the component for itself
(b)   more than the total cost of manufacturing the component for itself
(c)   more than the total marginal cost of production of the component plus the loss of contribution made on the product
(d)   less than the total marginal cost of production of the component plus the loss of contribution on the product

30 The 'pay back' method of capital appraisal involves calculating
(a)   the net return from an investment after deducting expenses

(b)   the point at which net cash inflow equals the amount of investment
(c)   the capital sum which has to be refunded to investors
(d)   the residual value of equipment at the end of the project.

In questions 31–40, answer:
A if responses a, b and c are all correct
B if responses a and b only are correct
C if responses b and c only are correct
D if response a only is correct
E if response b only is correct
F if response c only is correct

31 A rise in fixed costs will result in
(a)   an increase in the break-even point
(b)   a decrease in the margin of safety
(c)   a lower contribution sales ratio.

32 The greater the contribution, the
(a)   less the loss
(b)   greater the profit
(c)   larger the difference between selling price and variables.

33 The break-even point can be calculated by the formula(e)
(a)   fixed costs plus variable costs divided by sales revenue
(b)   fixed costs divided by the difference between unit selling price and unit variable
(c)   fixed costs multiplies by output divided by total sales revenue less total variables.

34 On a CVP graph, the cost curve at nil production indicates the
(a)   loss at this level of activity
(b)   total fixed costs
(c)   variable costs at this level of activity.

35 Contribution may be described in terms of
(a)   unit sales variable divided by unit variable
(b)   unit sales revenue *less* unit variable
(c)   total sales revenue *less* total variables.

36 Is it correct to say that
(a)   direct costs vary directly with output

(b) contribution is regarded as a constant percentage of sales revenue

(c) net profit at break-even point is nil?

37 The break-even point can be calculated
(a) arithmetically
(b) graphically
(c) arithmetically and graphically.

38 'Net cash income' includes
(a) receipts from cash sales
(b) payments made for arrears of such expenses as insurance
(c) allowances for such charges as depreciation.

39 The limitations of break-even analysis include
(a) a precise answer is never obtained
(b) variable costs are not always linear
(c) fixed and variable costs are not always distinguishable.

40 On a CVP graph, the intersection of cost curve and the x axis indicates
(a) the sum of the fixed and variable costs at that level of activity
(b) the break-even level of production
(c) the point at which neither profit nor loss is made.

MAJOR ASSIGNMENTS: PART IV

1. Part A

Newton & Co is a partnership run by the Ridley brothers. It produces electrical components and machine parts for the home market and for export abroad. In the past, the firm has only maintained routine financial accounts. You have recently been appointed as an accounting assistant with the specific responsibility of developing costing procedures. A new component – coded as ABJ1 – is planned and, following a careful analysis of the situation, you are satisfied that the following projected data is accurate:

Unit Costs:	£
Direct materials	5
Direct labour	3
Variable overhead	4
	12

The estimated fixed cost for the component as £15 000 and the proposed unit selling price is £20. John Ridley, who is mainly responsible for marketing, forecasts sales of 2500 units for the initial period.

Simon Ridley, in charge of production, has suggested that the company upgrade the product by using higher-grade materials at an increased material cost of £1.50 per unit. He believes that the selling price could be increased by £3 per unit subject to a reduction in overall demand of 10%. Fixed costs would remain constant.

REQUIRED:
1. (a) Draw a break-even graph for the original forecast.
   (b) Draw a profit-volume graph for the revised proposal.
      In both cases, calculate the break-even point in units for the original forecast and the revised proposal.
2.   Prepare a profit statement for both proposals assuming that sales are as forecast. Your statement should show total contribution.
3.   Prepare a background paper for the information of the Ridley brothers explaining the term *contribution* and outlining why it is useful in the decision-making process.

Part B

Further investigation into last year's records reveals the following data in respect of the firm's existing products.

Product Code	XB1	XB2	XB3	XB4
Sales (£000)	120	155	200	475
costs (000)	130	135	160	425
Profit (loss)	(10)	20	40	50

Of the costs, three-fifths are variable and two-fifths fixed in respect of each product. Total fixed costs have been allocated and apportioned over the three products using a suitable overhead absorption rate. Fixed costs will remain fixed regardless of the nature and level of production.

John Ridley has suggested that the product coded XB1 should be terminated because it is making a loss.

REQUIRED: Prepare a report, supported by relevant calculations, which examines all aspects of John's proposal. Your report should examine the non-financial implications of the proposal as well as the financial ones, and should conclude with a definite recommendation regarding what action, if any, the brothers should take.

Part C

The Ridley brothers are planning to develop a further new product – flashing lights for christmas trees – which will require the purchase of a specialised machine. Three models are on the market; each is produced by a different manufacturer. The machines vary in output and running costs, and the brothers are in some doubt which would be the best machine to buy. Research produces the following forecasted data:

	Machine 1 £	Machine 2 £	Machine 3 £
Purchase price	80 000	90 000	100 000
Trade-in value after four years	16 000	18 000	28 000
Revenue excluding depreciation:			
Year 1	20 000	23 000	20 000
Year 2	22 400	26 200	22 800
Year 3	29 200	32 600	28 000
Year 4	29 200	32 600	28 000

The trade will be seasonal, and it may be assumed that both the costs and the revenue accrue at the end of each year concerned. The cost of capital may be taken as 10%.

REQUIRED: The brothers are to make their decision at a meeting to be held towards the end of next week. They have requested you to produce a report which will brief them as regards the relevant facts which they should bear in mind, and to make a recommendation regarding the machine which, from a financial point of view, would appear to be the 'best buy'.

They have asked you to add any reservations which you might have, together with any additional factors which should be taken into consideration. You should also add a note summarising the problems in appraising capital projects of this type.

2. Price Norman Ltd manufacture a variety of products. The directors are concerned about the performance of a certain product line and Nicola Price, who is the financial director, has been asked to attend a board meeting to discuss the problem. Nicola has written the following memo to her assistant. Read the memo carefully; then prepare the draft report requested.

MEMORANDUM

To: Accounting Assistant

From: Financial Director

I have been asked to prepare a report regarding a number of proposals which have been put forward by Board members. I would like you to prepare a draft report which I can use as a basis for a full report to be prepared by myself next week. Your draft report should include the following in respect of the specific proposals:

(a) *Proposal 1.* A contribution statement and an explanation why contribution is important when making decisions to drop a product.
(b) *Proposal 2.* A profit statement and a break-even graph, together with any reservations you may have regarding the proposal.
(c) *Proposal 3.* A calculation, with comments, of the average rate of return, the pay back period and the net present value of the project over the five-year period for which data is given.

I attach background information regarding the three proposals.

APPENDICES:
Proposal 1
Iain Pyman, our marketing director, has suggested that product B is a loss-maker and he has suggested that it should be dropped from the range. The following costing data for the product range is available for the year ended 31 December 1993:

PRODUCT	A	B	C	TOTAL
SALES (£000)	250	400	550	1200
COSTS (£000)	180	450	390	1020
PROFIT (Loss)	70	(50)	160	180

Four-fifths of the costs for each product are variable, the remainder being fixed. Iain has suggested that the fixed costs presently apportioned to product B could be apportioned to products A and C in the ratio of one-third and two-thirds respectively.

Proposal 2
Susan Kenning, who was recently appointed to the Board, believes it is time to up-date product B. She has suggested that the material cost could be reduced by 20% if the company uses a substitute material which can be imported from the Far East. She also suggests that labour costs could be reduced by 30% if new machinery, which would increase fixed costs by £8000, were installed. Susan is convinced this will enable the company to reduce the unit selling price of the product by £5. Present unit costs for product B are material £20, labour £10 and variable overhead £6 (total £36). The maximum output of this product is 25 000 units and the present unit selling price is £40.

Proposal 3
The preference of the managing director is for a complete re-vamp of product B involving the purchase of new fixed assets and the introduction of extra working capital. This would involve an immediate investment of £500 000. Consultants have suggested that the costs and revenues resulting from this suggestion over the next five years would be:

Year	Revenue (£000)	Costs (£000)
1	600	510
2	650	552
3	720	612
4	850	722
5	920	782

The cost of capital to the company is currently 15%. The consultants believe that the profit figure for each year would have to be reduced by 15% to give a true reflection of the net cash flow for each year.

PART V UNDERSTANDING AND MONITORING FINAL ACCOUNTS

Planning a financial outcome is one task; monitoring its achievement is another. The principal financial results are summarised in the 'final accounts'. The form which these take may vary, in detail, from one organisation and another, but in terms of the principles involved there is little difference.

Part V of this book considers how it is possible to read meaning into the final accounts of commercial firms (the same principles apply in general to other organisations), and then to use that understanding to monitor the organisation's progress and its future viability.

A basic knowledge of accounting and of final accounts is assumed in this section.

18 BASIC UNDERSTANDING OF FINAL ACCOUNTS

Think about this . . . *There has been an increasing practice over recent years for companies to 'factor' (i.e. sell to a collecting agency) their book debts shortly before the end of their accounting year, and then to buy them back after the final accounts have been drawn up. What effect is this practice likely to have on the published balance sheet, why may a company wish to do it, and do you think it is a practice to be encouraged?*

18.1 NATURE AND USE OF MEASURES TO INTERPRET FINANCIAL INFORMATION

Accounts are of little use unless we can appreciate the real significance of them. The framework itself, and the procedures which are followed within it, are designed to throw up data which, if correctly interpreted, tell us a very great deal about the financial position, problems and potential of the organisation concerned. It is, of course, essential to understand the important distinction between capital and revenue if the final accounts are to present a true and fair view. If, in addition, certain basic measures are applied to the final account information, the data can tell us far more about the organisation than is immediately apparent.

The basic measures used to interpret (i.e. read more meaning into) balance sheets and revenue summaries fall into two principal groups. These are the measures of:

(i) liquidity, and
(ii) profitability.

These measures are of use 'as they stand', as comparisons with the figures from previous periods (trend analysis) and as comparisons with the figures of other similar organisations (inter-firm comparison).

18.2   MEASURES OF LIQUIDITY

The first group of measures, applied to the balance sheet, are known collectively as the measures of liquidity (or, alternatively, as the measures of solvency). They are applied to balance sheet data and provide a deeper insight into the financial strength and stability of an organisation.

Long-term Solvency

The long-term solvency of an organisation is given by the ratio of total assets to total liabilities and it indicates the ability of a firm,

Figure 18.1   Alpha Products: Balance Sheet as at 31 December 1994   *(£000)*

Fixed assets:			Capital: (see note 1)	300
Premises	120		Long-term liability:	
Equipment	80	200	Mortgage	150
Current assets:			Current liability:	
Stock	255		Trade creditor	50
Debtors	35			
Cash-at-bank	8			
in-hand	2	10	300	
		500		500

Trading and Profit and Loss Account, year ended 31 December 1994   *(£000)*

Opening stock	140		Sales	250
Purchases	130	270		
Less closing stock		120		
Cost of goods sold		150		
Gross Profit		c/d 100		
		250		250
Administrative expenses		25	Gross profit b/d	100
Selling costs		15		
Distribution costs		10		
Net profit		50		
		100		100

Note 1:   The capital includes £50 000 profit made during the year, all of which has been retained within the firm. Capital at 1 January 1994 was therefore £250 000. In the case of limited companies registered under the companies acts (which Alpha Products is not), profits retained within the firm are, in any case, shown under a separate heading from the share capital.

ultimately, to pay all of its debts. Consider the balance sheet of Alpha Products in Figure 18.1.

Since the item 'capital' is, by strict definition

the difference between total assets and total liabilities

it is in itself a measure of solvency. However, the relationship has more meaning if the assets are expressed either:

(i) as a simple ratio to liabilities, (i.e. 5 : 2 in the case of Alpha Products)
(ii) as a percentage of liabilities, (i.e. 250%).

In each case it becomes obvious that the assets 'cover' the liabilities 2½ times. Percentages tend to be the preferred way of expressing ratios since the common base makes the situation clearer when comparing different organisations.

If liabilities exceed assets, the organisation is insolvent. Care must be taken to distinguish insolvency from the term *bankruptcy* which can only be used when, after a lengthy legal process, a decree in bankruptcy has been issued by the courts. A person can be insolvent without being bankrupt even though he cannot be bankrupt unless he is also insolvent. It can amount to libel to describe a trader as bankrupt if no official decree has been issued, even if he is insolvent. In addition, it should be appreciated that bankruptcy proceedings can only be brought against individual persons; they cannot be brought against companies which, if insolvent, must be 'wound up'.

Short-term Solvency

The short-term solvency of an organisation is given by the ratio of current assets to current liabilities. It is an indication of the firm's ability to pay the debts which will fall due within the next year with the funds which will be available during that period.

Whilst it is important for any enterprise to be solvent in the long term, it is even more important that it should be solvent in the short term – that is, *that it can pay the debts which will fall due for payment in the immediate future*, with the funds which will be available in the immediate future – i.e. the current liabilities must be paid out of current assets. Hence the importance of showing these items as distinct sub-totals in the balance sheet.

The difference between current assets and current liabilities, in money terms, is known as the *working capital*. Again, however, it may be more useful to express the relationship as a straight ratio or as a percentage, in which case it is known as the current ratio. The working capital of the firm Alpha Products (see Figure 18.1) is:

$$£(300\,000 - 50\,000) = £250\,000$$

and the current ratio is

$$300\,000 : 50\,000 \text{ or } 600\%$$

i.e. current assets cover current liabilities 6 times.

If the current liabilities exceed the current assets, the firm is said to be *overtrading*

What the ratio should be at any given time depends upon the working capital requirements of the firm. Obviously it should normally be well in excess of 100% though special circumstances apply to some firms which make this unnecessary. Large supermarket chains are a case in point where their huge daily turnover for immediate cash enables them to work on current ratios as low as 60%. Whatever the desirable figure might be, however, a steady drop in the current ratio over several years (i.e. a trend analysis) and a low figure compared with other similar firms (i.e. an inter-firm comparison) can be danger signals signifying the need for action.

Quick Ratio (sometimes known as the acid test)

The quick ratio is calculated by expressing the current assets *less* stock as a ratio of current liabilities. It indicates the firm's ability to pay its debts in the near future (say the next one to three months) by eliminating stocks from the calculation which may have to be held for some time before being sold (and in fact may never be sold at all). Large stocks of slow-moving goods can give a misleading impression of the short-term solvency position. The quick ratio of Alpha Products is:

$$£(300\,000 - 255\,000) \text{ as a ratio of } £50\,000 = 4.5 : 5 \text{ or } 90\%$$

Again it is difficult to specify a recommended figure. Much will depend on the nature of the firm's work, the speed with which debtors pay their debts, and the number which default. A ratio of 110% (1.1 : 1) would obviously be safe; however, most firms seem to find that ratios in the region of 80–85% are sufficient.

Cash Ratio

The cash ratio of an organisation is the ratio of the cash and bank balances as a ratio of current liabilities. It represents the firm's ability to pay its debts in the immediate future. The cash ratio of Alpha Products is, therefore:

£10 000 as a ratio of £50 000 = 1:5 or 20%

In interpreting the cash ratio, the general liquidity of the current assets (the speed with which stock will change to debtors and these to cash) has to be borne in mind, together with the length of credit available from creditors and the needs for cash for other purposes, e.g. the payment of wages.

It is impossible to prescribe a precise figure for the cash ratio. What will be too high for one organisation (resulting in cash lying idle) may be too low for another firm (which consequently will have insufficient cash to pay its debts).

18.3 MEASURES OF PROFITABILITY

The profit and loss account shows the operating efficiency of the enterprise in terms of profit (or loss) over a period of time. The object of the measures of profitability is to give a deeper insight into this.

Return (i.e. Profit) on Capital Invested (ROCI)

This measure is obtained by calculating profit as a percentage of capital invested by the proprietor(s). It indicates the value of the firm to the owner(s) as an investment. Consider the profit and loss account of Alpha Products: the return on capital invested is

£50 000 as a percentage of £250 000 = 20%

Note: The return should be calculated on the capital at the beginning of the year, as this is the capital which produced the profit. (If capital invested has varied throughout the year, a more accurate result is obtained by taking a weighted average of capital invested during the year.)

Return on Capital Employed (ROCE)

This measure is obtained by calculating profit as a percentage of all funds invested on a long-term basis in the firm (i.e. capital plus long-term liabilities). It indicates how efficiently the assets have been managed.

The ROCE of Alpha Products is given by:

£50 000 as a percentage of £400 000 = 12.5%

Notes:
   (i) The term 'capital' is here used in a broader sense than in the strict accounting definition. The ratio assumes that the "profit producing assets", i.e. the fixed assets, have been financed primarily out of these long-term funds – an assumption which is not necessarily true.
 (ii) Capital employed is made up of the £250 000 capital at the beginning of the year, plus the £150 000 long-term loan. As with capital, if the amount on loan has varied throughout the year, the average should be taken.

Return on Total Assets (ROTA)

This is obtained by taking profit as a percentage of either

(i)   total assets less profit retained, or
(ii) capital (*less* profit retained) plus long-term and current liabilities.

It is a more exact measure than ROCE of how efficiently the assets have been managed. In the case of Alpha Products, the calculation is:

£50 000 as a percentage of £450 000 = 11.1%

Profit on Turnover (i.e. sales)

This ratio shows how successful the selling operation of the firm has been and is calculated by taking profit (gross or net) as a percentage of sales. In the case of Alpha Products,

gross profit on turnover: £100 000 as a percentage of £250 000 = 40%
net profit on turnover: £50 000 as a percentage of £250 000 = 20%

18.4   OTHER MEASURES

Rate of Turnover

This measure estimates the average number of times the normal stock-holding is sold and replaced in the course of a year. It is calculated by dividing the sales (*at cost*) by the *average* stock-holding for the period. If only final account data is available, the average has to be taken just of the opening and the closing stock. A more satisfactory result can be obtained if the average can be taken of a greater number of stock figures (say quarterly or monthly) In the case of Alpha Products, the calculation is:

$$\frac{250\,000}{(140\,000 + 120\,000) \div 2} = 1.9$$

This indicates that the stock was sold and replaced 1.9 times over the course of the year. Managers have to ask themselves whether it would be beneficial to hold a smaller stock and turn it over more often, or to hold more stock but turn it over less often.

TASK 18.1 Consider the implications for a firm:

(a) of holding a greater volume of stock and reducing stock turnover
(b) of holding a small volume of stock and increasing stock turnover
(c) if trend analysis shows that the rate of stock turnover is (a) rising and (b) falling.

Debtors' and Creditors' Turnover Periods

This is the average period of credit taken by debtors to pay their accounts and the average time taken by the firm itself to pay its creditors:

(a) Debtors' turnover period (in days):

$$\frac{\text{Average debtors} \times 365}{\text{Credit sales}}$$

(b) Creditors' payment period (in days):

$$\frac{\text{Average creditors} \times 365}{\text{Credit purchases}}$$

It is clearly to a firm's advantage to turn over its debtors quicker than paying its creditors, but this is not always possible. More important is the trend over time. If, for example, the time taken by debtors to pay their debts begins to increase without it being noticed, the firm could easily find itself short of working capital

PRACTICAL ASSIGNMENT

The accounting records of G.GaGa indicated that at 31 March last, the firm machinery worth £120 000, stocks of £50 000 and that debtors amounted to £20 000. The creditors stood at £90 000 and there was a long-term loan outstanding of £60 000. Cash in hand and at bank at that date was £10 000. The firm's premises were valued at £80 000.

The proprietor felt his liquidity position needed improving, so in the first week of April, the following transactions were arranged:

(i)   A further loan of £20 000 was taken and paid into the bank.
(ii)   Pressure was put on outstanding debtors, and £5000 cash was received from them.
(iii) Additional machinery was purchased on credit for £8000
(iv)   The proprietor paid in £10 000 cash as additional capital
(v)   Out-dated stock was sold for cash at cost, £8000.
(vi)   £7000 was paid to the firm's creditors.

REQUIRED:
(a) A summary of the firm's assets and liabilities in the form of a balance sheet both before, and after, the transactions with a statement of the overall difference in the long-term and the short-term solvency of the firm.
(b) A statement of the effect of each transaction on the working capital of the firm.
(c) A table of the liquidity ratios of the firm:
     (i)   before the transactions
     (ii) after the transactions.
(d) A reasoned comment of the extent to which the transactions have improved or worsened the financial position of the firm.

19 KEEPING AN EYE ON COMPANY ACCOUNTS – 1: RATIO ANALYSIS

Think about this . . . *Different people look at company accounts in different ways. Take, for example, a manager, an investor, and a banker. Consider in what particular aspects of a company's structure, performance and potential each of them will be interested in.*

This chapter considers techniques for 'reading more meaning' into company accounts. This involves, primarily, the application to company accounts of the general measures of liquidity and profitability dealt with in Chapter 18 but, because of the nature and format of company accounts, it is necessary to define certain of the measures more precisely. The figure for 'return' presents particular complications since it has to be defined in a way which is relevant to the purpose in hand. The overall 'return' to the firm is different from the 'return' received by the ordinary shareholders since this will be net of deductions for various items such as tax and preference dividends. The chapter considers, in addition, some further measures which have no relevance to the accounts of other bodies.

Each measure will be illustrated by reference to the accounts for UNI PLC set out in Figure 19.1.

19.1 THE INTERESTS OF MANAGEMENT: MANAGEMENT RATIOS

Managers are primarily interested in the financial viability of the organisation and how well it is running. The most important measures from their point of view are, therefore, the general liquidity and profitability measures dealt with in Chapter 18 (see Figure 19.2). Note, in some cases, the precise definitions which have to be applied when dealing with companies.

Figure 19.1 UNI PLC Consolidated Profit and Loss and Balance Sheet Accounts

Consolidated Profit and Loss Account, year ended 31 December 19-9 (£m)

19-8			19-9
17 136		Turnover	21 551
(15 600)		Operating Costs	(19 100)
1536		OPERATING PROFIT BEFORE INTEREST AND TAXATION	2451
(110)		Interest	(220)
1426		PROFIT ON ORDINARY ACTIVITIES BEFORE TAXATION	2231
(556)		Taxation	(870)
870		PROFIT ON ORDINARY ACTIVITIES AFTER TAXATION	1361
		Dividends	
	(5)	Preference Dividend	(6)
	(600)	Ordinary Dividend	(800)
605			806
265		RETAINED PROFIT FOR YEAR	555

Consolidated Balance Sheet as at 31 December 19-9 (£m)

19-8			19-9
		FIXED ASSETS	
	4197	Tangible Assets	5438
	200	Investments	237
4397			5675
		CURRENT ASSETS	
	2632	Stocks	3242
	2557	Debtors	3435
	1414	Cash in hand and at bank	534
	6603		7211
		Less	
	4631	Creditors due within one year	5867
1972		NET CURRENT ASSETS	1344
6369		TOTAL ASSETS *LESS* CURRENT LIABILITIES	7019
		Less	
		Creditors due in more than one year	
	415	Debentures	950
	300	Bank Loan	200
715			1150
5654		TOTAL ASSETS *LESS* TOTAL LIABILITIES	5869
FINANCED BY:			
		CALLED-UP SHARE CAPITAL	
	50	10% £5 Preference Shares	60
	300	£1 Ordinary Shares	400
350			460
		CAPITAL RESERVES	
	140	Share Premium	200
	20	Land Revaluation Reserve	20
160			220
		REVENUE RESERVES	
	1500	Revenue Reserve	2000
	3644	Retained Profits	3189
5144			5189
5654			5869

Notes: to Figure 19.1
1. Market value of ordinary shares at 31 December 19-8 was £10.25 and 31 December 19-9 £10.60
2. The number of ordinary shares (weighted average) on issue during 19-8 was 290m and during 19-9 380m
3. A dividend of £2 per share held at 31 December was declared in both 19-8 and 19-9

Figure 19.2   Financial Viability of the Business: Key Ratios in Company Accounts

MANAGEMENT RATIOS

Liquidity measures
Current ratio
Quick ratio
Cash ratio

Profitability ratios
Return on capital invested
Return on equity capital employed
Return on capital employed
Profit/sales ratio

LENDING RATIOS

Interest cover
Borrowing ratio
Debt ratio

INVESTMENT RATIOS

Earnings per share
Dividend/Yield
Dividend cover
Price/earnings ratio

Liquidity Measures

The general measures of liquidity (see Chapter 18) can be applied without modification. When applied to the accounts of UNI PLC set out in Figure 19.2, they give:

(%)	19-1	19-2
Current ratio	142.6	122.9
Quick ratio	85.7	67.6
Cash ratio	30.5	9.1

TASK 19.1   What is your interpretation of the meaning of the liquidity figures for Uni PLC summarised above?

As you consider the further ratios listed below, ask yourself to what extent they begin to build up a picture of the company.

Profitability Measures

Return on (total) capital invested (%)

This ratio measures the net return earned on total share capital. Note from the formula below that it is based on the profits originally earned, not on the amount distributed as dividends, and that the 'capital' is the total amount owned by the shareholders. In other words, it is a measure of the gross amount earned by the 'invested' capital. The formula is, therefore:

$$\frac{\text{Operating profit plus other income (if any) less tax}}{\text{Total issued share capital plus reserves}}$$

UNI PLC   19-1   19-2

$$\frac{£870m}{£5654m} = 15.39\% \qquad\qquad \frac{£1361m}{£5869m} = 23.19\%$$

Return on equity capital (%)

This ratio measures the return attributable to the *ordinary* (i.e. equity) share capital. For this reason, the amount attributable to the preference shareholders (i.e. the preference dividend) is deducted from the return on the upper line of the formula used above, just as the preference capital is excluded from the capital on the lower line. We therefore have:

$$\frac{\text{Operating profit plus other income }\textit{less}\text{ both tax and preference dividend}}{\text{Ordinary share capital plus reserves}}$$

UNI PLC   19-1   19-2

$$\frac{£(870 - 5)m}{£(300 + 5304)m} = 15.44\% \qquad \frac{£(1361 - 6)m}{£(400 + 5409)m} = 23.33\%$$

Return on capital employed (%)

This ratio measures the efficiency with which assets have been managed. This means taking the initial gross earnings before tax and interest and expressing it as a ratio of the total 'capital' assumed to be invested in profit-making assets. This includes the long-term loans as well as the total share capital as such. The formula is:

$$\frac{\text{Operating profit before tax and long-term interest}}{\text{Total share capital plus reserves plus long-term liabilities}}$$

UNI PLC: 19-1   19-2

$$\frac{£1536m}{£(5654 + 715)} = 24.12\% \qquad \frac{£2451m}{£(5869 + 1\,150)m} = 34.92\%$$

Return on total assets (%)

This formula provides an alternative way of assessing efficiency by comparing the return against the *total* assets employed within a firm, not just those financed by capital and longer-term liabilities. The formula used is:

$$\frac{\text{Operating profit before tax and long-term interest}}{\text{Total share capital plus reserves plus all liabilities}}$$

UNI PLC: 19-1   19-2

$$\frac{£1536m}{£(5654+715+4631)m} = 13.96\% \qquad \frac{£2451m}{£(5869+1150+5867)m} = 19.02\%$$

Note that the lower line of the formula in fact equals the total assets.

19.2 THE INTERESTS OF SHAREHOLDERS: INVESTMENT RATIOS

Although the operating efficiency and financial viability of a company is ultimately of concern to investors as well as to management, the former are more immediately concerned with certain other aspects – namely, how much they will receive as a return on their investment, and how easily the company will be able to pay it from the funds available.

Earnings per Share (EPS)

The earnings (i.e. dividend) of *preference* shares is, of course, a fixed commitment and does not vary annually. The dividend payable on ordinary shares depends on the company's profits and the number of shares which have a claim on them. Hence the idea of *earnings per share* (EPS), obtained by dividing the total profits which could be made available (i.e. the profits after all deductions including preference dividends) by the number of ordinary shares. In practice, this is a complicated calculation as a weighted average of shares on issue throughout the year has to be taken. The formula therefore is:

$$\frac{\text{Profits after tax } less \text{ preference dividend}}{\text{Number of ordinary shares (weighted average for year)}}$$

In the case of UNI PLC, note 2 to the balance sheet gives the weighted average of shares on issue during each of the two years. The calculation for UNI PLC is:

19-1
$$\frac{\pounds865m}{290m} = \pounds2.98$$

19-2
$$\frac{\pounds1355m}{380m} = \pounds3.57$$

If the shares on issue have not varied throughout the year, then it is not necessary to take a weighted average.

The EPS calculation is used in the price-earnings calculation (see below).

Dividend Yield (%)

The EPS only indicates the maximum dividend which could be paid on the basis of the year's profits. It is the practice of most companies not to distribute the whole of profits. The shareholder, therefore, is likely to be more interested in the actual amount which the company intends to pay (i.e. the dividend), and how this relates to the actual purchase price of a share (which is probably different from its nominal (or par) value). This gives him a measure of the return he is receiving, on the amount he invested. This is usually expressed as a percentage and the formula therefore is:

$$\frac{100 \text{ (Dividend per ordinary share)}}{\text{Current market price of ordinary shares}}$$

UNI PLC: 19-1
$$\frac{100 \times \pounds2}{\pounds10.25} = 19.51\%$$

19-2
$$\frac{100 \times \pounds2}{\pounds10.60} = 18.87\%$$

Dividend Cover (Times)

The purpose of this calculation is to measure how many times a company could cover (i.e. pay) the declared ordinary dividend out of the funds normally available to it – namely the profits for the year less all other charges including the preference dividend. Since companies tend not to distribute all their profits, the cover is usually greater than 1 – the higher it is, the 'safer' the dividend is. If the cover is less than 1, then the company would have to draw on its accumulated profits from previous years in order to meet the commitment. The formula therefore is:

$$\frac{\text{Profits after tax less preference dividend}}{\text{Ordinary dividend}}$$

UNI PLC 19-1

$$\frac{£865m}{£600m} = 1.44 \text{ times} \qquad \frac{£1355}{£800m} = 1.69 \text{ times}$$

19-2

Price/Earnings (P/E) Ratio (Factor)

Investors maintain a close watch on possible movements in share prices as well as on the prices themselves. The price/earnings ratio has been devised as a measure of the interest of the investing public in the shares. The formula used is:

$$\frac{\text{Current market price of ordinary shares}}{\text{Earnings per share (EPS)}}$$

Since the interest of investors affects the market price, a rise in that price in relation to the EPS will result in a rising P/E ratio, whereas a lessening of interest (reflected in a fall in the market price) will cause a drop in the P/E ratio. The P/E ratio (which is published for all quoted companies in the financial press) represents a good barometer of the way the market is moving.

Using the EPS figures calculated for UNI PLC above, the P/E ratios for the company in respect of each of the two years is:

19-1

$$\frac{10.25}{£2.98} = 3.44 \qquad \frac{£10.60}{£3.57} = 2.97$$

19-2

19.3 THE INTERESTS OF LENDERS: BORROWING RATIOS

The main interests of the longer term creditors will be the ability of the company to pay the amounts due out of the funds available together with its ability to repay the capital sum. This information is given by the following measures.

Interest Cover

This measure is the creditors' equivalent of the dividend cover of shareholders and is a guide to the company's ability to find the funds to pay the interest due. Since interest is payable before tax or dividends, and the formula used is

$$\frac{\text{Profits before tax and interest}}{\text{Interest charges}}$$

UNI PLC 19-1
$$\frac{£1536m}{£110m} = 13.96 \text{ times}$$

19-2
$$\frac{£2451}{£220m} = 11.14$$

Debt Ratio (%)

This ratio measures the ability of the firm to repay the debt as such and therefore indicates the extent to which it is safe to lend money to a firm. It is generally considered that total debts should be no more than half (i.e. 50%) the total assets available. The formula used is

$$\frac{\text{Total debt (i.e. long-term and current liabilities)}}{\text{Total assets}}$$

(alternatively, the total debt can be taken as a percentage of shareholders funds, in which case the ratio should not be more than 100% – which, of course, has the same implication as the 50% in terms of the first formula given).

UNI PLC   19-1
$$\frac{£(4631 + 715)m}{£(4397 + 6603)m} = 48.6\%$$

19-2
$$\frac{£(5867 + 1150)m}{£(5675 + 7211)m} = 54.45\%$$

Borrowing Ratio (%)

The purpose of this ratio is to eliminate the effect of the current liabilities from the debt ratio, and so focus attention on the longer-term position. The formula is

$$\frac{\text{Medium and long-term liabilities (including bank overdrafts)}}{\text{Net assets employed (total assets} - \text{current liabilities)}}$$

Note: It has become customary over recent years to include bank overdrafts on the argument that, although strictly a current liability, banks have offered the facility increasingly as a medium-term loan.

UNI PLC 19-1   19-2

$$\frac{£715m}{£6369m} = 11.23\% \qquad \frac{£1150m}{£7019m} = 16.38\%$$

PRACTICAL ASSIGNMENT

1 Prepare a reasoned comment on the position of Uni PLC as disclosed by the above calculations.

2 A company has an issued share capital of 1000 000 ordinary shares of £1 and 500 000 10% preference shares of £5. The shares were all paid up at the beginning of the financial year just ended. The long-term liabilities consisted of a debenture issue of 100 000 12% debentures of £3 each. The revenue reserves stand at £1 575 000.

The current market value of the ordinary shares stands at £1.50. Profit after interest charges but before tax for the last financial year amounted to £1 500 000 and tax was charged at 40% An interim dividend of 20p per share was paid during the year, and a final dividend of 34p per share is proposed, making a total dividend of 54p per share for the year.

Calculate the dividend yield, the dividend cover and the price/earnings ratio.

---

20 KEEPING AN EYE ON COMPANY ACCOUNTS – 2: GEARING

Think about this . . .   1.   *Would you prefer to invest your life's savings in the debentures or the ordinary shares of a company? Give a reason for your decision. Would it make any difference how well the company was doing?*

2.   *If you were running a company, would you prefer to have the majority of the firm's capital subscribed by debenture holders or ordinary shareholders? Would it make any difference how well the company was doing?*

Chapter 19 summarised the principal ratios which help us to 'read meaning' into company accounts. There is one more ratio which is of crucial importance to management, investors and creditors alike – though for different reasons. It is the 'gearing' of the company, known in the USA as the 'leverage'.

20.1 WHAT GEARING (LEVERAGE) IS ALL ABOUT

Companies obtain their funds from two main sources – ordinary shareholders and debenture holders. Shareholders are regarded as 'members' of the company who have made a permanent investment in it in the hope of receiving dividends. Debenture holders are regarded as having lent money to the company. They are therefore creditors, and are paid interest on the debt.

The difference between the two forms of finance are considerable and have far-reaching implications. Because of this, the ratio – known as the gearing ratio – between the two broad categories of finance is of central importance in understanding the position and relative strengths (and weaknesses) of different companies.

The gearing ratio is primarily concerned with the distinction between funding which carries a 'fixed charge' and that which does not. *Fixed charge capital* consists of preference shares, debentures, and the long- and medium-term loans. Some argument exists at the moment whether bank overdrafts should be included: strictly, these are short-term liabilities but there has been an increasing practice, in recent years, for banks to offer overdraft facilities in circumstances where formal loans would have been given in the past, and on these grounds some accountants would include them. In an examination, they are best excluded, but you should add a note to your solution explaining your decision.

Non-fixed charge capital consists of the ordinary shares plus all other funds due to the ordinary shareholders, i.e. capital and revenue reserves, and retained profits.

The formula most commonly used to calculate the gearing is:

$$\frac{100 \times \text{fixed charge capital}}{\text{total capital}}$$

(the term 'total capital', as used here, refers to fixed charge capital plus non-fixed charge capital).

Note the following:

1. The term 'capital' is used in its broader sense to include both share capital and loan capital. The items which make up (i) fixed charge capital and (ii) non-fixed charge capital (explained above) must be remembered.
2. In the USA, the term leverage is used instead of gearing
3. An alternative formula is sometimes used in which the fixed charge capital is a percentage of just the non-fixed capital, not of the total capital. It does not matter which is used as long as:
   (i) the result is interpreted within the context of the formula used;
   (ii) in examinations, the formula chosen is clearly stated.

There is no particular point at which a company becomes 'highly geared'. The concept is more often used in a comparative sense – e.g. in saying that one company is more (or less) highly geared than another.

EXAMPLE 20.1 *A Ltd* has an issued share capital of 280 000 £1 ordinary shares and 20 000 £1 10% preference shares. Reserves and retained profits amount to £100 000.

B Ltd has an issued shared capital of 240 000 £1 ordinary shares, 100 000 £1 10% preference shares and 60 000 £1 10% debentures.

Calculate the respective gearing ratios

$$\text{A Ltd:} \quad \frac{100 \times 20000}{20000 + (280000 + 100000)} = 5\%$$

$$\text{B Ltd:} \quad \frac{100 \times (100000 + 60000)}{(160000 + 240000)} = 40\%$$

Although there is the same total 'capital' in both companies (£400 000), B Ltd is much more highly geared than A Ltd.

20.2 IMPLICATIONS OF GEARING

The importance of the gearing ratio lies, not in itself, but in its implications – and its implications for management are different from those for investors. It is necessary, therefore, to look at the problem from both points of view.

Implications for Management

Management are primarily concerned with the efficient running of the company and they therefore look at gearing in that context. To them, a high gearing has the following advantages:

1. *Managerial control*
    Effective control of a company is obtained by ownership of more than 50% of the voting (i.e. ordinary) shares of a company. The more highly geared a company, the easier it is for the existing management to retain ownership of the necessary 50% and to prevent take-overs. The possible threat of a take-over bid is a constant problem to large successful companies.
2. *Servicing cost*
    Because of the difference in treatment of debenture interest and of share dividends in the P&L (interest is a charge *against* income before profits are ascertained; dividends are an *appropriation* of profits after they have been calculated) a highly geared company funded by way of debentures and loans rather than shares pays less tax than one funded primarily by shares.

The disadvantages of high gearing are:
1. *Possible cash-flow problems*
    Unlike dividends, debenture and loan interest must be paid irrespective of trading results. Also, both have, ultimately, to be paid back. These factors can create cash flow problems and have caused the downfall of a number of very well known companies over recent years.
2. *Drain on profits*
    As it is unusual for shares to be redeemed, the issue of shares instead of debentures creates a permanent drain on profits.

3. *Provision of security*
   Debentures are normally backed by security, such as a mortgage of the firm's premises. Some firms may not have assets which can be charged in this way.
4. *Rights issues*
   A highly geared company may find its ability to float a rights issue limited because of its comparatively few ordinary shareholders.
5. *Borrowing potential*
   A new, unknown company may find it difficult to borrow money.

Implications for Investors

Investors are primarily concerned with the company as an investment, and therefore with the return which they will receive on the funds invested.

1. If profits are low
It is better to hold fixed-charge investments. Interest on debentures must be paid even if losses are made. Preference shareholders will receive the current and arrears of dividend before ordinary shareholders receive anything.

2. If profits are high
It is better to hold ordinary shares in any company, but it is particularly true of high geared companies because, although a relatively larger proportion of the profits will be allocated to the owners of fixed charge capital, the slightly smaller remainder will be available to a much smaller ownership of non-fixed capital, giving a considerably larger return per share.

EXAMPLE 20.2 Two companies each have a total capital of £100 000. *X Ltd* has a capital of 80 000 10% £1 preference shares and £20 000 £1 ordinary shares. *Y Ltd* has a capital of 20 000 10% £1 preference shares and £80 000 £1 ordinary shares. *Note:* Of the two firms, X Ltd is more highly geared than B Ltd (80% compared with 20% respectively).

Each company makes a profit of £40 000 to be distributed in full to the shareholders.

What are the amounts received by the shareholders?

SOLUTION: X Ltd: Preference shareholders' share (10%): £8000
Ordinary shareholders' share £(40 000 - 8000) = £32 000

i.e. £32 000 — 20 000 = £1.60 per share

Y Ltd: Preference shareholders' share (10%): £2000
Ordinary shareholders' share £(40 000 – 2000) = £38 000

i.e. £38 000 – 80 000 = £0.475 per share

Look back at your answer to the Point to Ponder at the start of the Unit. Is your answer still the same?

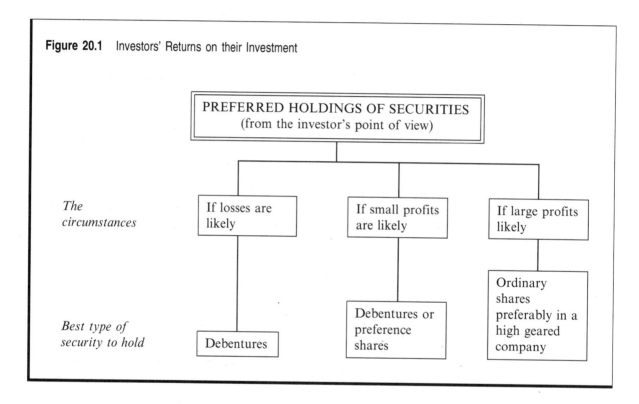

Figure 20.1   Investors' Returns on their Investment

PRACTICAL ASSIGNMENT

In its last published balance sheet, Suri Ltd disclosed that it had an authorised share capital consisting of 375 000 £1 ordinary shares of £1 and 500 000 10% preference shares of £1. Its issued capital amounted to 300 000 £1 ordinary shares and 450 000 preference shares. It had also issued 180 000 8% debentures of £5. It had a capital reserves £600 000 and retained earnings of £900 000.

Bala Ltd, in its balance sheet, disclosed an authorised capital of 600 000 ordinary £1 shares of which 300 000 had been issued. It had capital reserves amounting to £450 000 and had issued 450 000 £1 debentures.

REQUIRED:

(a) Explain what is meant by the term 'gearing' in relation to company accounts.

(b) Compare, and comment on, the gearing of Suri Ltd and Bala Ltd.

(c) What disadvantages can a company find in being highly geared?

(d) Explain to a potential investor why, in a period of high profits, he may be better advised to purchase ordinary shares in a highly geared company rather than in a similar but low geared company, even though the proportion of profits available to the ordinary shareholders will be lower.

REVISION QUESTIONS: PART V

In questions 1–20, note the option which best answers the stem question.

1 The working capital of an organisation measures the extent to which the current assets
(a) exceed the current liabilities
(b) are less than the total liabilities
(c) exceed the total liabilities
(d) are less than the current liabilities.

2 If profits are likely to be high, it is better for an investor to hold
(a) ordinary shares in a low geared company?
(b) preference shares in a high geared company?
(c) debenture stock in a low geared company?
(d) ordinary shares in a high geared company?

3 A firm is overtrading when its
(a) total assets exceed total liabilities
(b) current liabilities exceed current assets
(c) total liabilities exceed total assets
(d) current assets exceed current liabilities.

4 A dividend is
(a) an appropriation of profit
(b) a charge against profit
(c) an allocation to provisions
(d) a transfer to reserves.

5 If, at the end of a trading period, cash and bank balances are low, it means that the firm is
(a) overtrading
(b) making a loss
(c) making a profit
(d) may be making either a profit or a loss.

6 Capital employed is normally defined as
(a) issued share capital
(b) share capital and long-term liabilities
(c) share capital plus long-term and medium-term liabilities.
(d) share capital and all liabilities

7 High gearing usually results in
(a) reduced cash-flow problems
(b) lower annual fixed-charge on profits

(c) reduced risk of loss of management control
(d) ease in floating rights issues.

8 A company's profit calculation includes
(a) retained profits brought forward
(b) proposed dividends for the year
(c) debenture interest paid and accrued
(d) depreciation provisions on fixed assets.

9 A company's equity capital comprises
(a) ordinary share capital
(b) ordinary and preference share capital
(c) ordinary share capital and debentures
(d) ordinary and preference share capital and debentures.

10 Gearing is a measure of the relationship between
(a) ordinary and preference shares
(b) ordinary shares and debentures
(c) ordinary shares and preference shares plus debentures
(d) ordinary shares and preference shares plus all fixed-charge securities.

11 The acid test is another name for the
(a) cash ratio
(b) short-term solvency ratio
(c) quick ratio
(d) working capital.

12 Interest cover refers to the relationship between the interest charge for the year and profits
(a) before tax and interest
(b) after tax and interest
(c) after tax, interest and preference dividends
(d) after tax, interest and all dividends.

13 Which of the following would be regarded by a company as a current liability:
(a) retained profits for the year
(b) annual debenture interest paid
(c) proposed dividends for the year
(d) depreciation provision for the year.

14 The difference between the earnings per share (EPS) ratio and the dividend yield (D/Y) ratio is that
(a) EPS measures the maximum amount payable to shareholders out of the year's profits and D/Y the actual amount paid
(b) D/Y measures the maximum amount payable to shareholders out of the year's profits and EPS the actual amount paid
(c) EPS measures the minimum amount payable to shareholders out of the year's profits and D/Y the maximum amount
(d) D/Y measures the minimum amount payable to shareholders out of the year's profits and EPS the maximum amount.

15 Capital invested is equal to
(a) total assets *less* total liabilities
(b) total assets *less* current liabilities
(c) current assets *less* current liabilities
(d) current assets *less* total liabilities.

16 A dividend is
(a) a charge against profits
(b) an appropriation of profits
(c) a transfer to reserves
(d) a distribution of reserves.

17 Revenue reserves
(a) appear in the balance sheet as a liability
(b) can finance bonus issues
(c) arise from rights issues
(d) are regarded as an asset.

18 Dividend cover refers to the number of times the
(a) ordinary and preference dividends are covered by profits after tax and interest
(b) ordinary dividend is covered by profits before tax and interest cordinary and preference dividends are covered by profits before tax and interest
(d) ordinary dividend is covered by the profits after tax and interest.

19 The issue of debentures instead of shares
(a) results in a corporation tax advantage
(b) results in a corporation tax disadvantage
(c) does not affect the corporation tax position
(d) may affect corporation tax in various ways.

20 Debt ratio is the ratio between
(a) debtors and current assets
(b) current liabilities and current assets
(c) long-term liabilities and total assets
(d) total liabilities and total assets.

(*Questions 21–25 are based upon the following data extracted from the balance sheet of Ajax Ltd at 31 December last:*

Issued share capital £84m, fixed assets £92m, stock-holdings £26m, debtors £18m, cash balances £3m, debentures (maturing 2020) £40m, trade creditors £15m

21 Is the company
(a) insolvent and overtrading?
(b) solvent but overtrading?
(c) bankrupt and overtrading?
(d) solvent and not overtrading?

22 The company's cash ratio is approximately:
(a) 2.16%
(b) 6.38%
(c) 6.67%
(d) 20.0%.

23 The quick ratio of the company is approximately:
(a) 313%
(b) 140%
(c) 38%
(d) 15%.

24 The amount of the company's working capital is
(a) £2m
(b) £8m
(c) £32m
(d) £45m.

25 The capital employed and the capital invested in the company are respectively:
(a) £124m and £84m
(b) £84m and £139m
(c) £139m and £84m
(d) £84m and £124m.

MAJOR ASSIGNMENT: PART V

(Assume you are an accounting assistant employed by Murchison, Falls & Co, financial advisers. The firm has been approached by Sandra Evans, an eighteen-year old hair-dressing student at the local further education college. She has recently inherited £20 000 and wishes to invest it. Two companies have been mentioned to her, and she has approached your firm with a request for advice.

Joe Falls, one of the partners of the firm, has asked you to produce a report based on the available information concerning the two companies. You are aware that one reason for this is that the firm is anxious to assess your ability, initiative and competence as a financial adviser, and that other assistants within the firm will be receiving similar assignments. There have been suggestions that the firm will have to cut back on the number of assistants that it employs.

The information, which you suspect Mr Falls has deliberately muddled, is as follows:

Company 1: Bell Petroleum PLC

A long-established conglomerate with over 150 subsidiaries whose operations extend over more than 90 different countries. The corporation's main interests are oil exploration and the refining, production and marketing of a wide range of fuels. Other interests include the production and marketing of chemicals, gas, coal and various manufactured commodities. It has extensive marine interests.

Financial data:
At 31 December last, the corporation's fixed assets were valued at £44 500m, stocks stood at £5000m, debtors at £9000m and cash holdings at £4000m. There were current liabilities outstanding of £15 000m, and debentures (due to mature at various dates after 2010) amounting to £2300m. The corporation held capital and revenue reserves of £6000m and had an issued fully-paid capital of 36 200m ordinary shares of £1 each and 600m 10% preference shares of £5 each. The operating profit for the year was £8100m against which interest of £276m and tax provision of £2430 was charged. In addition to the preferred dividend, an ordinary dividend of 7p per share was declared.

At the previous year-end, the company had on issue 30 500m £1 ordinary shares and 600m 10% preference shares, both issues fully-paid. Reserves stood at £4500m and current liabilities at £14 000m. Cash holdings stood at £3000m, debtors at £6000m. Fixed assets were values at £38 000m and stocks at £6000m. The operating profit for that year had been £7705m, interest charges amounted to £180m and tax provision to £2311m. An ordinary dividend of 8p per share was paid.

Company 2: Slim-down Ltd

This company has been operating for just over two years and has a young and dynamic management. It produces a single principal product-line, a pre-frozen range of meals of low calorific value which the company claims stimulates the metabolic rate, thus resulting in slimming. The introduction of the product was backed by an intensive television and press advertising campaign and profits have been high.

Financial data:
At 28 February last, the company had on issue 180 000 ordinary shares of 50p and 200 000 10% preference shares of £1, all fully paid. There were two sets of debentures on issue: 150 000 8% debentures of £1 maturing in 2010, and 250 000 12% debentures maturing in 2030. Revenue reserves amounted to £20 000 and current liabilities stood at £350 000. Fixed assets stood at £165 000, stocks at £730 000 and debtors at £150 000. Cash balances amounted to £15 000.

The previous year's figures showed that fixed assets then stood at £180 000, stocks at £384 000, debtors at £90 000 and cash balances at £16 000. Ordinary share capital consisted of 180 000 ordinary shares of 50p each and 130 000 10% preference shares of £1, all fully paid. There was just one issue of debentures – namely the 150 000 8% issue of £1 each maturing in 2010. Revenue reserves stood at £100 000 and current liabilities of £200 000.

An 20% ordinary dividend was paid in the earlier of the two years. This was increased to 30% in the latter year.

REQUIRED: Your report to Mr Falls should summarise the above information and include such derived statistics as you think appropriate. You should assess each company on the grounds of investment potential. You should summarise the recommendations which you think should be put to Sandra Evans and, if you think appropriate, include suggestions of alternative avenues of investment which she might consider, bearing in mind her age, status and possible ambitions. You should note any additional information which you think it necessary to obtain before finalising the advice.

You are anxious to convince Mr Falls that you have the makings of a first-class accountant and that you are able to look further than the 'end of your nose'.

Answer Guide

The purpose of this guide is simply to provide a check on the answers to Tasks, Revision Questions and Practical Assignments in the text. The purpose is not to provide a model answer. It is emphasised that, in all cases, the important part of the exercise is the method and workings necessary to obtain the answer, not the answer itself.

The guidance is limited to answers to numerical-type questions. No guide is given to the major assignment answers in order to retain them as full tests which meet the requirements of the main assessment boards.

TASKS

Chapter 4
4.1 Budget month-end balances £14 000, £19 100, (£16 200)
4.2 Actual balance, 31 January £11 400.

Chapter 5
5.1 Net revenue: April £24 935, May £9950, June £15950.
5.2 Production levels for August and September revised to 5000 and 2000 units respectively.

Chapter 7
7.1 (1) £64m, (2) £96m, (3) £99m.
7.2 Profit margin £60m, cost of sales £240m, closing stock £36m, purchases £264m.

Chapter 8
8.3 (a) Opening balance, last quarter £82 000 (deficit)
(b) Closing balance for year £259 000
8.5 New opening balance £250 000.

Chapter 9
9.1 New average cost 16.63043p (correct to 5 places of decimals). Care has to be taken in rounding, particularly if multiplying afterwards – can you think why?
New average profit 3.36957p (correct to 5 decimal places).
Note the drop in the actual profit (£225) – more than the loss previously being incurred on the production of the loss-making brand.
9.2 (1) Overhead absorption rates   (2) Cost of job

(a) £1 per direct Labour-hour	£28
(b) £10 per machine-hour	£12.25
(c) £2 per unit output	£8

Chapter 15
15.1 (a) £315 000; (b) £75 000; (c) (i) 400 units, (ii) £140 000.
Price increase £(385–350) = £35 = 10% increase.
15.2 Break-even at 30 000 units (sales revenue £900 000); profit £300 000.
15.3

Task		Unit	Break-even	Actual production
		contribution	contribution	contribution
15.1	(a)	150	60 000	135 000
	(b)	165	66 000	148 500
15.2		10	300 000	600 000

15.4 Break-even (i) 432 units; (ii) sales revenue (obtained by proportion) £1 036 800.

Chapter 16
16.1 Curve should cut x axis at 6000 units (sales revenue £150 000).
16.2 (A) Break-even at 10 000 units.
(B) Break-even 8334 units.
16.3 A: Break-even at 9000 units.
B: Break-even at 4000 units.
C: Break-even at 5000 units.
16.4 (a) 40%
(b) +£2000, −£800, +£4800.
16.5

Production Programme Priority	C	B	A
Units	9000	11 000	1800
Contribution (£)	315 000	352 000	54 000

Chapter 17
17.1

	A	B
(a) Total profits	£16m	£20m
(b) Annual average rate of return	12.8%	10%

17.2
Franchise:

	A	B	C
Pay back point (00 yrs)	2.957	3.357	4.044

17.3 At a cost of capital of 9%, the discounted NCI shows a surplus of £44 437 over the discounted investment. Therefore it is worth undertaking.

17.4
Plot:
(approximately)

	A	B	C
	2.3%	15.2%	13.4%

PRACTICAL ASSIGNMENTS

Chapter 4
1. Closing balance 30 April £13 075
2. Closing balance 31 December £680 (deficit).
3. Closing balance 31 December £10 190. Profit forecast £17 168. Minimum return on capital required: 10.73%.
4. Closing balance 30 June £2596.
   (Note for monthly average for wages and expenses multiply weekly amount by 52 and divide by 12).
5. £24 240 (deficit).

Chapter 5
1.

Purchases:	A		B	
	kg	£	kg	£
July	389 840	389 840	390 000	585 000
August	240 000	240 000	480 000	720 000
September	198 000	198 000	396 000	594 000

Purchases:	A		B	
	kg	£	kg	£
October	252 000	252 000	504 000	756 000
November	160 000	160 000	320 000	480 000
December	140 000	140 000	280 000	420 000

2. Total sales 4300 units, turnover £554 160, net revenue £312 160.
3.

(b)	A	B
Total sales (units)	5568	3918
Turnover (£)	136 992	71 250
Net revenue	7682	9660

4. (a) 20 000 trees (b) monthly stock balances 10, 10, 30, (10), (10), 20
(c) Main problem – shortages in October, November. December surplus unlikely to meet the earlier demand.

Chapter 6
1. The individual variances should add up to a favourable variance of £40 000 in the gross profit but an adverse variance of £5000 in the net profit. The question therefore requires a close analysis and interpretation of the indirect variances.

Chapter 7
1. (a) Stock at month-ends (£): November 2000; December 2000; January 7000 February 1000.
   (b) Final cash balance £20 450 (overdrawn).
   (c) Gross profit £12 500; net profit £6120.
   (d) Note that the cash balance is overdrawn although there is a net profit.
2. (a) Final cash balance, £28 500 (overdrawn).
   (b) Gross profit £107 800; net profit £30 800.

Chapter 9
2. (a)

	X	Y	Z
Total costs (£)	865	993	692
Selling price (40% on cost) (£)	242.20	139.02	322.94
Selling price (£ at 20% on sales)	216.25	124.12	288.34

(b)

	X	Y
Total costs (£)	1174	936
Selling price (£ at 40% on cost)	328.72	436.80
Selling price (£ at 20% on cost)	293.50	390

3. Costings should indicate that acceptance of the supermarket proposal will result in the greatest increase in contribution. Broader marketing issues, such as challenge to the firm's own market, should also be considered.
4. If all overheads are re-allocated, total profits drop. The question is therefore one of to what extent the overheads will be avoided. Consideration should also be given to the longer-term issues such as growth potential.
5. (a)
   Gross profit: A £55 634; B £49 009; C £68 106.
   Net profit: A £17 149; B £4.82595; C £7.735575.

6. (a) OAR – Shaping dept: £8.1 per machine-hour; (or £5.4 per labour-hour)
Polishing dept: £2.5 per labour-hour
(b) Job EOTW6 – Dept costs: Shaping £335.04 (using OAR based on machine-hours); Polishing £211.20; Total job costs: £546.24

7. (a)

Department	Firm A	Firm B
Moulding	£17.5 per machine-hour	£15 per machine-hour
Machining	£10.5 per machine-hour	£13.5 per machine-hour
Polishing	£18.75 per machine-hour	£15.625 per machine-hour

(b) Total OH cost: Firm A £662.50 Firm B £675

8. (i) £2.7 per machine-hour
(ii) £1.7525773 per labour-hour
Note: Considerable caution should be exercised before rounding figures which may be 'multiplied up'.
(iii) A £45.43 B £54.97 C £28.82

9. (a) £3.94 per partner-hour
(b) £19.47 per partner-hour;
(c) extra salary £6266.67
Note: Despite the caution given in the previous question, the figures here have been rounded to the penny above to reflect what would be done in the practical situation – even more likely, they would be rounded to the £ above!

Chapter 10

1. (a)

(£)	Year 1	Year 2
Net profits: absorption costing	406 857*	306 031
marginal costing	380 000*	320 000

* stocks at year-end rounded

2. (a) (i) Total costs of production £1 045 000; (ii) absorption unit cost £26.125; (iii) total gross profit £320 000; net profit £75 000. (iv) unit gross profit £8; unit net profit £1.875.
(b) £20. (c) £2.73.

3. The difference in profit is minimal (no more than ± £1000). The decision would therefore have to rest on the various long-term and short-term market considerations depending on the reliability of the forecasts.

4. (a)

Net profit (£)	Year 1	Year 2
(i) total cost basis:	96 000	65 000
(ii) variable cost basis:	91 000	65 000

Chapter 11

1. Prime cost £5 030 500; cost of production £5 716 400; gross profit £2 297 600; net profit £1 834 900.

2. (a) Materials cost £64 050; prime cost £84 050; cost of production £94 850.
(b) Gross profit £203 750; net profit £180 950.

3. (a) Prime cost £249 500; cost of production £471 800; gross profit £173 375; net profit £92 375.
Note: Closing stock valuation:
5500 units   £92 675
+ rejects, lower of cost or NRV   <u>2500</u>   £95 175

4. (a) Cost of production £1428m; gross profit £490m; net profit £25.24m; retained earnings £16.04m.

5. Prime cost £105 560; cost of production £119 400; gross profit £76 600; net profit £36 600.

6. Prime cost £639 862; cost of production £979 415; gross profit £657 225; net profit £161 247.

7. (a) (i) *Note*: Importance of depreciation, possible bad debts, returns and wastage.
(ii) Costs £29 970 + profit £8991 to give £38 961; unit selling price £64.94 (allowing for depreciation at 20% p.a. straight line).
(iii) Costs £37 957 + profit £11 388 to give £49 435; unit selling price £61.69.

Chapter 12

1. (a)

(£)	Total	Aphondrine	Nephrex
Prime cost	330 000	135 000	195 000
Cost of production	428 000	188 800	239 200
Profit on manufacturing	85 600	37 760	47 840
Profit on trading	149 800	127 840	12 960
Net profit (Loss)	46 800	84 197	(37 397)

2. (a) Prime cost £60 000; cost of production £238 000; loss of manufacturing £40 000; profit on trading £172 000; net profit £48 000.

3. (a) Prime cost £765 000; cost of production £904 000; gross profit £328 640; net profit £190 640.

4. (a) Prime cost £1 096 160; cost of production £1 133 810; net profit £384 258.

5. (a) (i) Gross profit £38 000; (ii) 42% of turnover

(b) (i) Manufacturing loss £11 000; trading profit £49 000; 54.4% of turnover.
(ii) High trading profit covers up manufacturing loss in (a)(i) above. Figures in (b)(i) suggest 'buying out', but non-accounting factors may have to be considered.

6.

Profit(loss)(£)	1st Contract only	2nd Contract only	Both contracts
excluding pay award	155 650	(33 125)	194 421
adjusted for pay award	125 650	48 125	149 425
Profit/contract price (%)			
excluding pay award	31.1	–	28.8
adjusted for pay award	25.1	–	22.1

7. (a)

(£)		Standard	Super
(a)	Prime cost	80 645	148 900
	Cost of production	85 645	156 900
(b)	(i) Minimum unit selling price to give returning 20% on cost.	4.68	6.73
	(ii) Profit	9444	14 643

Chapter 13

2. (a) (i) Materials variances: usage £7800 (adv); price £4100 (adv); net £11 900 (adv).
(ii) Labour variances: efficiency £220 (fav); wage-rate £584 (adv); net £220 (fav).

Chapter 14

1. (b) Variances:
Materials usage: components A £1350 (adv); B £20 250 (adv).
Materials price: components A £1100 (fav); B £1450 (adv).
Labour efficiency: skilled £400 (adv); unskilled £250 (adv).
Labour wage-rate: skilled £425 (adv): unskilled £825 (adv).
Variable overhead: efficiency £1875 (fav); budget £1125 (adv).
Fixed overhead: volume £1500 (fav); budget £1500 (fav).

2. (a) It is possible to calculate the actual materials usage and the actual wage rate from the data given. It is also possible to flex the original budget on the basis of an output of 18 000 compared with 24 000 bags.

(b)

Variance	(i) Origina budget	(ii) Flexed budget
Materials volume	10 000 (fav)	5000 (adv)
Materials price	5000 (adv)	15 000 (adv)
Labour efficiency	80 000 (fav)	64 000 (adv)
Wage rate	62 000 (adv)	62 000 (adv)

Chapter 15

1. (a) The graph should show break-even points of 8334 and 3948 units.

2. (a) The original and revised forecasts should show profits of £400 000 and £205 000 respectively.
(b) 8572 and 12 337 units.

3. (a) (i) 5000 and 6106 units respectively.
(ii) Year 1 los £150 000; year 2 profit £85 000. Note that, without the development charge (a short-term expense), a profit would have been made in year 1.
(b) The projected increase in demand would not be sufficient to compensate for the reduction in price (a case of elastic demand) and profit would fall to £20 000.

4. (1) Break-even at 133 334 locks.
(2) Break-even at 195 834 locks. Calculation should indicate that a greater profit is obtained, but this would depend on proposals being realised. Other longer-term effects should also be mentioned.

5. (a) 191 boxes; (b) 477 boxes.

6. (a) Break-even points: 18 182 disks, 22 051 disks and 27 508 disks respectively.
(b) Profits £65 000, £144 500 and £154 506 respectively.

7. (a) 6429 clubs; (b) 8067 clubs; (c) Total contribution £132 500, net profit £61 250.

8. Break-even 1250 units. New unit selling price £87.12

9. (a) Break-even 13 750 units (£55 000).
(b) 17 500 units.
(c) Total contribution £200 000, profit £90 000.

Chapter 16

1. The accounting calculations should indicate it is more profitable to 'buy out' – but the report should mention other considerations which might be important. The question of re-allocation of the overheads should also be discussed.

2. Calculations should indicate that it is cheaper to 'buy in'.

3. This is a difficult question involving some complex calculations. You will find it helpful to bear in mind:

Variable admin, etc. costs: sales revenue *less* contribution = total variable. This, less the variables given = variable admin).

Contribution = 20% of sales revenue (same at break-even point).

Fixed manufacturing costs can be found by reconstructing a conventional trading account using given gross profit figure (same at break-even point).

Fixed admin costs – remember nil profit(loss) at break-even point.

5. (a) Buy from manufacturer. Saving (approx) £3.80 per unit.
   (b) Saving by buying out £104. Other factors to be considered include, among others, security of supplies and quality control.
6. Contribution A £48; B £216; C £384.
   (a) 37.5%; (b) £40 per unit; (c) £25 000; (d) 1667 units; (e) 466 680.

Chapter 17
1. Average annual rate of return 20.14%.
2. Pay back 1 year 1.02 weeks.
3. (i) Pay back (A) 3.39 years; (B) 2.94 years; (C) 2.54 years.
   (ii) Overall profit (A) £9000; (B) £1100; (C) £2200; (A modified) (£9500).
   (iii) Average annual rate of return (A) 6.25%; (B) 6.92%; (C) 1.05%; (A modified) 11.875%.
   The essence of the question is a reasoned report based on the above data (the calculations for which you should show) – not simply a X_num1 of calculations.
4. (b) Able shows the better NPV but Cain better overall profit – what other factors have to be considered?
5. Configuration B should be the best on all the tests.
6. The report should include the normal capital appraisal calculations, but should review these in the light of the club's situation and the broader problems associated with sport (e.g. the implications of injury early in the season).

7. Of the two main proposals, it should be found that Project Medico has the quicker pay-back and average annual rate of return. Best Seller (1) has the better average annual rate of return and NPV. The modified investment proposal for Best Seller gives an even better NPV.
   Remember: The importance lies in an intelligent report.

Chapter 18
(a) Calculations should indicate that the firm was long-term solvent both before and after the transactions. Also that it was insolvent short-term before, but solvent long-term after with working capital.
(b) Final effect of transactions on working capital plus £22 000 to give a net figure of £12 000.

(c)

Ratios (%)	(i) Before	(ii) After
Long-term solvency	186.7	181.9
Current ratio	88.9	113.2
Quick ratio	33.3	67.0
Cash ratio	11.1	50.5

Chapter 19
1. Comment should be made on the drop in liquidity, improvement in profitability and EPS although D/Y has dropped. This should be related to the lower P/E ratio and the higher dividend cover. The change in interest cover should be examined and interpreted.
2. D/Y 36%; dividend cover 1.2 times; P/E 2.31 times; EPS 65p per share.

Chapter 20
1. (b) (Gearing: Suri Ltd 72.2%; Bala Ltd 42.86%.)

REVISION QUESTIONS: PART I – PART V

REVISION QUESTIONS:

Part	I	II	III	IV	V
1.	b	F	D	T	a
2.	a	T	A	F	d
3.	d	T	B	F	b
4.	b	F	D	T	a
5.	c	T	B	T	d
6.	a	F	C	F	c
7.	d	F	D	T	c
8.	d	T	D	F	b
9.	a	F	A	T	a
10.	a	T	D	F	d
11.	b	A	b	D	c
12.	d	D	d	D	a
13.	b	F	a	D	c
14.	c	C	c	E	a
15.	a	B	d	D	a
16.		F	b	E	b
17.		E	d	D	b
18.		D	a	D	d
19.		E	d	D	a
20.		B	c	C	d
21.		A	a	a	d
22.		E	c	c	d
23.		E	c	c	b
24.		C	a	d	c
25.		F	d	a	a
26.			B	b	
27.			E	d	
28.			C	d	
29.			C	c	
30.			A	b	
31.			£1 060 000	B	
32.			£2 060 000	A	
33.			£840 000	C	
34.			£2 880 000	B	
35.			Profit £416 000	C	
36.				A	
37.				A	
38.				B	
39.				C	
40.				A	

Index